TRENDS IN LINGUISTICS

JANUA LINGUARUM

STUDIA MEMORIAE
NICOLAI VAN WIJK DEDICATA

edenda curat

CORNELIS H. VAN SCHOONEVELD
STANFORD UNIVERSITY

SERIES MINOR
NR. XLII

1965
MOUTON & CO.
LONDON · THE HAGUE · PARIS

TRENDS
IN
LINGUISTICS.

by

MILKA IVIĆ

NOVI SAD

translated by

MURIEL HEPPELL

1965

MOUTON & CO

LONDON · THE HAGUE · PARIS

Printed in The Netherlands by Mouton & Co., Printers, The Hague.

PREFACE

This book presents a condensed account of the history of linguistics from its first modest beginnings up to the most important achievements of the present day in the field of general theory and method. The evolution of man's knowledge about language is here conceived as indissolubly connected with the widening of his cultural and scientific horizons. The various linguistic trends of the past, as well as the approaches to language in our day, are explained in their mutual relations and with the reference to the cultural atmosphere which inspired them.

The tremendous upward surge of linguistic studies, especially in recent decades, has brought along a flood of new concepts and terms. Even for a well-trained scholar, it is not easy to keep pace with all the new achievements in the field of language research. For the beginner in linguistics it is still harder. It takes considerable time to escape the danger of being confused by different schools, since they use different terminology and usually do not explain thoroughly in which points they agree or disagree. The need has often been mentioned for a book which would provide basic information about the different approaches supported nowadays by the most outstanding linguists. This book is an attempt to fulfil such a need. Moreover, the presentation of facts in this work is in accordance with the author's intention to increase its practical value as much as possible, i.e. to make possible its use as a student's textbook.

The relatively unimportant deviations of the English translation from the Serbo-Croatian original (written in 1961/62, published in 1963) have been introduced by the author. The changes include the omission of some details which would be of interest to a Yugo-slav reader, but not to a broader public, and the use of different examples (since the original Serbo-Croatian word-forms would not be familiar for the reader of an English text).

M.I.

TABLE OF CONTENTS

LINGUISTIC RESEARCH IN THE
TWENTIETH CENTURY

LIST OF ABBREVIATIONS

Arens, *Sprachwissenschaft* = Hans Arens, *Sprachwissenschaft, der Gang ihrer Entwicklung von der Antike bis zur Gegenwart* (München, 1955).

Bloomfield, *Language* = Leonard Bloomfield, *Language* (New York, 1933).

CFS = the periodical *Cahiers Ferdinand de Saussure* (pub. "Société Genevoise de Linguistique", Geneva).

For Roman Jakobson = *For Roman Jakobson. Essays on the Occasion of His Sixtieth Birthday* (The Hague, 1956).

IJAL = the periodical *International Journal of American Linguistics* (Baltimore).

Lg = the periodical *Language (Journal of the Linguistic Society of America, Baltimore).

8th Proceedings = the collection *Proceedings of the Eighth International Congress of Linguists* (Oslo, 1958).

SIL = the periodical *Studies in Linguistics* (Norman, Okla).

TCLC = the periodical *Travaux du Cercle Linguistique de Copenhague* (Copenhagen).

TCLP = the periodical *Travaux du Cercle linguistique de Prague.*

Trends = the collection *Trends in European and American Linguistics 1930-1960* (Utrecht-Antwerp, 1961).

Vja = the periodical *Voprosy jazykoznanija* (Moscow).

Zvegincev, *Istorija jazykoznanija* = V. A. Zvegincev, *Istorija jazykoznanija XIX i XX vekov v očerkax i izvlečenijax*, Books I and II (Moscow, 1960).

LINGUISTIC RESEARCH
BEFORE THE NINETEENTH CENTURY

INTRODUCTION

1. Civilized people have shown an interest in linguistic problems from the earliest recorded times. The scope of this interest has, as a rule, been governed by the specific needs of social life.

2. In communities where religion has played a far-reaching social rôle, people have aspired to a knowledge of the language of their cult, particularly in the form in which that language has been written down in their religious texts. In this way, for instance, the Sanskrit language was described in detail in the remote past of the Hindu religion, some centuries before our era (see below § 17). Medieval Christendom devoted a considerable part of its energies to the study of Latin (see below §§ 24-27). The Jews studied Hebrew from the Bible (see below § 34). The Arabs founded grammatical centres with the basic aim of making it possible for the faithful to read the Koran correctly (see below § 31). The first precise grammatical descriptions and philological studies of texts, the first ideas about the codification of grammatical rules – all these in fact rest on distant, humble beginnings of this kind, dictated by the particular character of life in a civilized society and its specific customs.

3. The cultural atmosphere in Ancient Greece, a community distinguished by a high level of civilization and a relatively liberal religious outlook, gave birth to a lively interest in language. There linguistic investigations passed beyond the narrow confines of purely practical aims. They became part of the rich field of philosophical research to which Hellenic thought was so strongly inclined (see below § 8). The first fundamental notions about language categories, the principles governing the construction of sentences and the correlation existing between thought and speech processes have been established on the basis of this linguistic interest which

arose within the scope of philosophical studies. Indeed, all this represented only vague knowledge of the phenomenon of language. However it is just this first, early and somewhat naïve contact between linguistic and philosophical research that contains the roots of the long history of grammar, that is, classical grammar, on which were nurtured generations of linguists up to quite recent times, and which even today still has its adherents.

4. The era of the centralization of political power towards the end of the feudal period in Europe gave an impetus to work on normative grammar. The creation of powerful political units with a highly differentiated social system brought with it a desire to establish precisely and firmly the language of the privileged class. The rise of the French monarchy, for example, also saw the growth of the French tradition of elaborating the normative approach to language facts (see below § 38). In the course of time such a tradition, faithfully handed down from generation to generation, has also been adopted by other nations.

5. But all the linguistic work achieved before the beginning of the nineteenth century was either devoted to the solution of practical language problems in a particular community, or undertaken within the scope of wider, philosophical, i.e. non-linguistic interests. In a word, before the nineteenth century linguistics did not exist as a specific discipline, with a systematically established working method and a well-founded general theory.

6. When we look back carefully at what any people has given us in the field of our knowledge of language, we are struck not only by the fragmentary character of the interests expounded, but also by the simple and one-sided way in which all the investigators estimated their own language in relation to others: every nation has regarded its own language as the model language – the most complete documentation of a most successful synthesis of linguistic forms with the human spirit. Wider horizons of general knowledge and more profound contact between different nations were required to create the necessary intellectual basis for systematic and truly linguistic research.

LINGUISTIC RESEARCH IN ANCIENT GREECE

7. The Ancient Greeks initiated linguistic investigations in several directions. They were the first, and for a long time the only linguistic theoreticians in the world. They also have the credit of being the first Europeans to interest themselves in the accurate study of written texts, and also in fixing the norms concerning the language of their culture. Not only were they the founders of the principles of classical European grammar, but we are also indebted to them for the tradition of grammatical research which was faithfully preserved in later centuries.

8. Their work on linguistic theory developed from their philosophical interests. In order to complete or give more precise form to their philosophical viewpoints they made special efforts to observe the origin of language,[1] the direct relationship between its sound structure and the corresponding meaning, and the possibility of applying logical principles in explaining grammatical forms. All these problems first stated by the Greeks are still of interest in present-day linguistics.

[1] The origin of language has been the subject of human thought from time immemorial. The Ancient Greek historian Herodotus (in the fifth century B.C.) noted a story about an Egyptian king called Psametichus who ordered two newborn babies to be isolated from the rest of the world in order to find out what language they would speak spontaneously. Tradition relates that the children first pronounced the word *bekos*, which is the word for bread in Phrygian. So Phrygian was proclaimed the oldest language in the world. In recent times reflection on the origin of language has been primarily concerned with the question of the formation of the sounds of a language: perhaps they developed from a wish to imitate sounds in nature (the so-called *onomatopoeic* or *bow-wow* theory), or as a vocal response to every external impression received (the so-called *nativistic* or *ding-dong* theory), or, finally, in spontaneous cries uttered under the influence of intense emotion (the so-called *interjectional* or *pooh-pooh* theory). Glottogonistic problems (problems relating to the origin of language) are still discussed today.

9. Nearly all the most important ancient philosophers occupied themselves with theorizing about language, at least by the way. Philosophical discussions often included arguments with a direct bearing on linguistic problems. One of these discussions is particularly famous: the one as to whether there is a direct, logical connection between the meanings expressed by words and their sound forms, or whether this connection is arbitrary and the result of chance.[2]

According to the conception of the "analogists", language is a gift of nature and not dependent on human convention. It is in its essence regular and logical, which means that there is perfect harmony between the sound form of a word and the meaning concealed in it. In their desire to show this harmony and in their efforts to eliminate any obscuring of such an ideal connection (which had possibly occurred in the course of time), the analogists payed special attention to etymological research.[3] The etymological inclinations of these first etymologists never reached the point of the systematic study of linguistic changes.[4]

The "anomalists", on the other hand, did not believe in an ideal correlation between the formal and the semantic structure of a word. They pointed out the irregularities which appeared everywhere at all levels of linguistic relations.

The etymological enthusiasm of many generations of "analogists" was stimulated, for example, by the fact that a man of such lucid

[2] It is not known exactly who first began this discussion. Some people attribute it to Protagoras (c. 480-410 B.C.) and some to Pythagoras (c. 572-497 B.C.). The discussion lasted for centuries.
[3] Later Latin grammarians, following the example of the Greeks, also paid considerable attention to etymology – again without sufficient objectivity.
[4] Among the most ardent champions of etymological studies (which "reveal the truth about words") were the Stoic philosophers in the third century B.C. Apart from etymology, the Stoics achieved positive results in their linguistic investigations. The study of cases, for example, had its first noteworthy beginning with the Stoics. While for Aristotle the case was every form of a word which differed from what was regarded as the basic form (every verbal form, for example, was a "case" in relation to the present, etc.), the Stoics excluded verbs from the case category and limited this concept to nominal forms. They first introduced the classic distinction between the nominative and other cases (casus rectus/casus obliqui).

judgment as Heraclitus (c. 500 B.C.) insisted on the identity between human intellect as an organized whole and the basic structure of language. The "anomalists", for their part, swore by the ideas of the famous Democritus (c. 460-360 B.C.), who decisively repudiated the hypothesis of the divine origin of speech.[5] Nor was the subject neglected by Plato (427-347 B.C.).[6] Although he fought against the naïve etymological views based on literal interpretations of the assertions of Heraclitus, Plato nevertheless supported Heraclitus in his fundamental idea regarding the correlation of human intellect and linguistic structure.[7]

10. In general Plato's point of departure was the conviction that a word is the material form of an idea, and that in the idea lies the beginning of our knowledge about the world. This philosophical standpoint gave birth to the first attempts to define basic grammatical categories. Applying the criteria relevant to the operations of logic, Plato pointed to the noun as a thing about which something is stated (which corresponds to the later traditional definition of the subject, repeated by many people right up to the present day). He defined the verb as what is stated about a noun (and this later became the classic conception of the predicate, supported even today by adherents of traditional linguistics).

11. It was Aristotle (384-322 B.C.) who entered the history of linguistic scholarship as the main founder of classical European grammar. During later centuries his teaching about the categories of words changed only in details, not in its basic spirit. The traditional approach to grammar has its essential roots in Aristotle's

[5] His arguments were as follows: the imperfect nature of language was proved by the existence of homonyms and synonyms, by the fact that linguistic forms are subject to change, and also by the fact that there is no regularity in the grammatical behaviour of words (e.g. verbs can be derived from some nouns but not from all).

[6] He developed this theme in his work *Cratylus*, in the form of a discussion between Cratylus (a supporter of Heraclitus), Hermogenes (an anomalist) and the philosopher Socrates (who represents Plato's point of view and for the most part pleads for compromise).

[7] Plato keeps clear of primitivism in this correlation, and insists that it should not be sought in the concrete manifestation of a linguistic phenomenon. It exists in the sphere of human intellect, where the same logical principles are valid for linguistic structure as for the process of thought.

methods of observing the phenomenon of language, especially in the field of syntax. By qualifying grammatical forms according to whether they denoted substance, quality, quantity, relation, existence, change, etc., Aristotle in fact introduced into his reflections about language criteria peculiar to philosophical investigations. This heritage from philosophical conceptions proved to be exceptionally far-reaching and of long duration in the later development of linguistics.

It was Aristotle who first tried to work out a classification of parts of speech. He grouped together nouns (*onoma*) and verbs (*rhema*), since he considered that only these words have a distinct meaning by themselves, in contra-distinction to all other words which simply serve to link the logical processes of thinking (*syndesmoi*). The principle of his division was consistently maintained later, although the actual arrangement of the particular parts of speech within these two groups has been changed to some extent.

According to Aristotle's way of thinking, verbs differ from all other kinds of words by reason of their tense-forming properties. That is why the primary function of the verb is that of predication. Nevertheless Aristotle regarded the predicate as having a wider function than the verb. The predicate includes everything which gives information about the subject. Since people can be designated in terms of qualities, then these qualities, expressed by adjectives, are not true verbs, but they are predicates. This means both that there are sentences without verbs and that the predicate need not be a true verb.

Aristotle defined the sentence as a combination of sound elements which has a definite, independent meaning, but at the same time each of its component parts also means something by itself. But in general Aristotle's theory of the sentence was connected with his theory of judgment, which led him to assign a position of central importance to the question of predication.[8]

12. Certainly the Greek philosophers showed a sincere interest

---

[8] Predication consists in uniting or dividing two ideas. The basic element of predication lies in the verb *to be*; even when we say, for example, *the man goes*, these words in fact correspond to the logical judgment: the man is in a state of

in language phenomena, but they lacked a true awareness of their complicated and many-sided nature. Their knowledge was limited by the very fact that they regarded their own language as the best means of expressing human thought, and considered that theorizing about language in general could be carried out solely on the basis of Greek linguistic data.

13. The Ancient Greeks were also pioneers in the field of philological studies. They initiated the tradition of the precise description of the language of written texts. The most famous Greek philologist of antiquity was Aristarchus (216-144 B.C.) who studied the Iliad and the Odyssey from the linguistic point of view. In his methods he was one of the outstanding representatives of the so-called "Alexandrian school".

14. The term "Alexandrian school" refers to an exceptionally fruitful era of grammatical work in the centre for linguistic investigations which the Greeks founded at Alexandria (it was active as early as the third and second centuries B.C.). There were similar schools at other places in the Hellenistic world – in Asia Minor, at Pergamon and Tarsus.[9] However only the Alexandrian school acquired an exceptional reputation as a famous centre, unique in the Ancient World, in which generations of gifted grammarians were trained, and great traditions of grammatical fields of interest and methods of work were established. Before the time of the "Alexandrians" grammar had been simply a branch of Greek philosophical studies; from their time onwards it was an independent discipline nurtured by well-trained specialists, and even had its own specialized branches (*lexicographers* were concerned with collecting and observing the vocabulary; *glossators* explained difficult terms, dialectal forms and poetical expressions; *rhetoricians* studied language for the purpose of developing skill in oratory; *scholiasts* were specialists in textual commentary, etc.).

There was nothing particularly new in the contribution of the Alexandrians to linguistic theory. They embraced and developed

---

going. This theory of Aristotle's concerning judgment and predication remained fundamental in the history of logic.

[9]   Later there were schools of the same type in the Byzantine Empire.

further the philosophical conceptions of language inherited from their Greek masters. They also continued the investigation of parts of speech. Morphological studies flourished, and phonetics also entered the field of their linguistic interest.[10]

The Alexandrians showed an inclination to fixing the norms of the Greek language. They tried, for example, to introduce the characteristic forms of Old Ionic (in which the famous epic poems were written) into the everyday linguistic usage of their times. There was also an attempt to establish the language preserved in the famous choral songs of Doric origin as a linguistic model.

The Alexandrians elaborated a descriptive grammar of the Greek language which enjoyed widespread fame. However its value was lessened by the fact that the description was not sufficiently objective, for two reasons: the interpretation of linguistic phenomena was too philosophical, and there was an exaggerated attitude in regarding Greek as the most logical, ideal human language.

The author of the oldest Greek grammar which has been preserved (known by the name of *grammatikē technē*) was the famous Dionysius Thrax (second century B.C.).[11] Apollonius Dyskolus (second century A.D.), another outstanding Alexandrian, also worked on descriptive grammar, and was one of the first grammarians in the world who began to take a serious interest in the problems of syntax.[12] Dyskolus's son Herodian worked on linguistic history:

[10]   The Greeks had divided sounds into vowels and consonants. Vowels were defined as sound phenomena which can represent a sound unit by themselves and be either long or short, while consonants were treated as sound phenomena which can form a complete sound unit only in combination with vowels. Consonants were divided into half-voiced and voiceless. The articulatory features were not taken into account.

[11]   He was the first to formulate the well-known traditional definition of the sentence: a combination of words which expresses a complete thought. He divided nouns into common nouns and proper nouns. Thrax was also the first to give a detailed description of the morphological characteristics of the Greek verb.

[12]   He was the first to establish the scope of syntactical investigations: syntax should be concerned with the rules governing the combinations of words in a sentence. In stating these rules Dyskolus proceeded according to his views on parts of speech: he did not make a clear distinction between the occasional uses of words in the sentence and those standard grammatical functions which are implied by their basic lexical forms.

his studies of the language of ancient Greek writers (from the fifth century B.C.) included, for example, the first descriptions of Greek accents worthy of attention.

BIBLIOGRAPHICAL REFERENCES

15. For basic information, consult: Bloomfield, *Language*, the chapter "The Study of Language"; Zvegincev, *Istorija jazykozanija*, I, pp. 9-14; Arens, *Sprachwissenschaft*, pp. 5-28.

More detailed information is given in a collection of articles entitled *Antičnye teorii jazyka i stilja*, ed. O. M. Freidenberg (Moscow-Leningrad, 1936). See also H. Steinthal, *Geschichte der Sprachwissenschaft bei Griechen und Römern* (Berlin, 1863; second ed. 1890); E. Egger, *Apollonius Dyscole, Essai sur l'histoire des théories grammaticales de l'antiquité* (Paris, 1854); Anton Dobiaš, *Sintaksis Apollonija Diskola* (Kiev, 1882); R. H. Robins, *Ancient and Medieval Grammatical Theory in Europe, with Particular Reference to Modern Linguistic Doctrine* (London, 1951); W. S. Allen, "Ancient Ideas on the Origin and Development of Language", *Transactions of the Philological Society* (1948-49), pp. 35-60; Josef Derbolav, "Der Dialog 'Kratylos' im Rahmen der platonischen Sprach und Erkenntnisphilosophie", *Schriften der Univ. der Saarlandes* (Saarbrücken, West-Ost Verlag, 1953).

The exposition of the linguistic theories of antiquity given by the philosopher Ernst Cassirer may be of interest to linguistic scholars: Ernst Cassirer, *The Philosophy of Symbolic Forms* (New Haven, 1953), the chapter "The Problem of Language in the History of Philosophy", the section "The Problem of Language in the History of Philosophical Idealism (Plato, Descartes, Leibniz)", pp. 117-132.

3

THE INDIAN GRAMMATICAL SCHOOL

16. The Ancient Indians certainly deserve the widespread fame won by their exceptional gift for grammatical studies. They are remembered today with special esteem not so much because of the amazing volume of their work and the results they achieved as because of their feeling for the objective, precise description of linguistic facts. These old masters of grammar knew how to define phenomena with the highest degree of brevity and precision, almost mathematically. (Indeed they were strikingly anti-historical with respect to both linguistic interest and working procedure: they were reliable and precise only when approaching language on the field of synchrony.) For such a sense of exact method in analysis they are highly appreciated today by many modern linguists as the most remote forerunners of our present, structural and mathematical age in linguistics.

17. Interest in language appeared in Indian society some centuries before our era, in direct connection with the general social and cultural atmosphere prevailing there. In this society, divided as it was into castes, attention was early devoted to the language which expressed the culture of the highest, privileged class. In order to ensure the purity of this language, grammatical schools were established with the intention of providing a well-trained staff of grammarians able to observe and describe linguistic facts adequately. The roots of such grammatical work stretch far back into antiquity, but its traditions are still alive today.

References to the Indians' interest in grammar can be found even in their own ancient literature. In the so-called third group of Vedic texts some linguistic questions are discussed. Proof of a firmly established grammatical tradition is also afforded by the most reliable of witnesses – Pāṇini, who mentioned the names of a number of his predecessors. But it is his own work which shows more strikingly than anything else that he had a wonderful background of knowledge about language which enabled him to demonstrate his unique linguistic talent to the world.

18. Pāṇini[1] set himself the task of fixing the norms of classical Sanskrit,[2] the language which had long been famous as the means of expression of Indian culture at its best and richest.

Pāṇini's Sanskrit grammar has already been appropriately described by Bloomfield (see below § 325) as "one of the greatest monuments of human intelligence".[3] The feeling of this ancient Hindu in evaluating, describing and formulating things was truly amazing. His definitions are almost formulae, short and simple in a way only possible when perfectly lucid judgment rests on a firm basis of exactitude in observing facts. Pāṇini has described classical Sanskrit in 4,000 such definition-formulae. Undoubtedly he was fully aware that language is a system. He was even familiar with the concept which is today called zero-morpheme (for the term *morpheme* see below § 334). The linguistic scholars of our age, for their part, had to make considerable efforts in order to acquire their knowledge of the principles of morphophonemics (see below § 298). However for Pāṇini it was quite easy to penetrate into the secret of sound alternations used to denote differences in the grammatical meaning of linguistic forms. He was as unmistakably correct in observing morphophonemic phenomena as though his theoretical horizons had been shaped under the influence of structural linguistics in the twentieth century.

19. The impressive achievements of the Indians in the field of linguistic research did not end with Pāṇini. His heritage fell to descendants who were gifted enough not only to preserve it, but also to develop it further. Among many eminent grammarians, two deserve special mention: Patañjali (second century B.C.)

---

[1] It is not known for certain when Pāṇini lived. It is thought that it must have been some time at the beginning of the fourth century B.C.
[2] Sanskrit (*saṃskṛtá-*) means "language which has achieved perfection".
[3] L. Bloomfield, *Language* (New York, 1933), p. 11.

and Bhartṛhari (seventh century A.D.), much later in time but closely akin to Patañjali as regards the spirit of his work. They were both representatives of the grammatical school which constructed a theory of the permanent, unchangeable substratum of all the spoken variants of a particular language system. When applied to sounds, it refers to what has been called the *phoneme* in the present century, i.e. the invariant (not subject to the variations of individual pronunciation) sound value which exists as the unit of a particular language system and serves to mark the differences in the meanings of words.

20. The tasks of Indian grammar included the determination of the numerical relationships between the various words and syllables in a text. It is only in our days that the statistical method has been unanimously recognized as highly useful in linguistic research and has attained wide application.

21. The ancient Indians also occupied themselves with phonetic descriptions. They were among the first in the world (together with some other eastern nations, primarily the Chinese) who devoted the requisite attention to articulatory elements in describing sounds. Nor did they show themselves inferior as lexicographers. They were least successful in their etymological work. Untrained in historical grammar and synchronists by tradition, they were unable to penetrate all the evolutionary factors under the influence of which the constitution of actual word units took place.

22. The grammatical achievements of the ancient Indians remained unknown to the world beyond their borders. Centuries were to pass before Europeans became aware of all the wonderful linguistic work the Indians had done so long ago. In their isolation they missed the rare fame (so nearly within their grasp!) of being the immediate inspiration of what were later to be the greatest achievements in linguistics.

BIBLIOGRAPHICAL REFERENCES

23. For basic information, see Bloomfield, *Language*, the chapter

"The Study of Language", and Zvegincev, *Istorija jazykoznanija*, I, pp. 5-9, which is rather more detailed.

See also the following more specialized studies: John Brough, "Theories of General Linguistics in the Sanskrit Grammarians", *Transactions of the Philological Society* (1951), pp. 27-46; W. S. Allen, *Phonetics in Ancient India* (= *London Oriental Series*, 1,) (London, Oxford Univ. Press, 1953), pp. 1-96. See also O. Böhtlingk, *Pāṇinis Grammatik* (Leipzig, 1887, second ed.).

4

FROM THE DAYS OF THE ROMAN EMPIRE
TO THE END OF THE RENAISSANCE

24. The Romans followed faithfully in the footsteps of the Greeks, particularly the Alexandrians, in their language investigations. In the first century B.C. the grammarian Varro wrote a grammar of the Latin language, *De lingua latina*, highly esteemed both in his own time and later (in this book special attention was paid to morphology). His grammar served as a model for many generations of medieval specialists in language who worked diligently on the study of Latin – the language of their culture.

25. In the first century A.D. there are references to the names of several individuals who worked successfully on problems of Latin grammar (e.g. Remmius Palaemon, by origin a Greek). The most famous grammarians appeared somewhat later: Donatus, in the fourth century (author of *Ars grammatica*) and Priscian in the sixth (author of *Institutiones grammaticae*, who developed the ideas of Apollonius Dyskolus and exercized a great influence on the grammatical conceptions of his contemporaries).

26. At the end of the fourth century the efforts of grammarians were mainly concentrated on studying Latin orthoepy and prosody. As a rule there were no original viewpoints regarding language, nor was there any wider linguistic interest.[1] From the sixth century onwards (thanks to Priscian) new fields of language problems were approached: several studies were devoted to sounds (this section of grammar was called "De voce" or "Ortographia"); the phenomenon of the syllable was explained ("De syllaba" or "Prosodia"); words

---

[1] The Church Father St. Augustine (d. 430 A.D.) expounded some challenging ideas concerning the relationship between sound form and meaning in his *Principia dialecticae*. However they attracted relatively little attention at the time.

were classified as parts of speech ("De partibus orationis") and the first attempts were made to grapple with syntax ("Oratio", "Syntaxis"). It was not until the thirteenth century[2] that the inventory of both linguistic knowledge and interest became truly richer: the principles of word building were indicated, a start was made on describing the use of cases and the principles of congruency, and basic information was given as to what constitutes a unit of verse. By the end of the Middle Ages the elementary concepts concerning some basic grammatical phenomena were for the most part determined (for example a clear distinction was made between nouns and adjectives, the importance of the verb head for determining the case meaning of the subordinated noun was pointed out; the grammatical category called apposition was defined, etc.).

27. The linguistic theories of the Middle Ages acquired an interpretation which corresponded to the general cultural and philosophic thought of that age: the scholastic philosophers saw in the phenomenon of language first and foremost a direct manifestation of logical argument.

The famous Abailard (1079-1142), for example, declared himself in favour of the application of scholastic logic to grammar. In the eleventh century the scholastic school of Michael Psellos won considerable fame, and even exercised an influence on subsequent generations. The scholastic spirit in medieval grammar reached its culmination in the ideas of Raymond Lulle (1235-1315). Lulle considered that it would be useful to compose a universal philosophical language based on Latin, but so elaborated that the combination of linguistic elements would reflect to the highest possible degree the application of the principles of logic (in this Lulle was to some extent the forerunner of the present-day scholars who are working on the construction of metalanguage, see below § 388). The logical spirit in linguistic investigation remained characteristic above all of French grammarians, not only throughout the Middle Ages but also later (see the Port-Royal school, below § 38).

28. Some interesting observations on language were made in the

---

[2] In 1199 there appeared Alexander de Villa Dei's Latin grammar, which was well elaborated and very practical (this grammar was written in verse!).

Middle Ages, but they remained side issues, without significance for the development of linguistic studies. For example the philosopher Thomas Aquinas (1225-1274) came to the following conclusion: sounds exist in order to designate something (principaliter data ad significandum); if they have no connection with meaning, sounds are artificial human creations (significantia artificialiter) which have no purpose. These ideas which sound strangely modern (almost phonological; for phonology see below § 270), in fact fell on deaf ears and met with no response.

29. In the Middle Ages linguistic studies also flourished in communities where Indoeuropean languages were not spoken – among the Arabs and Jews, representatives of the Semitic language group.

30. The powerful medieval Arab states included heterogeneous national elements. With a truly amazing eclecticism, the Arabs selected the cultural achievements of the peoples they had conquered, and on the basis of these began to construct a culture of their own. They took their grammatical tradition from the Greeks. However since the language of the Arabs was of a quite different type from that of the Greeks, their grammatical investigations had to be conducted in a special way.

31. Here the immediate motive behind linguistic research was a practical one: the need to study the *Koran*, the "holy book of a holy religion". Tradition forbade the text of the *Koran* to be translated or changed. Thus it had to be studied in Arabic (which was particularly hard for those of the "faithful" whose mother tongue was not Arabic). The purity of the language of the *Koran* was the concern of language specialists. Grammatical schools sprang up to train young men in language problems (the most famous were the schools at Basra and Kufi in Mesopotamia).

32. The Arab grammarians were among the first to indicate the importance of detecting the connection between the actual syntactic function and the given form of a language unit. They paid special attention to the study of sounds (the words of the *Koran* had to be correctly pronounced!), taking into account both physiological and acoustic elements.

The Arab grammatical system was set out in the book *Al Kitab*, written by Sibawajhi of Basra (Kitāb Sībawaih). Both the writer and the book had a wide fame in their time.

33. The Arabs were renowned as lexicographers.[3] References to many diligent workers in this field have come down to us, most especially to Fīrūzābādy (1329-1414) who, according to tradition, wrote about a hundred volumes of dictionaries (a dictionary was called *Al-qāmūs*, which means approximately: a boundless ocean of words).

The type of this lexicographical work was largely determined by the social and cultural customs prevailing in the Arab states. There every individual, whatever his social position, could retain the dialectal features of his mother tongue without any fear for his personal reputation: the important thing was that he should also know the language of the *Koran* and be able to read it correctly. Hence the vocabulary of Arabic was enriched by the intensive and uncontrolled acquisition of a variety of lexemes which were used side by side, introduced from the different regions where Arabic was spoken. Lexicographers zealously noted these synonyms, without observing the differences in their origin, stylistic value, or the epoch in which they had arisen. In fact words from different dialects and periods, poetic neologisms as well as standard expressions, were all treated at the same level, without any sense of perspective.

34. The Arab states included many Jewish inhabitants. Hebrew, the language of the Jews, was related to Arabic. The Jews had noted this affinity as early as the tenth and eleventh centuries. As a result of comparing Hebrew not only with Arabic but also with Aramaic, they had come to the conclusion that these three languages had quite a lot in common. Thus the Jews have the credit of being the pioneers of comparative studies of language, although it was not until much later that their work acquired wide publicity in Europe; hence it had no immediate influence on the development of linguistic thought elsewhere.

---

[3]   The Chinese had also been excellent lexicographers for a very long time. But their work remained unknown to European linguists, so that it had no direct influence on the development of world linguistics.

The Jews took their methods of linguistic analysis from the Arabs, applying them to the language of the Bible.

35. It was only during the Renaissance that European grammarians gained a closer acquaintance with the tradition of linguistic research which had developed in the Semitic world. The concept of the *root* of a word was taken from this tradition into Indoeuropean grammar.

36. The interest in language during the period of the Renaissance was predominantly philological: Latin and Greek texts were intensively studied. It was only during the later part of the Renaissance that people began to study Hebrew and Arabic (especially Hebrew, which was regarded as the oldest language – in connection with the Biblical story of Noah and the Flood). Etymological studies were also in vogue at that time.

A number of original and inspiring ideas were already advanced then, but they remained without direct consequence for the general trend of linguistic thought. The sixteenth-century Italian Claudio Tolomei was, for example, the first grammarian to direct his attention to the consistency of the laws governing the change of language sounds. He was able to point out the development of the Latin *pl* into the Italian (Tuscan) *pi* – by comparing such examples as Ital. *pieno*: Latin *plenus*, Ital. *più*: Latin *plus* etc. Unfortunately he had no immediate successor in these investigations.

BIBLIOGRAPHICAL REFERENCES

37. As an introduction, see Bloomfield, *Language*, the section "The Study of Language"; Zvegincev, *Istorija jazykoznanija*, I, pp. 14-20. For more detailed information see Arens, *Sprachwissenschaft*, pp. 28-54. See also R. H. Robins, *Ancient and Medieval Grammatical Theory in Europe...* (see above § 15); Jean Collart, *Varron grammairien latin* (Paris, 1954); Louis Kukenheim, *Contributions à l'histoire de la grammaire grecque, latine et hebraïque à l'époque de la Renaissance* (Leiden, 1951).

5

FROM THE RENAISSANCE TO THE END
OF THE EIGHTEENTH CENTURY

38. The grammatical tradition of the seventeenth and eighteenth centuries was permeated by the heritage of the past. For instance the logical conception of language long remained the basic theoretical support of grammar, especially among French grammarians (who were held in high repute by their contemporaries). They were most worthily represented by the works of the grammatical centre at Port Royal. It was this centre which produced in 1600 the famous *Grammaire génerale et raisonnée* (by Cl. Lancelot and A. Arnauld). In this book the basic principle of the "Port Royalists" was very strikingly expressed: grammatical norms should conform as far as possible to the demands of logic; logic is single, universal, and common to all mankind; thus it is possible to construct a universal grammatical theory which would suit the essence of all the languages in the world. These ideas had many repercussions.[1] It was then, in fact that the rich tradition of normative grammar was initiated in almost the whole of Europe.

39. Even before the end of the Renaissance there appeared in some European centres an interest in studying texts which were not written in Latin or Greek but in some other Indoeuropean language (as the end of the eighteenth century approached this interest became much stronger). Franciscus Junius (1589-1677) was noted for his researches connected with Germanic languages (first of all

---

[1] The Port Royal grammar served as a model in the eighteenth century for the creation of "philosophical grammars" (i.e. universal grammars composed according to general logical principles). One of these was a work written by the Englishman James Harris: *Hermes or a Philosophical Inquiry Concerning Language and Universal Grammar* (published in 1751) which was extremely popular with the writer's contemporaries (it went through five editions in England by 1794, and was translated into German in 1788 and into French in 1796).

English, then the Scandinavian languages, Frisian, Dutch and Gothic). He was followed by George Hickes (1642-1715) who published a Gothic and Anglo-Saxon grammar[2] and a variety of information available at that time on English and related languages.

However it was not until the eighteenth century that the philological examination of texts acquired a serious methodological elaboration (the same method also began to be applied successfully in other fields – in the history of literature and the study of national customs).

40. In the eighteenth century normative grammar was definitely set on a theoretical basis which had its roots in the conception of linguistic stagnation: it was considered that grammarians were to blame for the changes suffered by the Latin language in the course of time – thanks to their lack of vigilance unlearned people had succeeded in spoiling the language (otherwise, left to itself, the language would not have changed).

41. The philosophical ideas of the eighteenth century influenced linguistic investigations considerably. The French rationalism of the time of the encyclopaedists (1751-1777) favoured a logical approach to linguistic facts and supported the tendency towards the universalization of grammar. The influence of the seventeenth-century English philosophers, the empiricists and inductivists, the psychologists and the pragmatists, showed itself in an interest in the spoken language among English grammarians (which was something quite new in the history of linguistic studies).

42. The eighteenth century was a period of intensive reflection about the origin of language (the hypothesis about Hebrew being the oldest language of mankind after the Flood, see above § 36, and many other equally arbitrary theories had existed much earlier than the eighteenth century).[3] It was then, for the most part, that knowledge of the diversity of linguistic structure began to be more widespread.

[2]   Under the title *Institutiones gramaticae anglo-saxonicae et moeso-goticae* (Oxford, 1689).
[3]   The Fleming Goropius Beccanus (sixteenth century) was led by the fervour of his patriotism to express the belief that all the languages of the world had developed from Flemish.

43. As early as the sixteenth century the first primitive descriptions of some American and Philipine languages began to percolate into Europe (from reports sent by Spanish missionaries). By the end of the eighteenth century the existence of about 200 languages was already known[4] and by the first decade of the nineteenth century the figure had reached about 500.[5]

44. The most important discovery, however, was not connected with any "exotic" non-Indoeuropean language. It was the discovery by the scholarly public of Europe of a hitherto unknown Indoeuropean language, Sanskrit.

The first great Sanskritologist was an Englishman, William Jones (1746-1794) who asserted that Sanskrit, Greek, Latin, Gothic and, probably, Celtic were closely related and had sprung from a common language now no longer in existence. This assertion of his did not immediately give rise to the epoch of comparative linguistics; this came somewhat later (see below § 53). Nevertheless Jones' theory prepared the ground of linguistic thought for the beginning of comparative linguistic studies.

45. At the end of the eighteenth century, the comparative study of the Finno-Ugric group of languages had already begun (mainly thanks to the services of the Hungarian linguist S. Gyarmathi).[6]

BIBLIOGRAPHICAL REFERENCES

46. Sources of basic information: Bloomfield, *Language*, the section "The Study of Language"; Zvegincev, *Istorija jazykoznanija*, I, pp. 21-24. More details may be found in Arens, *Sprachwissenschaft*,

---

[4]   At the instigation of the philosopher Leibniz and under the protection of the Russian empress Catherine II, P. S. Pallas (in the period between 1787 and 1789) published in St. Petersburg a kind of dictionary containing 285 words in 200 different languages from Europe and Asia, under the title *Linguarum totius orbis vocabularia comparativa Augustissimae cura collecta*. The second edition of this dictionary, which was enlarged (1790-91) by the Serb Teodor Janković-Mirijevski, included 80 more languages (some from Africa and America).
[5]   The time of the publication of Adelung's dictionary, see below § 50.
[6]   S. Gyarmathi, *Affinitas linguae hungaricae cum linguis fennicae originis grammatice demonstrata* (Göttingen, 1799).

pp. 58-132. See also Ernst Cassirer *The Philosophy of Symbolic Forms* (see above § 15), the sections: "The Position of the Problem of Language in the System of Empiricism...." (pp. 133-139) and "The Philosophy of French Enlightenment..." (pp. 139-147); P. Kuehner, *Theories on the Origin and Formation of Language in the Eighteenth Century in France* (Philadelphia, Univ. of Pennsylvania Press, 1944); G. G. Harnois, *Les Théories du langage en France de 1660 à 1821* (Paris, 1929); Otto Funke, *Studien zur Geschichte der Sprachphilosophie* (Berne, 1928) (Part I: "Zur Sprachphilosophie des 18 Jahrhunderts: J. Harris Hermes").

LINGUISTIC RESEARCH
IN THE NINETEENTH CENTURY

6

INTRODUCTION

47. Already at the beginning of the nineteenth century linguistic research was primarily concerned with concrete language data, and this vivid interest in concrete facts remained a striking characteristic of nineteenth century linguistics in general. It yielded a break with the eighteenth-century traditions of searching for universal, logical structures in language.

48. As early as the first decades of the nineteenth century, historicism began to develop in the investigation of language.[1] In the seventies and eighties (the era of the neo-grammarians) all linguistic work was primarily based on the conviction (explicitly formulated by Hermann Paul, the greatest theoretician among the neo-grammarians), that there could be no linguistics without historicism (see below § 98).

49. The discovery of Sanskrit[2] was a very important event for the advancement of linguistic studies. Sanskrit differed considerably from Latin and Greek (on which linguistic concepts had hitherto been founded). The knowledge of it gave rise to new views on linguistic phenomena, provided scholars with new problems, and led to the creation of a new discipline – comparative grammar.

In the first decades of nineteenth century linguistics was marked by intensive and successful comparative studies. The comparativists

[1] This referred primarily and most of all to studies of the Romance languages: the knowledge of Latin, from which the Romance languages had developed, gave exceptional opportunities for bringing to light historical perspective. As regards the interest in national languages, it was first awakened in Germany during the epoch of Romanticism.
[2] Although W. Jones had called attention to the importance of studying Sanskrit as early as 1786 (see above § 44), the linguistic public of Europe came into direct contact with this language much later, thanks to the services of F. Bopp, see below § 53.

of that epoch investigated primarily the Indoeuropean linguistic family. They were less interested in the affinities of other language groups (Semitic, Hamitic, Ugrian and Altaic) though these groups were also quite well-known at that time. In fact it was not until the end of the nineteenth century that the study of non-Indoeuropean linguistic problems was first approached seriously (for example Semitic linguistic studies began to flourish at that time, after the deciphering of Assyrian texts). The first comparativists, like Schleicher and his school (see below § 60) included theoreticians whose linguistic conceptions directly reflected the current trends of scholarly thought.

50. Europe in the nineteenth century was strewn with linguistic information from widely differing parts of the world. This was the time of the European expansion into other continents, which inevitably brought with it new fields of linguistic knowledge. Already in the first two decades of the century Adelung's dictionary[3] had aroused interest in hitherto unknown types of language, and had stimulated some individuals to reflect on general linguistic problems. One of the most gifted theoreticians in linguistics, the great W. von Humboldt (see below § 68) was directly inspired by his knowledge of non-Indoeuropean linguistic structures.

51. While the eighteenth century had been dominated by a logical conception of language, the linguistic theory of the nineteenth century was primarily characterized by the introduction of psychological criteria. "Psychologism" in linguistics already had its eminent champions in the fifties and sixties (see below § 80); their

---

[3] This dictionary (published by Johann Christoph Adelung in collaboration with other linguists, most of all Vater, but also Humboldt) was entitled *Mithridates oder Allgemeine Sprachenkunde, mit dem Vater unser als Sprachprobe in beinahe fünfhundert Sprachen und Mundarten.* It was printed in Berlin: the first volume in 1806, the second in 1809, the third 1812-1816 and the fourth in 1817. The dictionary contained a survey of all the languages in the world then known, together with indications of their structures and affinities and references to many earlier linguistic works. The languages were classified geographically. Although the affinities between Persian and German and Latin and Greek were pointed out, a firm conception of the unity of the Indoeuropean linguistic family is lacking. But with all its faults, in its day Adelung's dictionary contributed to the broadening of scientific horizons.

works decisively influenced the formation of the basic linguistic conceptions of many generations.

52. However the most important epoch came only towards the end of the century, in the seventies, when the neo-grammarians took the lead in linguistic studies (see below § 93). Then the comparative-historical method acquired its fully systematic and rigorous character and its theoretical foundations. The neo-grammarians left behind them serious works. Their achievements can be expanded and corrected; but the fact remains that they contain a basic fund of competently collected knowledge relating to the history of Indoeuropean languages, and this gives them an indisputable value.

7

THE EPOCH OF THE FIRST COMPARATIVISTS

53. The German Franz Bopp (1791-1867) is considered the founder of comparative grammar. The year 1816, when Bopp presented the linguistic public with language material from Sanskrit compared with some other Indoeuropean languages,[1] remains a historical date in linguistics: this was the beginning not only of the comparative epoch in language studies, but of linguistics itself as an organized, independent scientific discipline.

Sanskrit and its affinity with other Indoeuropean languages was known before Bopp's time: W. Jones had spoken of this in the eighteenth century (see above § 44). However Bop was the first to realize that the question of the mutual relations of Indoeuropean languages could become the subject of special studies, and this is his greatest merit.

54. It was the absence of this conception that deprived the Danish scholar Rasmus Kristian Rask (1787-1832) of Bopp's fame, although Rask worked on the comparative analysis of languages at about the same time as Bopp, even somewhat earlier.[2]

---

[1] In the study: *Über das Conjugationssystem der Sanskritsprache in Vergleichung mit jenen der griechischen, lateinischen, persischen und germanischen Sprache.* However Bopp's most important work is usually considered to be a book published in three volumes (between 1833 and 1852) with the title: *Vergleichende Grammatik des Sanskrit, Zend, Armenischen, Griechischen, Lateinischen, Litauischen, Altslavischen, Gotischen und Deutschen.* This book is regarded as the first textbook of comparative grammar.

[2] Rask had a knowledge of many languages. Among other things he was the author of a notable work on the Finno-Ugrian language group. His study of the Old Icelandic language *Undersøgelse om det gamle Nordiske eller Islandske Sprogs Oprindelse* (published in 1818), was especially significant. Here, for example, Rask showed that there was a consistent relationship between the sounds of Germanic words and those of the corresponding words in other Indoeuropean languages (for instance the Germanic *f* corresponds to the Latin *p* –

Since on many occasions he strongly insisted on the application of historical criteria in linguistic research, many people consider Rask the founder of *diachronic* (= historical) linguistics.

55. The epoch of the first comparativists is marked by many distinguished names. Jakob Grimm (1785-1863), the author of the work *German Grammar*,[3] is recognized as the founder of German linguistics. Actually in this work Grimm treats not only problems connected with the German language, but gives a comparative survey of the grammatical characteristics of the whole of the German linguistic group (the Gothic, German, Dutch, English, Frisian and Scandinavian languages). In the second edition of the first volume (1822) Grimm also included a systematic survey of the relationships between Germanic consonants and the corresponding ones in other Indoeuropean languages, and established the existence of fixed rules governing these relationships (known in linguistics under the name of *Grimm's law*).[4]

56. George Curtius (1820-1885), the author of the work *Grundzüge der griechischen Etymologie* (1858-1862), introduced the comparative method into classical philology. Johann Kaspar Zeuss (1806-1856) laid the foundation of Celtic studies by the publication of his *Grammatica Celtica* (1853). Romance studies were placed on a firm basis by Friedrich Diez (1794-1876); his work *Grammatik der romanischen Sprachen* (published between 1836 and 1844) made a considerable contribution to the development of

---

father/pater). The second part of this study (which enjoyed a wide popularity in the German translation of the linguist Vater) was entitled *Über die Thrakische Sprachklasse* (Halle, 1822). There the author indicates the connections between Germanic languages, Greek, Latin and the Baltic and Slavonic languages (Sanskrit is not considered). Although he insists on the affinities between these languages, Rask nevertheless lacked a sufficiently clear concept of the Indoeuropean family of languages.

[3] *Deutsche Grammatik* (first volume 1819, revised edition 1822; second volume 1826, third volume 1831, fourth 1837); this work embraces all fields of grammar except syntax.

[4] Latin: *p, t, k* correspond to Gothic *f, þ, h*; Greek θ, ϑ, χ – Gothic: *b, d, g*; Latin: *b, d, g* – Gothic *p, t, k* (e.g. Latin *caput*, Goth. *haubiþ*). Grimm's law is not always valid, particularly in the case of consonants in word-medial position. Later Grimm's law was completed by Verner (see below § 97).

historical perspective in linguistic studies. The first comparative investigations of the Slavic languages were achieved by the Czech J. Dobrovský (1753-1829), and the first systematic work on the sound system of Slavic was written by the Russian A. X. Vostokov. His book on Slavic phonetics (indeed the first book of its kind dealing with one of the Indoeuropean languages) was published in 1820 under the title *Rassuždenie o slavjanskom jazyke*. The work of the Slovenian Franz Miklosich (1813-1891) *Vergleichende Grammatik der Slavischen Sprachen* was of special significance for the development of Slavonic linguistic studies. It was published in the period between 1852 and 1875; the fourth and last volume deals with syntax and is still in use as a valuable collection of material.

57. Friedrich Pott (1802-1887) is considered the founder of serious etymological studies. He explained that etymological investigation should be concerned with a search for the older aspects of language data, but not for the original form and meaning of actual words (which was the subject of etymological studies in the days of antiquity); the works published by him between 1833 1836 initiated the successful growth of such a special branch of linguistic research.

58. The early comparativists were not only the pioneers of serious methods in linguistic analysis. They also provided detailed information on various Indoeuropean languages, and for the first time estimated the data collected from a comparative standpoint. They were the first linguistic scholars to devote special attention to the elaboration of a general linguistic theory (see August Schleicher and his followers, below § 60.

BIBLIOGRAPHICAL REFERENCES

59. Theodor Benfey, *Geschichte der Sprachwissenschaft und Philologie in Deutschland* (Munich, 1869); *Geschichte der indogermanischen Sprachwissenschaft seit ihrer Begründung durch F. Bopp* (written by a number of authors, under the leadership of W. Streit-

berg, Leipzig, 1916; an edition of the famous collection founded by K. Brugmann and A. Thumb: *Grundriss der indogermanischen Sprach- und Altertumskunde*); B. Delbrück, *Einleitung in das Sprachstudium*[5] (Leipzig, 1908); V. Thomsen, *Sprogvidenskabens Historie* (Copenhagen, 1902). German transl. by H. Pollak, *Geschichte der Sprachwissenschaft bis zum Ausgang des 19 Jahrhunderts* (Halle, 1927); H. Pedersen, *Sprogvidenskaben i det Nittende Aarhundrede: Metoder og Resultater* (Copenhagen, 1924). English transl. by John Webster Spargo, *The Discovery of Language: Linguistic Science in the Nineteenth Century* (Cambridge Mass., 1931; last edition 1962); Iorgu Jordan, *An Introduction to Romance Linguistics*, transl. John Orr (London, 1937); A. Meillet, *Introduction à l'étude comparative des langues indo-européennes*[3] (Paris, 1912); A. Meillet, *La méthode comparative en linguistique historique* (Oslo, 1925).

A clear exposition of the basic facts is given in the following books: Zvegincev, *Istorija jazykoznanija*, I, pp. 25-27; Bloomfield, *Language*, pp. 14-16.

A survey of the early results achieved in the field of comparative linguistic studies is given by A. Schleicher in *Compendium der vergleichenden Grammatik der indogermanischen Sprachen* (Weimar, 1861).

8

THE BIOLOGICAL NATURALISM OF
AUGUST SCHLEICHER

60. About the middle of the nineteenth century, an important event took place in the field of biological sciences: Darwin presented his challenging exposition of the theory of the evolution of the species. Darwin's views exercised a tremendous influence on his contemporaries. Many people became convinced that the principles of evolution laid down by Darwin for living creatures should also be brought to light in other forms of human activity, since they were universal. This conception was applied to linguistics by the Geerman August Schleicher, professor of Jena University.

61. Schleicher, an outstanding comparativist, was interested in problems connected with the reconstruction of the Indoeuropean parent language.[1] His method grew out of his conception that language was a living organism, independent of man, whose line of development was determined by the general biological laws of evolution: a language is born, lives for a certain time, gives life to another, younger language which in time replaces it, in its turn to be continued by one of its own offshoots; thus language, like man, has a "genealogical tree", i.e. a common ancestor from which numerous related progeny have developed as branches of the tree (hence Schleicher's theory is called the theory of biological naturalism in linguistics, and is known under the name of the "Stammbaum", or "pedigree" theory).

62. For Schleicher, language was thought expressed in sounds: there could be no language without thought, or thought without language. The meaning of a word lies in its roots, and can always be discovered.

[1] See: A. Schleicher, "Eine Fabel in indogermanischer Ursprache", *Beiträge zur vergl. Sprachforschung*, Bd. 5 (1868), p. 206.

63. Language is a natural organism, and in principle its development has the same forms that we find elsewhere in nature. There are three basic language types: *radical languages* (such as Chinese, where both grammatical relationships and syntactical functions are indicated predominantly or consistently by word order), *agglutinative* (e.g. Hungarian, where grammatical relationships are indicated by various linguistic elements which combine into a single word, and which always have a distinct, fixed meaning and an independent identity), *amalgamating flexional* (e.g. Latin, where the changes of grammatical meaning are indicated by linguistic elements which are additional to the root and which fuse with it but have no independent identity). According to Schleicher these three types stand in direct dependence to the degree of development achieved, and directly correspond (in the same order) to the basic forms of the created world: crystal, plants and animals.[2]

64. Schleicher's theory received considerable attention from his contemporaries, though it aroused critical comments. One of the first to have doubts about Schleicher's "family tree of languages" and to break through the whole theory was his pupil Johannes Schmidt (1843-1901).[3]

Schmidt asserted that linguistic innovations spring up in one speech environment, but do not spread to others, as envisaged by Schleicher, in the form of branches; on the contrary, their progress is similar to the impact of a wave; sometimes larger and sometimes smaller speech communities are caught by them, which is a matter of chance.[4] Hence three adjacent speech communities will never know an absolutely identical or absolutely different inventory of linguistic characteristics: a newly risen feature will in one case cross

---

[2] A similarly naïve though differently formulated conception of "stages" in linguistic development was advocated in the twentieth century by the Soviet linguist Marr, see below § 200.

[3] See J. Schmidt, *Die Verwandtschaftsverhältnisse der indogermanischen Sprachen* (Weimar, 1872).

[4] H. Schuchardt (see below § 108) had similar ideas about the spread of linguistic innovations, see his studies *Der Vokalismus des Vulgärlateins* (Leipzig, 1866-67) and *Über die Klassifikation der romanischen Mundarten* (Graz, 1900) (later reprinted in Schuchardt-Brevier, see below § 113). Nevertheless it was Schmidt who fully worked out and established the "theory of waves".

the boundary of community A and embrace that of community B; in another case it will embrace C, and in a third B and C, while in the fourth case the innovation will not go beyond the boundaries of community A. (In a detailed exposition of his ideas Schmidt made use of a diagram of concentric circles; because of his "waves", the theory itself became known in scholarly circles as the *theory of waves*.) In order to illustrate his conceptions Schmidt pointed out several *isoglosses* (= the limits of the extension of a linguistic characteristic), on the basis of which the Germanic and Balto-Slavonic language groups on the one hand, and Greek and Sanskrit on the other, are joined into a single family. In both cases Schmidt's isoglosses cut across the line which divides Indoeuropean languages into two main groups, the "centum" and "satem" groups. Modern dialectological research has provided fresh confirmation of Schmidt's hypothesis.

65. Schleicher's ideas were advocated in a modified form by the Oxford professor Max Müller (1823-1900). Müller agreed with Schleicher that linguistics should be given a place among the natural sciences, since the past of languages should not be regarded as an historical event but as a spontaneous process of growth common to all natural phenomena. He also agreed with him in his determination of the relationship between language and thought: for Müller too language was the direct organ of human thought. However he diverged from Schleicher's conception at one point of vital importance: he did not bestow on language the property of a living, autonomous organism, but insisted that it was indissolubly connected with the human speech process (what has been said can never be repeated: the speech phenomenon dies at the very moment of utterance).

Müller performed valuable services in popularizing the ideas of biological naturalism among his contemporaries. His lectures in this field (*Lectures on the Science of Language*) delivered at Oxford between 1861 and 1863 were received with great interest (they went through several English editions and were also translated into other languages).

66. The adherents of this school estimated that the direct con-

nection between language and thought was most clearly manifested in the phenomenon of speech. Hence they turned their attention towards the problems of spoken language, which was a positive achievement.

Their idea that linguistic evolution was conditioned by natural laws and consequently not subject to the control of the human will was accepted by the most eminent representatives of nineteenth century linguistics – the neo-grammarians.

BIBLIOGRAPHICAL REFERENCES

67. See Schleicher's works: *Sprachvergleichende Untersuchungen*: *Zur vergleichenden Sprachgeschichte* (Bonn, 1848); *Linguistische Untersuchungen*: *Die Sprachen Europas in Systematischer Übersicht* (Bonn, 1850); *Die deutsche Sprache* (Bonn, 1859); *Compendium der vergleichenden Grammatik der indogermanischen Sprachen* (Weimar, 1861-1862); *Die Darwinische Theorie und die Sprachwissenschaft* (Weimar, 1863); *Über die Bedeutung der Sprache für die Naturgeschichte des Menschen* (Weimar, 1865). See also B. Delbrück, *Einleitung in das Sprachstudium* (see above § 59); V. Thomsen, *Geschichte der Sprachwissenschaft*...(see above § 59); A. V. Desnickaja, *Voprosy izučenija rodstva indoevropejskix jazykov* (Moscow-Leningrad, AN SSSR, 1955); V. Pisani, "August Schleicher und einige Richtungen der heutigen Sprachwissenschaft", *Lingua*, vol. IV, 4 (1954-55), pp. 337-368; A. S. Čikobava, *Problema jazyka kak predmeta jazykoznanija* (Moscow, 1959); Zvegincev, *Istorija jazykoznanija*, I, pp. 89-104.

9

"HUMBOLDTISM" IN LINGUISTICS
(THE "WELTANSCHAUUNG" THEORY)

68. The greatest linguistic theoretician of the nineteenth century was the German Wilhelm von Humboldt (1767-1835); he is regarded as the founder of *general linguistics* (= the discipline which examines the phenomenon of language in the light of data collected from a great variety of concrete languages).

69. W. von Humboldt was the first scholar to study an Indonesian language: the Kawi language from the island of Java.[1] This contact with linguistic properties so radically different from those characterizing Indoeuropean language structures enabled Humboldt to approach language and its rôle in the life of man from a quite new standpoint.

70. The originality of Humboldt's talent as a scholar was manifested both in his methods of research and in his theoretical views. The beginning of language investigation in the nineteenth century was as a rule marked by the illumination of linguistic facts from a historical perspective, and the search for the parent language of the great Indoeuropean family (see above § 49). However Humboldt did not insist on *diachrony* (= history of language). On the contrary; his attention was primarily concentrated on bringing to light linguistic data occurring in a given period of time, that is, on observing languages in their *synchronic* aspect (see below § 260). He carried out the comparison of languages analytically, without enter-

---

See W. von Humboldt, *Über die Kawi-Sprache auf der Insel Java* (Berlin, 1836-1839) (posthumus edition). Kawi is the Old Javanese language (it became extinct in the thirteenth century) in which the oldest Javanese texts were written (dating from the ninth century). The phonemic and morphological structure of this language had a pronounced Indonesian character, but its vocabulary obviously owed much to the influence of Sanskrit (which can be linked with the historical rôle of Indian culture in Javanese life).

ing into the question of genetic kinship. He did not concern himself with the reconstruction of the parent language. He did not even consider that Indoeuropean languages deserved more attention than other language families.

71. Humboldt expressed himself against universal grammar constructed according to the classic, scholastic mould, and emphasized that grammatical rules should be sought inductively, from the specific facts of each particular language. He defined language as a dynamic phenomenon (according to Greek terminology: language is *energeia* and not *ergon*) and insisted that the static aspect of language is only apparent. He laid special emphasis on the conection between language and thought: intellectual activity necessarily strives towards unification with the sound (= speech) phenomenon; without the association of thought and sounds the world of images cannot pass into the world of concepts; i.e. there can be no true thinking. With this was connected his theory of the *inner form* ("innere Form") of languages, which was later discussed by many eminent representatives of linguistic theory (particularly the adherents of "psychological linguistics", such as Marty, see below § 89): by the term *inner language form* should be understood the specific psychological structure of individual speakers, on which depends the actual organization of the sound and meaning aspects of their language.[2]

72. The problem of the relations between language structure and national mentality occupies a central position in Humboldt's linguistic theory. In his opinion, language is "a specific emanation of the spirit of a particular nation", the external expression of an "interior form" which reveals a particular view of the world ("Weltanschauung"; hence Humboldt's theory is usually called the "Weltanschauung" theory).

73. The stage of development of a language is directly related to the mentality, culture and general outlook of the people speaking

---

[2] Humboldt formulated his idea of "inner form" on a number of occasions, and not always in the same way, which later gave rise to misunderstandings. On this see: O. Funke, *Innere Sprachform. Eine Einführung in A. Martys Sprachphilosophie* (Reichenberg, 1924), pp. 111-113.

it. Hence the history of language must be closely connected with the history of national culture. Such a simplification of actual facts proceeded from Humboldt's failure to make an adequate distinction between those factors which influence the formation of vocabulary and phraseology and the specific conditions which regulate the development of phonemic and morphological phenomena.

74. Humboldt supported his theory that language is a characteristic emanation of the human spirit by recalling that people find it difficult to understand each other completely. In fact, he insisted, this is because their world views are not identical (today the term *the linguistic relativism of the Humboldt school* is used to denote that part of Humboldt's teaching which indicates the unreliability of language as a means of ensuring perfect mutual understanding).

75. In connection with his general conception of language, Humboldt expounded his thoughts on the evolution of language: every change in language takes place in harmony with the forward movement of the human spirit; in fact changes always lead to the one fundamental aim (Humboldt uses the term "Vollendung") of language as an instrument through which the human spirit expresses itself.

76. A great event in its time was Humboldt's lecture delivered on June 29, 1820 at the Berlin Academy of Sciences on the comparative study of languages with respect to the different phases of their development. Here Humboldt for the first time publicly expounded his main views on language. From then on Humboldt excercised a powerful influence on the linguistic views of many generations. His fullest exposition of his theory is in his study "Über die Verschiedenheit des menschlichen Sprachbaues und ihren Einfluss auf die geistige Entwicklung des Menschengeschlechts" (1830-1836; this was intended to be the introduction to a large work on the Kawi language, and was later published by the Berlin Academy in *W. von Humboldts gesammelte Schriften*, vol. VII).

77. Twentieth century linguists who support Humboldt's basic theoretical standpoints, above all his "Weltanschauung" theory, are called *neo-Humboldtians*. They are mostly lexicologists (such as

L. Weisgerber, J. Trier, G. Ipsen, F. Dornseif, A. Jolles, W. Porzig, W. von Wartburg, etc.).[3]

In American linguistics, ideas on language also connected with the problem of Weltanschauung have developed in the middle of the twentieth century independently of European Humboldtism, see below § 348.

BIBLIOGRAPHICAL REFERENCES

78. See A. Fr. Pott *Wilhelm von Humboldt und die Sprachwissenschaft* (Berlin, 1876); Otto Funke, *Studien zur Geschichte der Sprachphilosophie* (Berne, 1928) (Part II, under the title: "Zur Sprachphilosophie der Gegenwart", pp. 51-55); G. Ipsen, *Sprachphilosophie der Gegenwart* (Berlin, 1930).

Extracts from Humboldt's study *Über die Verschiedenheit....* (see above § 76) are given (in Russian) in V. A. Zvegincev, *Istorija jazykoznanija*, I, pp. 68-86.

Among the works of L. Weisgerber, the greatest popularizer of Humboldt's ideas, the following book is recommended: *Vom Weltbild der deutschen Sprache*[2] (Düsseldorf, 1953). Further information on Weisgerber's linguistic views is given by M. M. Guxman in the study: "Lingvističeskaja teorija L. Vejsgerbera" in the collection *Voprosy teorii jazyka v sovremennoj zarubežnoj lingvistike* (Moscow, AN SSSR, 1961, pp. 123-162).

For a closer acquaintance with the methods and basic theoretical standpoints of the neo-Humboldtians, see: W. von Wartburg, *Einführung in die Problematik und Methodik der Sprachwissenschaft* (Halle, 1943; French translation, 1946); W. Porzig, *Das Wunder der Sprache* (Berne, 1950).

See also: H. Basilius, "Neo-Humboldtian Ethno-linguistics", *Word*, 8 (1952), pp. 95-105.

---

[3] The most eminent representative of neo-Humboldtism is Leo Weisgerber (a bibliography of his works can be found in the collection published in honour of his sixtieth birthday under the title of *Sprache – Schlüssel zur Welt. Festschrift für L. Weisgerber*, Düsseldorf 1959).

10

PSYCHOLOGISM IN LINGUISTICS

79. Humboldt's teaching (above § 72) struck root in German linguistics. So H. Steinthal (1823-1899), the founder of linguistic psychologism, was indebted to Humboldt's theories for his basic linguistic training.

80. As regards Steinthal's knowledge of psychological phenomena, this was mainly founded on the views of the psychologist and pedagogue Herbart:[1] he adopted Herbart's ideas concerning the "associative" organization of the human spirit (i.e. thoughts, stimulated by an external impression, develop spontaneously in the human brain one after another: one thought arises from another, following subconscious associations). In his "psychological grammar": *Grammatik, Logik und Psychologie, ihre Principien und ihr Verhältniss zu einander* (Berlin, 1855) Steinthal strove to describe grammatical facts from a psychological point of view, at the same time subjecting the earlier conception of logical universalism in grammar to criticism. This work of Steinthal's was highly appreciated by his contemporaries, as was the book *Das Leben der Seele* (Berlin, 1855) written by M. Lazarus, a collaborator of Steinthal in the propagation of the psychological interpretation of the language phenomenon. However the most important landmark in the popularization of psychologism in linguistics was the foundation of the periodical *Zeitschrift für Völkerpsychologie und Sprachwissenschaft* (1860-1890) in which its founders, Steinthal and Lazarus, together with their disciples, had the leading say. The linguists connected with this periodical were also the faithful proponents of Humboldt's theory concerning the

---

[1] Johann Friedrich Herbart (1776-1841), best known as the founder of scientific pedagogy based on psychological studies.

relationship between language and national psychology (it was precisely at that time that the expression "Völkerpsychologie" became very popular among German intellectuals interested in questions of national culture).

81. While in principle adopting Humboldt's ideas on language, Steinthal extended their theoretical framework by also introducing the notion of the individual speech act into the field of scientific interest: if language is the organ through which the human spirit manifests itself, then the language of the whole speaking society is the expression of the collective psychology, just as the language of an individual is the expression of individual psychology. Steinthal also propounded the idea (later advocated by other linguists, notably those of Vossler's school, see below § 171) that the meanings of words are not rigidly determined: each individual, when he utters a word, stamps it with his own personal experience, his own individual psychology, so that words acquire their actual sense only at the moment when they are spoken.

82. Steinthal was the first to determine the framework of linguistic investigations explicitly in such a way that they would contribute to knowledge of "national psychology". These investigations were to be concerned not only with the history of actual languages but also with establishing their origin as well as the affinities and differences in their structures. In connection with this, work was begun on the first comprehensive descriptions of linguistic types (a fair number of non-Indoeuropean languages were already known at that time).[2] While working on the first classifications of known languages linguists were guided by Steinthal's psychological criteria: they tried to demonstrate that spiritual affinities between nations are shown by related forms of linguistic structure, and vice versa.

83. The founder of the first laboratory for experimental psychology, Wilhelm Wundt (1832-1920) was also interested in the problem of "national psychology". This German scholar, a

---

[2]   A survey of basic linguistic types was given by Steinthal in 1860 in his work: *Charackteristik der hauptsächlichsten Typen des Sprachbaues* (Berlin, 1860). This work was revised by Fr. Misteli and published (under the same title) in Berlin in 1893.

physician by training and a psychologist as regards his main interests and achievements, was the author of the first serious discussions on the psychological background of language.

84. Wundt's psychological orientation was different from that of Steinthal who was an "associationist" (a follower of Herbart, see above § 80). Wundt supported the "apperceptionalist" theory, according to which the human brain is established on impressions from the external world received through the senses, while language serves to express ideas determined in this way (i.e. by the sensory factor).[3]

85. Wundt did not believe that language expressed the "spirit of a nation" although he himself was strongly interested in the problem of national psychology. The particular psychology of a speaking society, Wundt insisted, was shaped by the type of collective life. In order to investigate this psychology, it was necessary to know about all the manifestations of this common life – the language of a nation, its customs, its ideology – in short, its culture in its entirety.

86. Wundt's classic work *Völkerpsychologie* was printed in ten volumes. The first two books, entitled *Die Sprache* (see below § 92) were devoted to linguistic problems. Here Wundt made a series of interesting observations (e.g. on the perception of speech, sentence constructions and the formation of complex sentences, etc.). His exposition of sound changes was particularly successful.[4]

87. Wundt's contemporaries the neo-grammarians showed a critical attitude towards the value of his works on language, and stressed that the psychological approach he advocated was of no

[3] Wundt propounded the distinction between elementary and complex psychological processes. Elementary processes are directly connected with physiological ones; they are, in fact, psychophysiological (Wundt's experimental research was actually concerned with such processes). Wundt regarded as complex processes those immediately connected with thought (emotions, ideologies, etc.) which could not for this reason be studied by experimental methods.

[4] In emphasizing that sound changes were primarily the result of particular psychological processes, Wundt explained, for example, the assimilation and dissimilation of sounds and threw light on the crucial rôle of associative impulses in such cases.

real significance for linguistic studies. In our day Wundt's work has been much more favourably estimated, especially by the neo-Humboldtians (see above § 77) and the representatives of anthropological linguistics (see below § 342). In the history of experimental psychology Wundt won a particularly distinguished place.[5]

88. All the other nineteenth-century scholars who were concerned with linguistic theory in general kept within the scope of psychological interpretations of language phenomena, though without insisting on "national psychology". One of these was the German Georg von der Gabelentz (1840-1893) who explicitly stated that there was no such thing as a primitive language, and that every language was complete in its own way (this is clearly expounded in his work *Die Sprachwissenschaft* see below § 92). Another was the Slavist A. A. Potebnja (1835-1891) who on a number of occasions pointed out the deep-seated connection between the organization of thinking and the structure of language, and to whom linguists are indebted for a series of valuable works on the meaning and use of grammatical categories in Russian (the most important are collected in the work *Iz zapisok po russkoj grammatike*, see below § 92).

89. During the last decades of the nineteenth and the beginning of the twentieth century A. Marty (1847-1914) developed his psychological "philosophy of language". Marty wished to construct general linguistic principles on a psychological foundation. He started from the assertion that the meaning of linguistic forms is concerned with ensuring both the expression of the psychological states of the speaker and the stimulation of appropriate reactions in the listener. Hence this falls within the field of psychological studies, Marty advanced the conclusion that a fundamental theory about language – a philosophy of language – must in the last resort be psychological. Although his theory was not accepted in its entirety, some of his ideas, which were often interesting and original,

---

[5]   The influence of his doctrines was felt not only in Europe but also in America. There his experimental psychology enjoyed a high reputation in the first decades of the twentieth century. The popularization of Wundt's ideas in the U.S.A. owed most to the American psychologist E. B. Titchener.

influenced the formation of the views on general linguistics current in the first decades of the twentieth century.

90. At the end of the nineteenth century a psychological orientation appeared in French linguistic circles, which reached its fullest extent at the beginning of the twentieth century (see below § 161). The end of the nineteenth century also saw the beginning of *semantic* studies (see below § 404) which grew up in the same atmosphere of interest in the relationship between the psychic world and linguistic forms.

91. The traditions of the psychological approach to language have been continued in the twentieth century by eminent linguistic theoreticians and semanticians (A. Gardiner, K. Bühler and others).

BIBLIOGRAPHICAL REFERENCES

92. Information about Steinthal and Wundt is given by Otto Funke in *Studien zur Geschichte der Sprachphilosophie*, pp. 55-57 (see above, § 78) and also in Arens, *Sprachwissenschaft* (about Steinthal, pp. 252-260 and Wundt, pp. 360-370). Data relating to the representatives of psychologism (primarily Steinthal, Wundt and Marty) can also be found in Čikobava's, *Problema jazyka kak predmeta jazykoznanija* (Moscow, 1959), pp. 21-31. See also Zvegincev, *Istorija jazykoznanija*, I, section IV, "Psyxologizm v jazykoznanii", pp. 105-107; extracts from works by Steinthal and Potebnja are appended.

See the above-mentioned works: H. Steinthal, *Grammatik, Logik und Psychologie, ihre Prinzipien und ihr Verhältniss zur einander* (Berlin, 1855), and Potebnja's *Iz zapisok po russkoj grammatike* (first two books published in 1888, the third in 1899 and the fourth in 1941) and Wundt's *Die Sprache* (Leipzig, first ed. 1900, third ed. 1912). For a closer acquaintance with the attitude of the neogrammarians to Wundt's doctrines see B. Delbrück, *Grundfragen der Sprachforschung mit Rücksicht auf W. Wundts Sprachpsychologie* (Strassburg, 1901); W. Wundt, *Sprachgeschichte und Sprachpsychologie, mit Rücksicht auf B. Delbrücks Grundfragen der Sprachforschung* (Leipzig, 1901).

See G. von der Gabelentz *Die Sprachwissenschaft* (Leipzig, 1891, 1901²); A. Marty, *Untersuchungen zur Grundlegung der allgemeinen Grammatik und Sprachphilosophie* (Halle, 1908) and *Gesammelte Schrifte* (Halle, I, 1916, II, 1, 1918, II, 2, 1920); Otto Funke, *Innere Sprachform*; *Eine Einführung in A. Martys Sprachphilosophie* (Reichenberg, 1924).

Psychological investigations have been continued in the twentieth century; in what aspect and with what results can be see from the following works: A. Gardiner, *The Theory of Speech and Language* (Oxford, 1932, 1951²); K. Bühler, *Sprachtheorie. Die Darstellungsfunktion der Sprache* (Jena, 1934); Otto Ernst, *Sprachwissenschaft und Philosophie* (Berlin, 1949); Fr. Kainz, *Psychologie der Sprache*, in four books (Vienna, 1951-1956).

11

THE NEO-GRAMMARIANS

93. In the seventies of the last century there appeared at Leipzig University (in Germany) a group of gifted and diligent linguists whose rôle in the development of linguistic studies has been exceptionally important. At first this group was known as the "Leipzig school". Today, however, the name *neo-grammarians* ("Junggrammatiker") is most widely known; it is applied not only to this group but to all later linguists with the same methodological conceptions. The name was coined when the Leipzig group, consisting of members of the young generation, was conducting a campaign against the conservative ideas of older linguists (who included some famous names; for example one of the strenuous opponents of the "young" group was Curtius, see above § 56). The older generation introduced the term "young" ("Junggrammatiker") in order to depreciate the real value of the newly established, antagonistic standpoint in linguistics. But the Leipzig group was pleased with this name, which evokes a new, fresh approach. So the name "Junggrammatiker" was readily accepted by both parties, and has remained to the present day as the symbol of a serious, diligent school which deserves an honourable place in the history of linguistics.

94. The greatest merit of the neo-grammarians was that they gave full rigour to the already established comparative-historical method. This was first achieved within the study of sound changes. Of course, regularities in sound changes had already been observed.[1] But no generation before them had explicitly insisted upon the absolute consistency of the rules governing the occurrence of pho-

[1] Schleicher, for example, spoke of the consistency of sound laws in *Die Darwinische Theorie* (Weimar, 1863).

netic phenomena: sounds change in accordance with fixed laws to which there are no exceptions; the exceptions arise subsequently by *analogy* (i.e. as a consequence of the intervention of psychological factors: the normal result of a sound change in a given linguistic form is eliminated under the influence of a related form subconsciously associated with the former, where, however, the change did not occur because the conditions for it were not fulfilled).

95. The slavist August Leskien (1840-1916) and the Indoeuropeanist Karl Brugmann (1849-1919) were the first scholars to state, with a specific neo-grammarian emphasis, the regularity displayed in the manifestation of phonetic laws. Leskien's work *Die Lautgesetze kennen keine Ausnahme* (1876) received wide attention. But the most significant event was the publication of the study *Morphologische Untersuchungen* by K. Brugmann and H. Osthoff (Leipzig, 1878); this was regarded as the manifesto of neo-grammarian ideology, the definitive foundation of the school.

96. The idea of consistent language laws, underlying the convictions of the neo-grammarians, together with the comparative-historical orientation of their linguistic interests, determined the basic form of their work on language: patiently and with minute attention to detail they examined every linguistic fact through all its evolutionary phases, carefully noting the laws operating at every stage, and trying to find a suitable explanation for every exception to the rules stated. They "atomized" language, so said new generations later as they abandoned the neo-grammarian tradition in linguistic methods and conceptions. Indeed it is true that in their enthusiasm for all linguistic details, even unimportant ones, the neo-grammarians frequently lost sight of the whole picture of the language structure, in which nothing exists for itself, but only in combination with other parts of the whole. But it is also true that their diligent work resulted in the accumulation of much knowledge of concrete linguistic facts, sufficient to provide a solid basis for the new theoretical viewpoints which grew up later.

97. It was only under the leadership of the neo-grammarians that comparative-historical studies acquired full rigour as regards their methodological approach. Some earlier interpretations of

linguistic facts were revised and expanded (for example Grimm's law).[2]

The reconstruction of the oldest phases of Indoeuropean languages was more firmly and comprehensively carried out, primarily thanks to the merits of K. Brugmann[3] (morphological and phonetic problems received the best treatment; the first large and classic work on syntax was written by B. Delbrück).[4] Considerable attention was also devoted to the history of living Indoeuropean languages.

98. The neo-grammarians occupied themselves with history of language, firmly convinced that historicism in scholarship provided the methodological approach best suited to the lofty aims of the scientific pursuit of knowledge. They emphasized this attitude on a

---

[2] Grimm's law (see above § 55) was completed by K. Verner in 1877 in his study "Eine Ausnahme der ersten Lautverschiebung", Kuhn's *Zeitschrift für vergleichende Sprachforschung*, XXIII. The expansion consisted of the explanation that voiceless Germanic spirants in word-medial position which correspond to the old Indoeuropean voiceless *p, *t, *k, remain voiceless if the vowel immediately preceding them is accented; if the accent does not fall on the vowel immediately preceding the spirant, then the voiceless sound becomes voiced (this also holds good for the sound s in Germanic languages). Verner's law was later presented in a somewhat different form by the comparativist A. Meillet, in the study *Caractères généraux des langues germaniques* (Paris, 1917). According to Meillet's definition the above-mentioned spirants and the sound s become voiced between two voiced elements of which the first is the vowel in word-initial position; but if this first syllable is accented no voicing takes place.

[3] K. Brugmann was the author of the well-known handbook: *Kurze vergleichende Grammatik der indogermanischen Sprachen* (Strassburg, 1902-1904). Together with B. Delbrück he prepared the first edition of the classic work on Indoeuropean studies: *Grundriss der vergleichenden Grammatik der indogermanischen Sprachen*; Books I and II were prepared by Brugmann between 1886 and 1892, and Books III, IV and V by B. Delbrück; these were published between 1893 and 1900 under the title *Vergleichende Syntax der indogermanischen Sprachen*. Brugmann alone was the author of the second and revised edition of this work: Book I entitled *Einleitung und Lautlehre* (1897), Book II entitled *Lehre von den Wortformen und ihrem Gebrauch* (published in parts: first part 1906; second part 1909-1911; third part, 1st section 1913, third part, 2nd section 1916).

[4] Berthold Delbrück (1842-1922), Brugmann's closest collaborator, is specially noted for his work on syntax, in which the neo-grammarians had relatively little interest. His work *Vergleichende Syntax...* is still today a valuable source of knowledge concerning the historical syntax of Indoeuropean languages.

variety of occasions.[5] Its most emphatic advocate was Hermann Paul (1846-1921), an eminent theoretician of the neo-grammarian school.

99. While the other neo-grammarians usually gave practical demonstrations of their methodological conceptions, Paul was predominantly interested in the theoretical elaboration of methodological problems. His classic work, *Principien der Sprachgeschichte* (see below § 107) received both enthusiastic praise and sharp criticism. In it both the greatness of the neo-grammarian scholarly effort and all their weaknesses in the field of linguistic theory and methods are most strikingly manifested.

100. Paul explicitly declared himself against the simple description of a particular linguistic state without reference to historical perspective, for which twentieth-century linguistics, mostly devoted to synchrony (see below § 131), has never forgiven him. It has been forgotten that Paul's *Principien der Sprachgeschichte* contains some excellent observations which directly hint at many innovations which were to come after his time. He is mainly remembered as a tireless apostle of historicism.

101. Paul started from the conviction that linguistics was a branch of scholarship concerned with the study of human culture. In order to understand actual types of culture, it was above all necessary to know the historical conditions under whose immediate influence they took shape. Following such a basic conviction, Paul was so incautious as to insist on the following statement, which was adversely judged by later generations: what is not historical in linguistics is not scientific.

102. The study of culture implies the study of society. Language should be regarded above all as the property of the whole speaking community. Such collective language represents the linguistic average peculiar to the given society, i.e. its most typical speech manifestation, which could be established by observing the speech of different individuals, representatives of the whole community,

---

[5]   See, for example, the views expounded by K. Brugmann and W. Streitberg in the study: "Zu Fr. Bopps hundertjährigen Geburtstage", *Indogermanische Forschungen*, I, (1892), p. VII et passim.

and by seeking an average type. (Paul used the term "Sprachusus" for this linguistic average.) However, he insisted, the true linguistic reality is not the language of the speaking group. "Collective language" is only a psychological entity, a notion in us. The only reality is the language of the individual, its actual speech manifestation. What Paul said (although in a roundabout and longwinded way) was to appear later in the roots of the theory of the revolutionary De Saussure (see below § 259).

103. The neo-grammarians were firmly convinced of the consistency of the laws governing linguistic evolution, and considered that these laws were beyond human control. Some scholars, such as Brugmann, were inclined to seek the causes of different trends of language evolution primarily in man's physiological construction (in the organization of the speech apparatus). Meanwhile others, influenced by psychological ideas about language (mostly in the spirit of Wundt's teaching, see above § 84), looked in the first place for psychological reasons to explain changes in language. The most definite statements on this subject were made by Paul, who in this respect presented the most successful synthesis of the general ideas of his time.

104. Paul gave priority to the psychological factor, since he believed that there was a direct connection between the development of culture and the evolution of the human inner world. Moreover he insisted that the language we speak exists in us in the form of a network of particular acoustic-motoric sensations which are in a state of constant connection. By listening and thinking, man enriches his stock of linguistic associations. Every man registers the linguistic practices of his environment in his subconscious as a model, but he does not reproduce it exactly. The associative paths in each individual lead to a variety of slight divergencies from the norm. If these divergencies are transferred to other individuals, there is an increasing possibility that the divergence will acquire greater significance, even to the extent of causing noticeable changes in the language.

105. However Paul did not confine himself to psychological explanations in this matter. He also laid special stress on the im-

portance of the physiological element: man feels a desire for easier articulatory movements and unconsciously satisfies it. What movement will be most convenient for which individual depends on the actual structure of the speech organs. He also gave some thought to the importance of man's objective living conditions (climatic, geographical and social). Although he was far from establishing a definitive theory of linguistic evolution, Paul nevertheless contributed a series of remarkable observations in this direction, which served as a fruitful stimulus to the reflections of the twentieth-century pioneers in linguistic theory.

106. The neo-grammarians were the first to take a serious interest in the question of extant dialects, since they considered that the consistency of the ceaseless process of linguistic development (which was for them the central theme of scientific interest) could be best observed within the framework of a living linguistic organism. However in this field they did not achieve the results they had expected. Not only was this theory not supported by new arguments, but in fact the first convincing criticisms of their methods were heard from the ranks of the dialectologists (see below § 141). The linguistic geographers emphasized something which the eminent representatives of historical grammar had failed to stress sufficiently: the great importance of geographical, social and historical factors in shaping the dialectal scene (see below § 147). The introduction into linguistic method of the new criteria forged by the dialectologists considerably enriched both linguistic theory and practice at the beginning of the twentieth century.

BIBLIOGRAPHICAL REFERENCES

107. The best and fullest survey of the work of the neo-grammarians which has appeared so far is by A. V. Desnickaja in *Voprosy izučenija rodstva indoevropejskix jazykov* (Moscow-Leningrad, AN SSSR, 1955), chapter II: "Iz istorii sravnitel'nogo izučenija indoevropejskix jazykov". Cf. also the books of Thomsen and Pedersen (see above § 59).

The basic points in Paul's doctrine are expounded in the above mentioned book by Čikobava: *Problema jazyka kak predmeta jazykoznanija* (see above § 92). See also Hr. Zimmer, *Junggrammatische Streifzüge im Gebiete der Syntax* (Colberg, 1882), K. Brugmann, *Zum heutigen Stand der Sprachwissenschaft* (Strassburg, 1885).

Paul's book on the principles of the history of language is specially recommended: *Principien der Sprachgeschichte* (Halle, 1880) (There were four subsequent editions, the last in 1920).

12

HUGO SCHUCHARDT, A REPRESENTATIVE OF
THE "INDEPENDENTS"

108. The term "Independents" is used to describe the contemporaries of the Leipzig group who diverged from the neo-grammarian linguistic circle and followed an independent course of linguistic ideas of their own. There were not many of them. If we except the linguistic geographers (see below § 139) and the representatives of the Kazan school (see below § 186) only one prominent personality remains, a man of challenging and original linguistic ideas: Hugo Schuchardt (1842-1928).

109. Although he belonged to the same generation as the neo-grammarians, Schuchardt did not join forces with them. He was on the other side, in the ranks of their critics. But he did not criticize them from a conservative standpoint; on the contrary. A man of independent views and ideas, Schuchardt could not accept the conception that occupied the central place in the linguistic theories of the neo-grammarians: that changes in language take place according to fixed and consistent rules, similar to the blind force of natural laws. His penetrating mind saw that they were other possible explanations: he was among the first to bring to light the significance of the geographical element in linguistic evolution; he was also one of the first to indicate the rôle of individuals in the initiation of linguistic changes: an individual creation may be generalized by imitation.

110. Schuchardt expounded particularly challenging ideas about "mixed" languages. According to the traditional conceptions of the comparativists, genetic relations were "pure" (i.e. every language was connected as regards its origin with a single linguistic family). However Schuchardt directed his attention to the so-called *pidgin language*, that is, to languages which had arisen as a result of the

interweaving of completely unrelated linguistic structures (for example the language spoken by some African natives on a basis of English, but with typological features from their own language).[1] His investigations led him to conclusions which clashed sharply with the traditional conceptions of the comparativists. Even today, when scholars have gone much further into these problems than Schuchardt did in his pioneer works,[2] many of his observations in this branch of research are still classic.

111. Schuchardt's originality is also reflected in his lively interest in the problems of the meaning of words (which was quite alien to the neo-grammarians). When the periodical *Wörter und Sachen* was founded in 1909, in which semantic as well as etymological questions were treated, Schuchardt became an eminent contributor whose work considerably influenced the rise of interest in those fields of linguistic investigation.

112. Nevertheless much more was heard of Schuchardt's ideas after his death than during his lifetime. The era in which he lived belonged to the neo-grammarians. In fact this gifted scholar was fully accepted only by later generations whose ideas he had anticipated.

BIBLIOGRAPHICAL REFERENCES

113. Schuchardt's criticism of the neo-grammarians is best expounded in his work: *Über die Lautgesetze gegen die Junggrammatiker* (Berlin, 1885). This work (somewhat shortened) and other important works by Schuchardt (chosen by Leo Spitzer, the editor of the anthology) can be found in a book entitled *Hugo Schuchardt-Brevier, Ein Vademecum der allgemeinen Sprachwissenschaft* (second revised ed., Halle, 1928). A Russian translation of this book (with a variety of additions) came out in Moscow in 1950, edited by R. A. Budagov, with the title: *G. Šuxardt, izbrannye stati po jazykoznaniju.*

[1] On the problem of "mixed language" see A. Meillet *La méthode comparative en linguistique historique* (Oslo, 1925).
[2] For example today it is known that the theoretical distinction between "pure" and "mixed" has no real foundation: all languages are more or less "mixed".

LINGUISTIC RESEARCH
IN THE TWENTIETH CENTURY

13

INTRODUCTION

THE BASIC CHARACTERISTICS OF TWENTIETH
CENTURY SCHOLARSHIP

114. After the nineteenth century, during which scholars with a positivist outlook had taken historicism as the main motto of their theoretical standpoint, a reaction set in; and the twentieth century has seen the development of a completely new trend in scientific thought. An epoch spent in accumulating facts was succeeded by an epoch devoted to the deeper interpretation of the knowledge acquired. Only then did new points of view develop regarding the complicated nature of phenomena which had been the subject of scientific investigation. Thanks to these new points of view, which have sprung from the systematization of facts accumulated, mankind has entered upon an era of civilization and culture hitherto unforeseeable.

115. As early as the end of the nineteenth century, the work of scholars had yielded valuable results, which have ensured exceptionally dynamic progress since that time. Physics has begun the great age of its quantum theory; biology developed the theory of mutation; while psychology was building up its "Gestalt-theory" (the theory of the general, basic structures of entities) etc.

The first decades of the twentieth century enriched our knowledge with such concepts as relativity, electronics, colloidal chemistry, psycho-analysis and behaviourism. Since the Second World War, we have been confronted with yet more new scientific concepts: atomics, cybernetics, the theory of communication... We are certainly witnessing a tremendous upward surge of man's knowledge.

116. In the twentieth century the general trends of a new scientific

method have been laid down. In its work of systematization and generalization, scientific research has begun to insist on the importance of detecting the invariant characteristics of phenomena. It has therefore been necessary, while observing a series of related data, to find their typical representative (what biological sciences would term the genotype in relation to the phenotype). The typical "ideal" representative of its kind is obtained by bringing to light the common, essential characteristics in a series of particular phenomena, and setting aside the individual, variable, haphazard and therefore non-essential characteristics. Thus the scientific method of analysis has begun to veer towards the abstraction of the invariants from the actual variants.

117. Indeed the basic contrast between the research of the nineteenth century and that of the twentieth lies in the fact that the preoccupation with abstracting invariant features has been substituted for the previous almost exclusive interest in the concrete nature of facts.

118. Those whose intellectual outlook was entirely grounded in the conceptions of traditional nineteenth century scholarship (which until recently was almost exclusively represented in schools) show a certain reserve, frequently amounting to suspicion, towards the abstract method of modern scientific work. However it is only the application of the abstract method which has led to the most practical results, and these have finally ensured the level of our present-day civilization.

119. A more profound observation of facts leads to an unshakable conviction that this world is not a chaotic conglomeration of details, but a *system* (i.e. an organized whole). In asserting this truth, twentieth century scholarship has taken as its working slogan the following principle: in order to complete our knowledge of the world, we should search for the *structure* of the system, that is, the relationship between the members of the system. Thus there has arisen the era of *structuralism* in scientific research, marked by such events as Einstein's working out of modern physics, from which there has begun to emerge an entirely new civilization for mankind – the "atomic" civilization.

120. Right at the beginning of their pioneering advance in scholarship the champions of structuralism had to overcome the resistance of the "traditionalists" to such new and unusual trends of scientific thought as structuralism demanded (for, in the well-chosen words of a later critic,[1] the scientific rôle of such men as Copernicus, and in our own times Einstein, does not lie primarily in the discovery of new facts, but rather in finding new ways of looking at old data). The period of distrust, undeserved criticism and underestimation is now long past. The present level of the results achieved has fully justified the conviction that scholarship which rests exclusively on the concrete nature of facts represents only the first stage of our knowledge, while the more mature stage can be attained only by structural research.

121. A characteristic conception of twentieth century scholars is that scientific work as a whole should be indissolubly bound up with a theory of knowledge – *epistemology*. Since the concept of structure has been placed at the centre of epistomological investigations, scholars have examined the possibility of finding the most efficient procedures for describing the structure in scientific terms. Human speech is not suited to such purposes, since it is not absolutely precise and logical. Scholars have therefore combined their forces in order to undertake the task of establishing the principles of *metalanguage* – the most highly logical language of scientific analysis. The task has been undertaken by those most fit for it – mathematicians, logicians and linguists. Thus the twentieth century has become an age of interdisciplinary co-operation.

122. All this had led to a change in the formation of the specialist in individual fields. While the traditional linguistic education had a pronounced humanistic character, the modern linguist is equipped in addition with knowledge obtained from the exact sciences. In short, the whole type of culture is essentially different, and demands from the scholar far wider horizons of knowledge than one could have dreamt of in earlier (what we might call "pre-structural") times.

[1] See: G. J. Warnock, "Analysis and Imagination", *The Revolution in Philosophy* (London, 1956), p. 121.

THE TREND OF DEVELOPMENT IN LINGUISTICS

123. The fundamental characteristics in the development of linguistics correspond to those of twentieth century scholarship as a whole: revolutionary achievements in the field of scientific method have considerably widened the horizons of scholarly thought. The great upward surge of linguistic theory has yielded practical results which are making a significant contribution to our culture and civilization.

124. Linguistics in our time differs from that of the nineteenth century in the following ways: in the systematization of knowledge, and a new interpretation of the facts known; in a considerable widening of the scope of its interests; in the engagement of scholars in inter-disciplinary co-operation in large-scale tasks of research and in the successful transplanting of methodological procedures from other branches of scholarship to the analysis of linguistic phenomena.

125. The most fruitful, hitherto unforseeable period in the growth of linguistic studies actually started when the structuralists began to take the lead.

The adherents of structural linguistics have the advantage of being consistently aware of the upward surge of human knowledge in general and aspiring after fresh methodological approaches, after all that is new. They have shown the greatest ability in joining forces with the general trends of development in scholarship and finding a place in the front ranks.

Traditional linguistics was almost always under the influence of other disciplines (psychology, logic, biology and sociology), and could not by itself contribute much to the advance of scientific thought. Structuralism brought about a fundamental change: at present linguistics is not only on an equality with other disciplines in the working out of research methods, but its experience is often used by others.

126. The coming of structuralism has not resulted in the uprooting of traditional linguistics. Even today its proponents are doing useful linguistic work. Nevertheless it is only the structural

approach to language which has given to linguistics in the first half of the twentieth century its own particular and typical hall-mark. All the other non-structural trends, which have remained from the past or appeared subsequently, were of marginal importance in determining the fundamental line of its growth.

127. In the twentieth century, as in the nineteenth, sounds have been the object of most intensive study. As the simplest linguistic elements, and the most susceptible to investigation, they have represented the most worthwhile field of work and the most suitable soil for the building of theories.

128. The typical grammatical research of the twentieth century is distinguished not only by an exceptional growth in intensity, but also by another vitally important factor. In traditional linguistics historical and contemporary grammar were so closely interwoven that an actual linguistic situation was interpreted primarily in the light of earlier changes in language; whereas structural grammar insists on a clear-cut distinction between synchrony and diachrony (see below § 260).

129. While nineteenth-century linguistics was almost exclusively concerned with Indoeuropean languages, twentieth-century linguistics shows as much if not more, interest in non-Indoeuropean linguistic problems. The first modern (i.e. structural) grammatical descriptions were concerned with "exotic" languages. At one time there were justified complaints that the language of the Navaho Indian tribe, for example, was described more thoroughly than any Indoeuropean language. But that was in the very earliest stages of structural linguistics. Today, such works as Hall's description of the structure of the French and Italian languages (1948),[2] and *Outline of English Structure* by Trager and Smith are already classics.[3] The first descriptive grammar of a Slavonic language, made according to modern methods, was published in 1952 by Horace G. Lunt,[4] a representative of the Harvard School (see below § 236).

[2] Robert A. Hall, Jr., "French", *Language Monographs*, No. 24 (1948); "Descriptive Italian Grammar", *Cornell Romance Studies*, Vol. 2 (1948).
[3] G. L. Trager and H. L. Smith Jr., "An Outline of English Structure", *SIL*, *Occasional Papers*, No. 3 (Norman, Okla., 1951).
[4] Horace G. Lunt, *Grammar of the Macedonian Literary Language* (Skopje, 1952).

130. As a result of moving away from Indoeuropean linguistic material and abandoning classical grammatical criteria in the work of analysis, the linguists of our day have come face to face with a hitherto undreamt–of variety in the actual types of linguistic structures. Studies on the *typology* of language now represent a new and important branch within the scope of linguistic disciplines.

131. At one time the history of language was neglected by the majority of the structuralists. Thus those who are not adequately informed have the impression that one of the most marked contrasts between nineteenth and twentieth-century linguistics lies in the fact that the former put the emphasis on historicism, and underestimated the scientific value of descriptions of the contemporary state of a language, while exactly the opposite is true of the other; history of language is neglected, and the main efforts are concentrated on studying the present-day linguistic situation. Even if such an interpretation of the attitude of nineteenth-century linguistics is correct, the same cannot be said of linguistics in the twentieth century, apart from the first years of the development of structuralism. The history of language was left in the background only while the battle for the rights of synchronic linguistic description was being waged; later it took its appropriate place within the scope of scholarly interests.

The history of language has acquired a quite different content in our times. Earlier its rôle consisted in throwing light on the evolutionary progress of various linguistic particularities. Today the history of language is expected to explain linguistic evolution as a whole; that is, not the history of one detail, but the study of the causes which have led to the replacement of one particular linguistic system by another (see below § 312).

132. Nor have comparative linguistic studies been neglected in our times. But the actual type of scientific interests and the methods of work differ considerably from everything traditional. Types of linguistic structures and their mutual relations occupy the centre of attention, while mathematical criteria have been introduced into the analysis of affinity (see below § 445).

133. Etymological studies are still the most traditional. How-

ever there too, thanks primarily to the work of linguistic geographers (see below § 147) a significant advance can be noticed in comparison with what was achieved during the past century: new social, cultural and historical criteria have been introduced in reconstructing the origin of words.

134. At the beginning of the twentieth century dialectology was the most progressive linguistic discipline. Today too it is developing vigorously and keeps pace with the modern trends in linguistic method. However, in this field the possibility remains open for big leaps into the unknown with the help of a bolder application of structural viewpoints and statistical procedure.

135. Syntax and semantics, the most complicated linguistic studies, came to maturity only in the twentieth century (see below § 419 and § 404). Stylistics has also fully developed in the twentieth century (see below § 165) – not to mention such branches of linguistics as semiology (see below § 397), glottochronology (see below § 445), psycholinguistics (see below § 352), logistic grammar (see below § 394), generative grammar (see below § 422), paralinguistics (see below § 349) or kinesics (see below § 350) whose research programme could not have been imagined in the nineteenth century.

136. Even philological studies themselves have changed quite considerably in respect of the themes they embrace. Modern philology has added to its traditional repertoire of problems the cultural history of language, the investigation of the language of particular social environments (e.g. of slang) and comprehensive studies of folklore.

137. Linguistics at the present moment of development (the beginning of the sixties of the twentieth century) is marked by two essential features: the victory of structuralism over the neo-grammarian conception of language and the large-scale co-operation with other disciplines.

The victory of the structural approach to language is most clearly seen in the fact that there is scarcely a single scholar among those whose work is of serious significance for the development of linguistic theory who would not adopt the basic axiom of structuralism, i.e. the belief that language is a communicative system, the structure of which has to be investigated.

In those places where structuralism has developed without interruption from the very beginning (such as the U.S.A.) there are only a few linguists who are not familiar with the main principles of the structural approach to language. Where the spread of structuralism began much later (e.g. in the U.S.S.R.), representatives of traditional grammar are found today only among the older generation; all the younger scholars have enthusiastically accepted the achievements of the structural method. At the present time structuralistic methods are also rapidly penetrating to those centres which were, for some reason, until recently outside the main current of the development of linguistics.

There are quite a number of contemporary linguists who do not belong to any particular school. They have been taught according to the principles of traditional linguistics, and work in the classic fields of linguistic problems, but have adopted the fundamental structural views on language (e.g. Avanesov and Shevelov in Slavistics, Kuryłowicz in Indoeuropean studies and linguistic theory; Tesnière and de Groot in the field of syntactical research, etc.).

The generations which have been consistently educated in the spirit of structural research are today to an increasing extent departing from classic linguistic problems. The greatest interest is shown in those fields of research which offer the best opportunities for co-operation with other disciplines.

The intensive co-operation of linguistic scholars with those of other disciplines is no longer subjected to wide-spread criticism. We now have a number of studies, intended for a linguistic public, in which linguistic phenomena are qualified and classified not only in linguistic terms but according to criteria appropriate to other branches of scholarship.[5] Linguistic scholars, working together with representatives of other disciplines, publish books on scientific themes which they have studied in common.[6] They

[5] J. Greenberg's book *Essays in Linguistics* (Chicago, 1957) is typical in this respect; in it we meet anthropological and mathematical as well as linguistic conceptions.

[6] E.g. the book *The First Five Minutes. A Sample of Microscopic Interview*

also publish scientific periodicals whose contributors are drawn from quite different branches of research.[7] It is to be hoped that this type of activity will increase in the future.

BIBLIOGRAPHICAL REFERENCES

138. A clear and brief account of the basic facts concerning some of the main trends in twentieth-century linguistics with extracts from the most representative works of different schools is given by V. A. Zvegincev in *Istorija jazykoznanija XIX i XX vekov v očerkax i izvlečenijax*, II (Moscow, 1960). The collection *Trends in European and American Linguistics 1930-1960* (Utrecht-Antwerp, 1961) reviews the basic linguistic trends in the U.S.A. As regards European schools, there are accounts of the work of the glossematicians, French linguistics (in part) and the Geneva School (only in relation to the further development of De Saussure's teaching). The present state of Indoeuropean studies is described, and some information is given about the present level of development in Italian linguistics.

The most exact information about the broad repertoire of important problems treated in twentieth-century linguistics is to be found in the reports of international congresses: for example the Fourth International Congress held at Copenhagen in 1936 (*Actes du IV Congrès International des Linguistes*, Copenhagen, 1938), the Sixth International Congress held at Paris in 1948 (*Actes du VI Congrès International des Linguistes*, Paris, 1949), the Seventh International Congress held in London in 1952 (*Seventh International Congress of Linguists, Preliminary Reports*, London, 1952), and the Eighth International Congress held at Oslo (*Proceedings of the Eighth International Congress of Linguists*, Oslo, 1958).

Analysis (New York, 1960), published by the American linguistic scholar Charles F. Hockett in co-operation with R. F. Pittenger and J. J. Danhy, specialists in problems of psycho-analysis. The book deals with the diagnosis of a particular psychological case which is achieved by studying the verbal behaviour of the person subjected to psycho-analysis.

[7] A scientific periodical *The Journal of Auditory Research* was recently started in U.S.A. whose contributors include specialists in acoustics, neurology, linguistics, communication, musicology and psychology.

14

NON-STRUCTURAL LINGUISTICS

LINGUISTIC GEOGRAPHY

The Foundation of Methods

139. Linguistic geography is based on dialectological research – on the accumulation of information concerning the dialectal features of a given language and the geographical diffusion of individual language characteristics. As well as being subjected to the descriptive method, the dialectal phenomena are also considered in a historical light.

140. Linguistic research conducted in this way has provided material for new and more exact explanations of linguistic changes. The information accumulated has enriched our knowledge of cultural history, and the whole type of field research work has indicated various methodological problems and spurred linguists to devote themselves to hitherto untouched fields of study.

141. It was only at the dawn of the twentieth century that linguistic geography began to reach its full maturity and to influence the formation of linguistic concepts, though its roots lie in the nineteenth century. It originated c. 1870, when the neo-grammarians became interested in dialects, because of their conviction that dialectal phenomena would best afford proof of their theories concerning the consistency of linguistic laws (see above § 106). However instead of providing the proof required, these investigations confronted the learned public with evidence that dialects contained as many irregularities as literary language.

142. The theoretical achievements of linguistic geography proceeded directly from practical field work. In fact this school grew up in the course of the preparation of dialectological atlases. From

the first French dialectologists were pioneers in this work. Later important results were contributed by Italian scholars, adherents of the *neo-linguistic* school (in dialectology this trend is best known under the name of *areal linguistics*, see below § 176).

143. The end of the nineteenth century saw the beginning of an era of fruitful work on the dialectological atlases of individual European languages, primarily Romance and Germanic. The first of the great atlases, *Deutscher Sprachatlas* (published as early as 1876) was the work of the German linguist George Wenker. It is significant as the first serious achievement, although it is not without methodological weaknesses.[1]

144. The famous proponent of linguistic geography, Jules Gilliéron (1854-1926) formed his basic ideas on language under the influence of the French linguistic school.[2] His work *L'Altas linguistique de France* was published (in parts, between 1902 and 1912) on the basis of material collected between 1897 and 1901.[3] This atlas is now a classic work in dialectology.

145. Gilliéron's example was followed by other Romanists (Louis Gauchat, J. Jeanjaquet, E. Tappolet and others). Valuable contributions were made by two Swiss scholars: K. Jaberg and J. Jud who (between 1925 and 1940) worked on the *Sprach und Sachatlas Italiens und der Südschweiz*. They investigated both peasant and urban speech. The dialectological method elaborated by them was highly stimulating and fruitful.

146. The main achievements of linguistic geography emerged in lexical studies. In examining existing words and their diffusion in popular speech, linguistic geographers have set themselves the aim of reconstructing the history of these words, taking into consideration their semantics, flexion and syntactical function.

147. A tradition was established in explaining the history of

---

[1] Wenker entrusted his dialectal questionnaires to untrained village school-teachers; hence the results were not always reliable.
[2] He was the pupil of a group of outstanding French linguists in the seventies and eighties: Gaston Paris, Arsène Darmesteter, Louis Havet and Paul Meyer. Gaston Paris especially had considerable influence on Gilliéron's linguistic development.
[3] Gilliéron composed a questionnaire with 2,000 questions and used only one field investigator, but an excellent one, E. Edmont.

words with the help of knowledge concerning geographical, social and historical factors. National psychology has been studied, and past and present linguistic documents carefully examined. In fact the adherents of linguistic geography maintained that it is necessary to know all the various phenomena on which the life of a language depends. This method of approaching facts remains an outstanding achievement of modern dialectology.

The students of Romance languages were the first to take advantage of this new methodological trend. For example the conditions which preceded the romanization of western Europe in the first centuries of our era were seen in a new light (a distinction was now made between Christian and pagan Latin, in addition to the already established distinction between vulgar and classical Latin; this was important in the work of explaining the development of French vocabulary).

148. Certain assertions of the linguistic geographers are now regarded as axiomatic in modern dialectology; for example the following:

A. Dialectal differences are found most frequently in the fields of vocabulary and phonetics and least often in flexion and syntactical characteristics.

B. Social-historical factors are of decisive importance in linguistic differentiation (under the feudal system the number of dialects increased, which was the direct result of the isolation of individual autonomous regions; during the period of political centralization the degree of differentiation decreased).

C. Geographical conditions also have a vital influence on linguistic differentiation. A mountainous district is a linguistic periphery in comparison with a plain: while linguistic innovations can spread extensively in the plain because of easier communications, the speech of mountain districts, on account of their position, remains isolated from the main currents of development spreading through the plain.

D. The disappearance of dialects has been hastened in recent times by the efforts of peasants to adopt the cultural patterns of town populations.

149. Among the most important contributions of linguistic geography to the theory of language are explanations of the basic laws of lexical development. The main merit in this field belongs to Gilliéron, who indicated two factors causing innovations in vocabulary: homonymical conflicts and unsuitable structure of words.

150. The term "homonymical conflict" means a situation in which two homonyms, whose different meanings are usually established by a difference of context, begin to be used in the same context, which hinders precise understanding. Then a new word takes on itself one of the two meanings and the homonymical situation disappears.[4]

151. The phonetic structure of words changes in the course of time. It happens that a word which was originally quite suited to its function becomes too short or too long, or acquires some sound element evoking a different association from what one would expect. In such cases it is usually replaced by a new, more convenient word.[5]

152. Gilliéron's works made the greatest contribution towards revising the doctrine of the absolute regularity of sound laws. Gilliéron set out his most cogent arguments in his study *La faillite de l'étymologie phonétique* (Neuville, 1919).

Bibliographical References

153. In addition to the works of Gilliéron already cited, see also Jaberg's studies: *Sprachgeographie* (Aarau, 1908), *Aspects géographiques du langage* (Paris, 1936) and *Der Sprachatlas als*

[4] For example, in the Gascon dialect the word *gat* used to have two meanings: 1, cat (<cattus); 2, cock (<gattus). In a sentence such as "le chien a étranglé le gat," it was not clear whether the speaker meant that the dog had strangled a cat or a cock. This conflict was resolved by introducing the word *vicaire* for "cock", so that the name *gat* came to be used only for "cat". (See Gilliéron-Roques, "Études de géographie linguistique, XII. Mots en collision. A. Le coq et le chat", *Revue de philologie française*, 4, 1910, pp. 278-288).
[5] Gilliéron showed that the original word for "bee" *apis* was replaced by other words in those French dialects in which phonetic development had reduced the form "apis" to a single sound – é. The work in which Gilliéron discusses this: *Généalogie des mots qui désignent l'abeille, d'après l'Atlas linguistique de France* (Paris, 1918) is regarded as one of the classics of linguistic geography.

Forschungsinstrument (in collaboration with Jud) (Halle, 1928). The following write on linguistic geography: A. Dauzat, *La geographie linguistique* (Paris, 1922), E. Gamillscheg, *Die Sprachgeographie* (Bielefeld, 1928); G. Bottiglioni, "Linguistic Geography", *Linguistics Today* (New York, 1954) pp. 255-267.

The most comprehensive work on the history of dialectological research is Sever Pop, *La dialectologie: Aperçu historique et méthodes d'enquêtes linguistiques*, two volumes (Louvain, 1950).

A survey of literature on linguistic geography in the first decades of its development can be found in J. Schrijnen, *Essai de bibliographie de géographie linguistique générale* (Nimwegen, 1933).

A bibliography of Gilliéron's works has been published by Mario Roques, *Bibliographie des travaux de Jules Gilliéron* (Paris, 1930).

Modern Dialectology

154. Structuralism has not neglected dialectological studies. The interest shown by the first, classical representatives of structuralism in the possibility of applying the new method in the field of dialectology[6] has only been strengthened in later generations. Today we have an increasing number of descriptions of dialectal *systems*, which means that dialectal characteristics are not presented simply as a collection of details, but the principles according to which particular details come into definite relations with each other are brought to light. Then corresponding systems in different dialects are compared, which throws new light on the phenomena of affinity and differentiation among dialects, and opens up new horizons of linguistic theory. In the structural epoch in dialectology new terms and concepts have been worked out, for example the *diasystem* (= the graphic presentation of two systems so that both similarities and differences are brought into prominence), and *idiolect* (= the whole of the speech characteristics of an individual, including all personal nuances).

[6]   N. S. Trubetzkoy, for example, sets out his ideas as to the value of introducing phonological criteria into dialectology in his work "Phonologie et géographie linguistique", *TCLP*, IV (1931), pp. 228-234.

155. Under the aegis of linguistic geography there has developed the investigation of *languages in contact*,[7] that is the problem of the language system in a *bilingual* community (a community where two languages are spoken side by side). The survey of the mutual influence of different language structures compelled to live in direct contact with each other has made it possible to draw conclusions of wide general-linguistic significance. Therefore modern linguistic theoreticians are paying considerable attention to these problems. Psycholinguists in particular (see below § 352), being specially interested in the question of the process of communication, find in this field common ground with the dialectologists, and pass on to them their own experience in the study of linguistic phenomena.[8]

156. American dialectologists (Hans Kurath, Raven McDavid, William Labov) have opened up an important new line of investigation by concentrating their attention on variations connected with social strata rather than with geography. Mathematical methods, or statistics, are today being applied with increasing enthusiasm in the work of qualifying and classifying dialects. The possibilities opened up by the wider use of mathematical procedures in dialectology, and also the question of the real value of structural criteria for the classification of dialects, are now of topical interest.

The Polish School of W. Doroszewski has worked out a method of studying the so-called *quantitative isoglosses*. These isoglosses mark the frequencies of linguistic phenomena which are subject to variation within the same speech community.

Bibliographical References

157. An introduction to the problems of modern dialectological method can be found in the following works: Uriel Weinreich "Is a Structural Dialectology Possible?", *Word*, 10 (1954), pp. 388-400;

[7] The idea of "languages in contact" and the term itself has been popularized in scholarly circles by the American linguist Uriel Weinreich in his work *Languages in Contact* (New York, 1953). The same problems have also been treated by Einar Haugen; see his work, *The Norwegian Language in America, A Study in Bilingual Behavior* (Philadelphia, 1953).

[8] Hence dialectologists today are to an increasing extent adopting terminology from the theory of information (see below § 449) such as *code corn* (that which

Jean Fourquet, "Linguistique structurale et dialectologie", *Fragen und Forschungen im Bereich und im Kreis der germanische Philologie* (Berlin, Deutsche Akademie der Wissenschaften, 1956); Witold Doroszewski, Le structuralisme linguistique et les études de géographie dialectale", *8th Proceedings*, pp. 540-564; Edward Stankiewicz, "On Discreteness and Continuity in Structural Dialectology", *Word*, 13 (1957), pp. 44-59; Pavle Ivić, "On the Structure of Dialectal Differentiation", *Word*, 18 (1962), pp. 33-53; C. F. Voegelin and Zellig S. Harris, "Methods for Determining Intelligibility Among Dialects of Natural Language", *Proceedings of the American Philosophical Society*, 95 (1951), pp. 322-329; J. H. Greenberg, "The Measurement of Linguistic Diversity", *Lg*, 32 (1956), pp. 109-115.

On the problems of "languages in contact", in addition to the above-mentioned works of Weinreich and Haugen, see the studies published by both of these scholars in the *8th Proceedings*: Uriel Weinreich, "Research Frontiers in Bilingual Studies" (pp. 786-797, with an excellent bibliography); Einar Haugen, "Language Contact", pp. 771-785.

The first brief survey of the dialects of a language made with use of structural criteria was "Nařečí česká" by B. Havránek in *Československá vlastivěda*, III (Prague, 1934). A model of a structural description of a local dialect was given by A. V. Isačenko: *Narečje vasi Sele na Rožu* (Ljubljana, 1939). The first detailed dialectological study of a language, done on the structural principle, is Pavle Ivić's book on Serbo-Croatian dialects: *Die Serbokroatischen Dialekte*, I. Band (The Hague, 1958).

THE FRENCH LINGUISTIC SCHOOL

The Psychophysiological, Psychological and Sociological Investigation of Language

158. The tradition of phonetic investigation had developed in

---

is common in language, and therefore equally understandable by all speakers), or *code noise* (that which is not a general linguistic norm, so that it remains strange and unintelligible to some speakers).

France ever since the time of Rousselot (see below § 217). There was also a strong interest in the problems of word meaning from the time of Michel Bréal (see below § 404), which increased during the heyday of linguistic geography and its assiduous attention to the history of vocabulary (see above § 146). By the end of the nineteenth century, there was a firmly established inclination to link linguistic facts with social phenomena, thanks to the suggestive influence of Ferdinand de Saussure (see below § 242; De Saussure lectured in Paris from 1881-1891). The interaction of all these influences gave a specific hall-mark to the development of French linguistics in the twentieth century.

159. Psychophysiological studies of language (i.e. an examinaion dissimilation or assimilation, in the influence of psychological and physiological factors which condition them) experienced their classical epoch at the end of the nineteenth century when Maurice Grammont published (1895) his study, *La dissimilation consonantique dans les langues indo-européennes et dans les langues romanes.* Grammont sought the causes of phonetic processes, such as dissimilation or assimilation, in the influence of psychological and physiological circumstances. This tradition of psychophysiological investigation still exists in France (and at the present moment has been stimulated by the rapid development of similar researches in the U.S.A. within the framework of psycholinguistic studies; see below § 352).

160. The psychophysiological approach to language has led to greater attention being paid to the language of children (i.e. the question of the beginning of speech). The first scholars to include the complicated phenomena of *bilingualism* in the study of these problems were the Frenchman Ronjat (1913) and the Yugoslav Pavlović (1920).

161. The psychological interpretation of linguistic facts is particularly evident in the works of J. Vendryes, an eminent adherent of that school. Many people describe his linguistics as *affective.* He approached language with the conviction that every act of speech has an emotional tinge: it is not simply a statement, but the expression of a particular affect, so that no one ever gives the same

information twice in the same way (here Vendryes is in agreement with Bally, see below § 265 – and the proponents of aesthetic idealism, see below § 172).

162. The sociological study of language is based on the establishment of the correlation between linguistic and social phenomena. An outstanding adherent of "sociological linguistics" was Antoine Meillet (1866-1936), a specialist in comparative Indoeuropean studies. He made a great contribution to working out a sociological theory of language, which embraces the following basic ideas.

Language is not a simple phenomenon: it is a complex of different strata (styles) which acquires its form from particular social milieux (the language of the guild, the street, the office, the army, etc.). The process of formation is influenced not only by the cultural standard and way of living in a particular social environment, but more especially by the economic and technical activity of the people.

The main rôle in the change of the meaning of words is played by "social borrowings" ("emprunts sociaux"): words passing from one social class to another acquire new shades of meaning – a general word may become special, and vice versa. Semantic evolution proceeds from the application of two interacting principles: generalization and specialization.

163. The elaboration of the sociological theory enriched semantic studies (to which the French have paid active attention from the nineteenth century to the present day, see below § 404). History of language began to be seen in a new light.[9] However these conceptions had their most striking effect in the rapid rise of interest in the stylistic study of language.

Bibliographical References

164. See the classic works of A. Meillet, *Linguistique historique et linguistique générale* Vol. I (Paris, 1921), Vol. II (Paris, 1938) and

---

[9]   This tendency is strikingly illustrated in F. Brunot's work: *Histoire de la langue française des origines à 1900* (Paris, 1905): facts from the past of a language are set out with the aim of bringing to light moments which reflect the cultural atmosphere of former ages.

M. Grammont, *Traité de phonétique* (Paris, 1933; 1956[5]). See also J. Vendryes, *Le Language* (Paris, 1950; first ed. 1921); F. Brunot, *La Pensée et la langue* (Paris, 1936; first ed. 1922); H. Delacroix, *Le language et la pensée* (Paris, 1924); M. Cohen, *Pour une sociologie du langage* (Paris, 1956); G. Matoré, *La méthode en lexicologie. Domaine Français* (Paris, 1953).

A survey of the investigations of the French school (primarily those in the field of psychophysiology) is given by Alf Sommerfelt in "The French School of Linguistics", *Trends*, pp. 283-293.

Stylistic Research

165. Stylistic research can relate to a variety of phenomena. For example, classic stylistics is concerned with the investigation of the linguistic means by which an individual expresses his character, temperament, abilities and outlook on life (style is analysed in this sense by the exponents of "classical" literary theory; some linguists do the same, especially the adherents of aesthetic idealism, see below § 173). Stylistics can also be "social" – if interest is centred on those linguistic forms which reflect the type of culture of a community. The representatives of the French linguistic school are most active in this kind of study. In fact, if stylistics is strictly interpreted in this sense, it may be said that the whole of French sociological linguistics is, basically, stylistics.

166. With the spread of Bally's ideas (see below § 264), certain authors belonging to the French school began to prefer a broader conception of stylistics, in the spirit of De Saussure's classic distinction between the individual linguistic creation ("parole"), and language as the property of a whole social group ("language", see below § 259), to which a third distinction was added: "language" = the total concept of language, including both "langue" and "parole" (this idea was worked out by Delacroix). *Individual stylistics* (which corresponds to the idea of "parole") traces what gives an individual his identity in the linguistic sense; *group stylistics* embraces the sociological investigation of language (the field designated as

"langue"), while *general stylistics* is concerned with establishing all the means by which the fundamental categories of the human spirit acquire linguistic form (a more universal approach, reflecting the idea of "language").[10]

167. In practice the French linguists examine style according to the principle of including in a stylistic description all linguistic phenomena which deviate from the typical grammatical norm of a language. The explanation of these deviations is most often sought in psychological motives. Statistical methods have been increasingly used in this field during recent years (see below § 442).

168. The exponents of structural linguistics, in particular the Harvard School, are now developing a quite new type of stylistic research (see below § 236). Their theoretical starting point is the axiom that language is a means of communication. Thus only the minimum of expression by means of which communication is ensured belongs to linguistics in the narrowest sense of the word; everything else which, strictly speaking, is simply something added to the minimum in order to safeguard intelligibility or to emphasize or illuminate the message – belongs to stylistics. Interesting research is now in progress in this field.

Bibliographical References

169. See Pierre Guiraud, *La stylistique* (= *Que sais-je?*, No. 646) (Paris, 1957); J. Marouzeau, *Précis de stylistique française* (Paris, 1946); M. Cohen, *Grammaire et style* (Paris, 1954); M. Riffaterre, "Problèmes d'analyse du style littéraire" in *Romance Philology*, vol. XIV, No. 3 (1961), pp. 216-227.

For an examination of modern methodological procedure in stylistic analysis see P. Guiraud, *Language et versification d'après l'oeuvre de Paul Valéry. Étude sur la forme poétique dans ses rapports avec la structure de la langue* (Paris, 1953).

---

[10]   The French were the first to accept what goes by the name of *phonostylistics* (from the works of Trubetzkoy): the investigation of the expressive function of sounds. As early as 1913 Grammont spoke of the use made of sound factors in expressing emotion (in *Les vers français, ses moyens d'expression, son harmonie*).

A theory of style worked out in the spirit of the teaching of the Prague school can be found in F. Trávníček's book *O jazykovém slohu* (Prague, 1953). The views of the Harvard school are set out in the studies published in the collection *Style in Language*, ed. Thomas A. Sebeok (Cambridge Mass., 1960): R. Jakobson, *Linguistics and Poetics*, pp. 350-377, and E. Stankiewicz, *Linguistics and the Study of Poetic Language*, pp. 69-81.

AESTHETIC IDEALISM IN LINGUISTICS

Introduction

170. The beginning of the twentieth century saw the rise of a strong anti-rational movement in European philosophic thought, expressed above all in the intuitive doctrine of Bergson,[11] and the aesthetic teaching of Benedetto Croco.[12] The representatives of these philosophical ideas emphasized the importance of the rôle of the individual and his personal psychology in the creation of language. Some linguistic circles in western Europe were interested in this idea, the more so as similar ideas had already been expressed in linguistics. For example Hugo Schuchardt (see above § 109) represented a point of view which may be summarized as follows: language is the creation of the individual, which the group generalizes by imitation; individual psychology is the decisive factor in the creation of language, and this is determined by the external circumstances under which a person lives and which inevitably form his personality; since language is essentially the individual manifestation of a particular psychology, it should be defined as a stylistic phenomenon and approached in this way in scientific research. Thus under the influence of those ideas a new approach to language

---

[11] Henri Bergson (1859-1941) was one of the most influential West European philosophers of the first half of the twentieth century.

[12] Benedetto Croce (1866-1952) was one of the founders of the Italian school of neo-idealism in philosophy. His most important work, which is also well-known to linguistic scholars, is: *Estetica come scienza dell espressione e linguistica generale* (Bari, 1922).

was established and propounded by the German linguistic school of "aesthetic idealism" (Vossler's school) and by the Italian "neo-linguists".

Vossler's school

171. Karl Vossler (1872-1947), a professor of Munich University, was one of the most bitter opponents of the neo-grammarians. His theories were most often expounded in conflicts with them. Completely permeated with the idealistic philosophy of his times, Vossler was particularly impressed by the aesthetic writings of Croce. In linguistics he was closest to Humboldt (see above § 68), because of their mutual belief that language has the most direct connection with people's mentality.

172. Vossler, an idealist by conviction, method and his own definition, built his linguistic theory mainly on the following conceptions.

A. Different material forms of life have no meaning by themselves. Their basic significance lies in people's ideas about them. In everything created, one must seek for the only thing that has any value: the *idea* of the creator, his inner impulse, he himself. For in fact every work is simply the expression of someone's personality.

B. Language is an instrument of the spirit, the material phenomenon through which a man gives utterance to his personal ideas and feelings. Hence the investigation of language has real point only in so far as it is a search for *style*, i.e. that which most directly characterizes an idea and its creator: man.

C. A man is active with respect to his language, i.e. he chooses what he will say and how he will say it. This choice will be conditioned by the particular psychological make-up of the speaker. Hence it must always be emphasized and borne in mind that there is the relationship of the *principle of causality* between a man as the bearer of a particular psychological world and the language which reproduces it.

D. In his language we see the essence of a man (just as in a mirror), and this essence is the aspiration to an aesthetic ideal. Style is in fact the individual expression of a man's aesthetic ideal at the moment of most direct self-revelation.

E. A man conveys something of himself in everything he says, and every moment finds himself in a different emotional atmosphere. Hence what has once been said can never be repeated: in the process of repetition the speaker reproduces approximately, but never exactly, the original shade of meaning.[13]

173. Vossler's most prominent followers are Eugen Lerch and Leo Spitzer. Like Vossler himself, Eugen Lerch, a specialist in the French language, looked for a direct connection between linguistic structures and national mentality.[14]

Leo Spitzer worked on the stylistics, semantics and etymology of Romance languages. He is well known as the creator of *idealistic stylistics* and the so-called *stylistic criticism*.[15] He has expounded

[13] Vossler published his theory in the work *Positivismus und Idealismus in der Sprachwissenschaft* (Heidelberg, 1904). It was further developed in *Sprache als Schöpfung und Entwicklung. Eine theoretische Untersuchungen mit praktischen Beispielen* (Heidelberg, 1905), *Gesammelte Aufsätze zur Sprachphilosophie* (Munich, 1923), *Geist und Kultur in der Sprache* (Munich, 1925). Vossler's theory is practically demonstrated in his *Frankreichs Kultur im Spiegel seiner Sprachentwicklung* (Heidelberg, 1913; the second edition, entitled *Frankreichs Kultur und Sprache* was published in 1929). He maintains, for example that the word order: subject-verb-object, which is characteristic of the French language, is a clear indication of the French love of order and logic.

[14] The French are sociable people – so Lerch insists on the basis of linguistic analysis, but they are inclined to despise their fellow men; they like to use a future instead of the imperative, as in *tu viendras demain*.

[15] His views on how a work of literature should be approached are most fully set out in his book: *Linguistics and Literary History: Essays in Stylistics* (Princeton, 1948). Here he stresses the fact that all literary achievements cannot be treated in the same way. Each work has its own specific character, which should determine the choice of critical approach (this view is in fact a direct echo of the once popular ideas of Bergson and Croce). A work should first be grasped intuitively, though this subjective impression should be checked by analysis. Completely objective criticism is a Utopian dream: a man reacts to a work he reads in the light of his own experience, and the nature of this experience is largely determined by his individual psychological constitution. Every work is a whole, the centre of which is the spirit of the author. Every detail leads to this spirit-centre, because every detail is ideologically motivated. A work is invariably part of a larger, more general whole to the extent to which the spirit of the writer expresses the spirit of a nation (here Spitzer shows himself a faithful interpreter of one of Vossler's basic ideas).

the view that literary works should be estimated in their full complexity, from the linguistic as well as from the literary and aesthetic standpoint. He has vigorously championed the fusion of the experience and methods of linguistic theoreticians with those of literary theoreticians (for which reason some people call his linguistic school *the school of literary stylistics*).

174. Vossler and his followers have been justly criticized. Their basic idea of the purpose and scope of linguistics cannot be approved. As has already been pointed out, their one-sided and inadequate theoretical views led to some arbitrary interpretations of linguistic facts. Yet Vossler's school was not without merit. Its members stimulated a more active interest in the problems of style and have made some challenging observations in this field.

Bibliographical References

175. See the above-mentioned works of Vossler (§ 172) and Spitzer (§ 173). Spitzer's books, *Stilstudien* (Munich, 1928), and *Essays in Historical Semantics* (New York, 1948) also give a very good presentation of the neo-linguistic position. Lerch's views are clearly apparent in his *Handbuch des Frankreichkunde* (Frankfurt – Diestweg, 1933) and in his study "Nationkunde durch Stilistik", *Festschrift für E. Wechssler* (1929). See also the collection *Idealistische Neuphilologie, Festschrift für Karl Vossler* (Heidelberg, 1922), which contains studies by B. Croce, K. Bühler, E. Lerch and L. Spitzer.

Fuller information about Vossler's works is given in Theodor Ostermann, *Bibliographie der Schriften Karl Vossler*, 1897-1951 (Munich, 1951).

There have been many critical reviews of Vossler's school. Prominent among recent and more comprehensive polemical studies is: V. A. Zvegincev, *Estetičeskij idealizm v jazykoznanii: K. Fossler iego škola* (Moscow University, 1956).

Neolinguistics

176. The neolinguistic school is represented by a group of Italian scholars whose linguistic conceptions grew out of the ideas of Humboldt, Schuchardt, Croce and Vossler. In addition the works of the linguistic geographers, particularly Gilliéron, are highly estimated in their circles. We are certainly indebted to them for their work in helping to popularize the criteria of linguistic geography (this school also came to be known under the name of *geographical* or *areal* linguistics, see above § 142). The neolinguists, like the followers of Vossler, fiercely criticized the neo-grammarians, and in doing so were often one-sided and even unjust.

177. An article published in 1910, "Alle fonti del neolatino", *Miscellanea in onore de Attillio Hortis* (1910), pp. 889-913, by Matteo Giulio Bartoli (1873-1946), one of the first and most outstanding neolinguists, may be regarded as the manifesto of this trend. This article contains all the basic principles of the school, together with examples of their methodological application. In addition to this article, two books, both published in 1925, played a paramount rôle in the formation of the school: M. Bartoli, *Introduzione alla neolinguistica (Principi - Scopi - Metodi)* (Geneva, 1925); Matteo Bartoli e Giulio Bertoni, *Breviario di neolinguistica* (Parte I: "Principi generali", de Giulio Bertoni; Parte II: "Criteri tecnici", di Matteo G. Bartoli) (Modena, 1925).

178. Vittorio Pisani and Giuliano Bonfante were also outstanding adherents of this school. When the school, which was frequently criticized, experienced a particularly crushing attack from the American linguistic scholar Robert Hall,[16] Bonfante replied by giving a detailed analysis of its theoretical standpoints.[17] His clear survey of the problems throws into striking prominence the roots of neolinguistics: German aesthetic idealism and French linguistic geography.

---

[16] Hall's principal criticism (*Lg*, 22, 1946, pp. 273-283) was directed against lack of originality in ideas and methods.

[17] "The Neolinguistics Position (A Reply to Hall's Criticism of Neolinguistics)", *Lg*, 23, No. 4 (1947), pp. 344-375.

179. The theoretical position of the neolinguists may be briefly summarized as follows:

Man creates language in a spiritual as well as a physical sense – by his will, imagination, thoughts and feelings. Language mirrors its human creator. Everything connected with language is the result of both a spiritual and physiological process.

Physiology alone cannot explain anything in linguistics. It can only bring about the conditions under which a particular phenomenon is created. The causes behind linguistic phenomena lie in man's spiritual activity.

The "speaking society" does not exist. It is a fiction, just the same as the "average man". The only reality is the "speaking person". Every linguistic innovation is initiated by him.

A linguistic innovation created by an individual is more surely, completely and quickly grasped by a society if the author of the change is a person of importance (with a good social position, outstanding creative gifts, conversational skill, etc.).

Nothing in language can be regarded as incorrect. Everything which exists is correct by the very fact of its existence.

Language is basically the expression of aesthetic feeling, which is variable; in fact changes in fashion may be observed here as well as in other aspects of life equally dependent on aesthetic feeling (art, literature, clothes).

Changes in the meanings of words arise as a result of poetic metaphors. The investigation of these changes is valuable as a means of getting to know the workings of the human imagination.

Changes in linguistic structure arise as a result of ethnic intermixture, not in the sense of the intermixture of races, but of spiritual cultures.

In actual fact language is the storm centre of different trends of development which frequently contradict each other. If we wish to understand them, we must approach linguistic phenomena from widely different angles. In the first place we must take into consideration the fact that the evolution of a particular language is conditioned primarily by geographical and historical circumstances. (For example the history of the French language cannot be properly investigated without reference to the history of France – taking into account the part played by Christianity, German expansion, feudalism, Italian influence, the atmosphere at Court, the work of the Academy, the Revolution, the Romantic movement, etc.).

180. These theoretical standpoints have determined the fields of practical work undertaken by the neolinguists. They have made a considerable contribution to the advance of lexicological studies, and deserve particular credit for their serious work in dialectology, which has had a well-established tradition in Italy ever since the publication of Ascoli's works.[18]

181. In dialectology the neolinguists worked out methods of applying historical, social and geographical criteria to linguistic problems. They have shown a strong interest in the comparative investigation of forms existing in related dialects, and have paid particular attention to the geographical factors determining the areas of dialectal phenomena (hence the term *areal linguistics*, see above § 176).

182. These areal studies resulted in certain theoretical statements which have remained classic in modern dialectology. One of them, for instance, concerns the distinction between central and peripheral areas, which is of crucial importance for dialectological classification.

The term central is used for every speech region in which a linguistic innovation arises. But linguistic changes do not invariably occur in the same places. No speech region is the central area in respect of all its linguistic features. The ideas of "central" and "peripheral" must here be considered as relative.

The peripheries (in a geographical sense) of linguistic regions usually preserve a number of archaic features, but this does not

---

[18]   Graziadio Isaia Ascoli (1829-1907), an original figure in his day, was distinguished by a very strong interest in the life of dialects and a critical attitude towards the neo-grammarians. His conceptions, which had considerable influence in moulding the outlook of Italian linguistic scholars, were in some respects akin to those of the French linguistic geographers (there is a view, held mainly by Italians, that he was in fact the founder of linguistic geography). His main works were published in the periodical *Archivio glottologico Italiano*, from Vol. 1 (1873) to Vol. 16 (1902-1905).

mean that all linguistic characteristics found on a periphery are archaic. However if two different peripheral zones show the same linguistic form, it is in most cases archaic.

183. The neolinguists were among the first to call attention to the phenomenon which was further investigated by the Prague school and called the "association of languages" (see below § 297). They worked on the so-called *substratum theory* (the idea that if a population abandons its mother tongue in favour of another language, this latter is inevitably changed under the influence of the former, which then represents the linguistic substratum). The value of these theoretical achievements cannot be denied.

184. Among the idealistic attitudes which provoked the greatest amount of criticism was the fact that the neo-linguists expressed more or less explicit agreement with the theory of the *monogenesis* of language, i.e. the hypothesis that all the languages of the world developed from a single common language.[19]

Bibliographical References

185. In addition to the above-mentioned works of Bartoli and Bertoni, see also M. Bartoli, *Saggi di linguistica spaziale* (Torino, 1945); G. Bertoni, *La geografia linguistica* (Udine, 1925), and also the above-mentioned polemical works of Hall and Bonfante.

A good indication of the general formation of the Italian linguistic school during the early development of areal linguistics, that is c. 1930, is given in the collection *Silloge linguistica dedicata alla memoria di Graziadio Isaia Ascoli nel primo centenario della nascita* (Torino, 1929).

See also V. Bertoldi, *La parola quale mezzo d'espressione* (Naples, 1946); G. Bonfante, "On Reconstruction and Linguistic Method",

[19] This view was inspired by Christian teaching on the origin of mankind. It found its most devoted champion in the Italian scholar Alfredo Trombetti (whose ideas are expounded in his book *L'unita d'origine del linguaggio*, Bologna, 1905; he tried to find arguments in the fact that words with approximately the same meaning in different languages may accidentally show some similarities in sound structure).

Word, 1 (1945), pp. 131-161; V. Pisani, *L'Etimologia*: *storia, questioni, metodo* (Milan, 1947); V. Bertoldi, *L'arte dell'etimologia* (Naples, 1952).

THE PROGRESSIVE SLAVIST SCHOOLS

The Kazan School

186. The label *Kazan school* is used today to denote the linguistic ideas developed in the seventies of the last century by two Poles: Jan Baudouin de Courtenay (1845-1929) and Mikołaj Kruszewski (1851-1887). The most significant of these ideas were worked out while Baudouin de Courtenay was lecturing at the University of Kazan in Russia – which explains the origin of the term. In spite of chronological data the Kazan school belongs to twentieth-century linguistics. The views held by both Baudouin de Courtenay and Kruszewski in those remote Kazan days represented a quite new, fresh and peculiar world of ideas which grew to maturity much later, in the present century; it is in fact in our times that these challenging views from the past have been discovered, understood and admired.

187. Although Kazan was an unlikely place for a man with serious scholarly ambitions to work in it proved, however, to be a fairly active centre of research and as such exercized a favourable influence on Baudouin de Courtenay's work. Before long the young professor found an ideal companion with whom to discuss linguistic subjects in Kruszewski, a gifted student who wished to defend his doctoral thesis with him. Their conversations gave rise to many ideas about language hitherto unheard of, but they had no opportunity to elaborate a well-founded general linguistic theory, or to establish a school: Baudouin de Courtenay was soon obliged to leave Kazan and to continue his restless life as a fervent Polish nationalist, suspected by the Russian government,[20] and Kruszewski

---

[20]   After being several times moved from one university to another (St. Petersburg, Kazan, Dorpat, Cracow and then St. Petersburg again), in 1918 Baudouin de Courtenay at last obtained a university chair in his native country, in Warsaw.

died before he had time to give definite shape to his ideas. Only the memories of his teacher saved him from oblivion; Baudouin de Courtenay both wrote and spoke of him,[21] and pointed out the importance of the ideas expounded in his doctoral thesis.[22] The parting with Kruszewski was a great loss to Baudouin de Courtenay; never again did he find such a partner for the development of novel, large-scale theories. Baudouin de Courtenay's later works, though interesting and important in many directions, never again had the freshness of the Kazan days.[23] Hence the suitability of the term "Kazan school" rather than "Baudouin de Courtenay school".

188. The first formulations of many of the basic ideas of modern linguistics can be found in the views of these two Poles. For example they stressed the need to distinguish both the language belonging to a whole social group (in the sense of De Saussure's "langue", see below § 259) from individual speech ("parole"), and the evolutionary survey of linguistic facts from linguistic observation at a particular point of time (Baudouin de Courtenay was one of the first scholars who concerned themselves with describing the contemporary state of a language). They understood language as the meeting place of contradictory tendencies which condition its development: conservative forces which desire to preserve the existing situation and progressive forces making for innovation. Even the first modern conception of the phoneme began to develop in the days of the famous linguistic comradeship at Kazan (though Baudouin de Courtenay later abandoned it, see below § 275).

However all these efforts were insufficiently systematic – valuable observations are frequently lost in a flood of redundant, vaguely

---

[21] See Baudouin de Courtenay, "Mikołaj Kruszewski, jego życie i prace naukowe", *Prace filologiczne*, II, Fasc., 3 (1888), pp. 837-849 and III, Fasc., 1 (1889), pp. 116-175.

[22] Today the introduction to this thesis, which was separately published in 1881 under the title *Über die Lautabwechslung*, is regarded as a classic work of the Kazan school, in which its progressive conceptions of the phoneme are most clearly expressed.

[23] Baudouin de Courtenay later plunged into psychologism (see above §§ 88-92), which captured European linguistic circles at the end of the nineteenth and the beginning of the twentieth centuries. Even his ideas on the phoneme acquired a new, psychological interpretation.

expressed, and often contradictory statements. An excessive number of terminological innovations also make it more difficult to grasp the basic trend of the original ideas.

189. The greatest merit of the Kazan school lies in the fact that its ideas stimulated the development of the revolutionary theories of both Ferdinand de Saussure and of the Prague Circle (see below § 244). It was only much later that people realized how powerful this influence was (particularly in the case of De Saussure). The contemporaries of Baudouin de Courtenay and Kruszewski, on the other hand, were almost completely unaware of the wonderful achievements at Kazan. Unfortunately linguistic publications from a remote province of the Russian empire, written in a Slavonic language, were not sufficiently accessible to west European linguistic circles which in the nineteenth century had the main say in establishing linguistic theories.

190. Even in the Slavic world the interest in this new and stimulating way of linguistic thinking was not as great as it might have been if the collaboration of Baudouin de Courtenay and Kruszewski had lasted long enough for them to systematize and condense their original ideas and establish a new theoretical basis. However the Kazan school did not disappear without leaving any traces in the Slavic countries. Baudouin de Courtenay had many gifted pupils who were able to adopt his progressive views on language and to develop them in practice. Especially in St. Petersburg (where Baudouin de Courtenay was twice professor), there were developments in linguistic activity worthy of attention. Of course there were no striking discoveries of new views on linguistics, but the master's teaching was faithfully nurtured within the framework of Slavistics. The term *Petersburg school* in fact refers to the generation of Slavists trained according to Baudouin de Courtenay's teaching: L. V. Ščerba, L. P. Jakubinskij, E. D. Polivanov and many others (including the eminent Soviet slavists V. V. Vinogradov and S. B. Bernstein). Baudouin de Courtenay's pupil L. V. Ščerba (1880-1944) was the most prominent representative of the Petersburg school.

Bibliographical references

191. R. Jakobson gives a brilliant account of the Kazan school in "Kazańska szkoła polskiej lingwistyki i jej miejsce w światowym rozwoju fonologii", *Biuletyn polskiego towarzystwa językoznawczego*, zesz. XIX (Wroclaw-Crakow, 1960), pp. 3-34. A. A. Leont'ev's article "Obščelingvističeskie vzgljady I. A. Boduena de Kurtene", *V Ja*, VIII, 6 (1959), pp. 115-127 deserves close attention. More extensive information can be found in the collection of studies published by the Soviet Academy of Sciences to commemorate the thirtieth anniversary of Baudouin de Courtenay's death: *I. A. Boduen de Kurtene 1845-1919* (contributors A. A. Leont'ev, V. N. Toporov, Vjač. V. Ivanov, A. S. Posvjanskaja, V. P. Grigor'ev and N. S. Tolstoj; L. E. Bokareva and A. A. Leont'ev have appended an exhaustive bibliography of Baudouin de Courtenay's works).

The work of the Petersburg school is best illustrated in the linguistic studies of L. V. Ščerba. See L. V. Ščerba, *Izbrannye raboty po jazykoznaniju i fonetike*, I (Leningrad, 1958). See also: A. A. Leont'ev, "I. A. Boduen de Kurtene i Peterburgskaja škola russkoj lingvistike", *V Ja*, X, 4 (1961), pp. 116-124.

The Fortunatov (Moscow) School

192. The Moscow professor of Comparative Grammar, Filip Fedorovič Fortunatov (1848-1914) was a contemporary of Baudouin de Courtenay. For that time his ideas about language were also progressive, though not to the same extent as those of Baudouin de Courtenay in the Kazan days. Fortunatov was above all a man of practice and occupied himself primarily with work on actual linguistic data. But the way in which he approached particular phenomena in language revealed an exceptional sense of scholarly perspective (he understood, for instance, the need to distinguish diachrony from synchrony, see below § 260), and was able by intui-

tion to make the right choice of criteria for analysis (e.g. he successfully avoided introducing psychology into linguistics).

193. Fortunatov did not leave a large number of works, but he nevertheless established a notable linguistic school (his methodological ideas inspired the work of such outstanding slavists as Peškovskij, Šaxmatov, Belić and others); his famous university lectures were a specially potent source of influence.

Bibliographical references

194. See: F. F. Fortunatov, *Izbrannye trudy* (Moscow, I, 1956; II, 1957) which contain among other things information about Fortunatov's life and work. See also what Zvegincev says in *Istorija jazykoznanija I* (section VI).

The Linguistic Views of Belić

195. The most prominent Yugoslav linguist, Alexandar Belić (1876-1960), under whose scholarly leadership the majority of specialists in the Serbo-Croatian language grew up, was a student of F. F. Fortunatov (his teachers included such eminent neo-grammarians as Leskien, Brugmann and Sievers). In his early linguistic work Belić was primarily a slavist, but his later research was mainly concerned with linguistic theory. All the good qualities of the neo-grammarians, especially the most progressive of them, are also represented in his work. His own original ideas, which for the most part grew out of his diligent study of the Serbo-Croatian language, are concerned with the theory of syntagmatics (the science of word combinations at the syntactic level). Belić was among the pioneers in this field of linguistic research. His main contribution lay in calling attention to the need for investigating the syntactic function of words in order to be able to understand both the differences in their morphological structure and the principles of their concatenation.

Bibliographical references

196. Belić's views on general linguistics are most fully set out in his work *O jezičkoj prirodi i jezičkom razvitku* (Belgrade, Vol. I, 1941-45, second ed. 1958; Vol. II, 1959).

MARRISM

197. In the first years after the Russian Revolution the traditions of Fortunatov's school were still continued in the SovietUnion. However before long a new ideological trend began to dominate Soviet linguistics, the so-called Marrism whose creator was Nikolaj Jakovlevič Marr (1864-1934).

198. Marr began his scholarly career in the tradition of the neo-grammarians. He soon became well-known as a prominent specialist in Caucasian languages who published a number of notable works on this subject. In addition he interested himself in general linguistic theory, but with much less success.

199. His direct contact with non-Indoeuropean linguistic data stimulated him to reflect on the mutual relations of languages, especially their genetic relations.

Marr's ideas on the origin of language coincided basically with the so-called *monogenesis* theory (which was held by some linguistic theoreticians with an idealistic outlook, most of all by Trombetti, see above note to § 184): he thought that all the present-day types of language had proceeded from one basic language. In his view, people first made themselves understood by means of gestures, the first words being uttered only as an aid to magic, in mystic rituals. Marr even "discovered" that the sound combinations *sal, ber, jon* and *roš* were the basic phonetic elements from which all the languages of the world later arose by a process of interaction. He was also convinced that the primordial language structure of mankind (from which all the languages of the world were later derived) could be perceived even today through the existing variety of linguistic phenomena.

200. This monogenetic conception gave rise to his theory of *stadialism*, i.e. the idea that all languages develop by virtue of stadial transformation, reaching successively higher stages of evolutionary rank in the course of time.[24] The typological differences in linguistic structure which are so clearly evident today are connected with the fact that some languages have already attained the highest stage of development, while others have not. There is, then, an obvious hierarchical order among languages: some are higher in the scale and others lower in respect of the degree of development achieved. Marr tried to identify this hierarchical order. In his estimation, the Indoeuropean and Semitic linguistic families had attained the highest degree of evolution.

201. As early as 1908 Marr began to establish his stadial theory by separating the so-called "Japhetic" group of languages which, in his opinion, were at a lower evolutionary stage than the Indoeuropean and Semitic. Since all languages passed through the same levels of development, Marr affirmed that the study of the Japhetic group would afford valuable information about the long past, prehistoric periods of the Indoeuropean linguistic family.

202. In the course of time Marr changed many details in his theory. He was particularly inconsistent as to which languages should be regarded as "Japhetic". At first he limited these to the Caucasian group, but by 1920 he had included a much larger stock of languages.

203. In 1924 Marr proclaimed himself a champion of Marxism linguistics. Although in 1926 he refuted the ideas of his earlier works, his new ideological outlook did not mean the abandonment of his theories concerning monogenesis, stadialism, or "Japhetidism". In fact he simply added to his earlier ideas the conception that language is a social and economic edifice with an obvious class character. A particular phase of linguistic development is conditioned by a particular social and economic situation: thus the structure of a language changes with the structure of society and its economic basis. Since linguistic categories, like all other forms of superstruc-

---

[24] This corresponds to some conceptions in German nineteenth century linguistics, particularly Schleicher's theory, see above § 63.

ture, reflect actual social relations, linguistic development invariably moves in revolutionary leaps from one evolutionary stage to another. New ideologies, linked with a change of cultural patterns and level of civilization, lead directly to the creation of a new linguistic system.

204. In this last Marxist period of his work Marr definitively elaborated his theory about language mixture. In his opinion, what is in classical grammar called the "parent language" is nothing but a worthless fiction; hence this term and all it implies should be completely rejected (this caused the collapse of both classical comparative grammar and history of language during the whole reign of Marrism in the U.S.S.R.). Languages arise by a process of interweaving and combining, he asserted. They keep in step with the growth of political bodies (states). The universal principle of linguistic development is fulfilled in the constant mixing of different languages.

205. Marr considered that national languages did not exist, but only the languages of social classes. He believed that every language, created by a process of intermixing, contains two co-existing languages, just as every culture implies the existence of two cultural layers: one belonging to the exploiters and the other to the exploited. According to the laws of social development, the language of the exploited is predestined to oust the language exploiters.

206. After Marr's death in 1934 the further elaboration of his ideas was undertaken by the members of the "Institute of Language and Thought", among whom the leading spirit was I. I. Meščaninov. The definitive theory of Marrism was worked out in the period between 1930 and 1940, that is for the most part after Marr's death. Then, among other things, Marrism came to be applied to a wider linguistic field, for instance to syntax (with which Marr himself had not been particularly concerned).

207. Of all the heterogeneous ideas that the theory of Marrism embraces, the most prominent are the following assertions: language is monogenetic and always passes through the same degrees of development; it is a social and economic superstructure, with a clearly marked class character.

208. Serious scholarly criticism has for a long time countered the

monogenetic theory with the much more acceptable theory of polygenesis: language grew up among human beings in the process of work, on different parts of the earth's surface, and acquired its form in a variety of ways, but always had the same basic function of serving as a means of mutual understanding. Marr's basic postulation was in fact at variance with the Marxist explanation of the origin of language. When they realized how unacceptable the monogenetic view was, the Marrists themselves openly admitted the possibility of a critical attitude in this respect.

209. Although the Marrists for the most part kept silent as regards Marr's strange ideas about the "four elements" (*sal, roš, jon, ber*), they conceded that his explanation of the stadial transformation of language should be thoroughly revised.

210. The assertion that language is conditioned by social and economic factors was, however, accepted as an axiom which it was not permitted to doubt.

Because of the conviction that this attitude was in the closest possible accordance with Marxism, for many years no serious criticism was heard in the U.S.S.R. which might have shown that Marr's teaching was in many cases unrealistic. Outside the U.S.S.R. Marrism was rejected as unscientific, as a result of serious, well-documented criticism. Among other things it was demonstrated by practical examples that Marr's axiomatic statement concerning the subjection of the language belonging to the exploiters by the language of the exploited does not correspond to actual facts.

211. Public criticism of Marrism in the Soviet Union began only when the highest political authority (Stalin) began to interest himself in the unsatisfactory condition of Soviet linguistics.[25]

Marr's theories were demolished by the simple statement that language, as a specific phenomenon, cannot be directly connected with either a base or a superstructure. The following four viewpoints, which proceed from the above statement, completely overthrow all the ideas underlying Marrism.

---

[25] It is thought that this happened because certain prominent linguistic scholars, who disagreed with Marr's ideas, realizing that they were powerless to improve matters, sought help in the highest quarters.

1. It is well-known that every base has its superstructure, which is so indissolubly bound up with it that the destruction of the base means the disappearance of the superstructure. In Russia, from the time of the revolution onwards, capitalism has been abolished and socialism established; yet the language has not entered a new stage.

2. Every superstructure serves its own base which means, in this particular case, that every social class should have its own language. But in modern European states the same language is spoken by the capitalists and the proletariat.

3. A superstructure is connected with its base as regards time, which means that it cannot outlast it. But the Russian language used by Pushkin outlived both feudalism and capitalism, and even under socialism still serves as an example of the highest linguistic achievement.

4. A superstructure is not directly connected with man's productive activity, but language is. New advances in civilization bring new terms into the life of a society, although the base remains unchanged.

Such critical remarks, by which Marr's theories were finally disqualified on Marxist grounds, were followed, during the period when Marrism was under the full fire of criticism, by other wellfounded arguments.[26]

212. Marrism meant a long break with tradition in the development of classsic linguistics in the Soviet Union, and also isolation from all the main linguistic events which were taking place in the rest of the world. This was the greatest loss which Soviet linguistics suffered from Marrism, even greater than the fact that many years of work were devoted to developing a scientific theory which was basically erroneous.

The positive results of the Marrist epoch were indeed few; but they did include the use of studies relating to all the different ways in which word semantics have reflected different forms of social life,

[26] It was only then, for example, that a fact long since wellknown was publicly asserted, namely that Engels had pointed out that it was impossible to explain phonetic changes by economic conditions.

and also an increased interest in the numerous non-Indoeuropean languages of the Soviet Union.

Bibliographical references

213. Marr's collected works (in five volumes) were published between 1933 and 1937 in Leningrad under the title of *Izbrannye raboty* (AN SSSR, Gosud. akademija istorii material'noj kul'tury). For the ideas of the later exponents of Marrism, see I. I. Meščaninov *Novoe učenie o jazyke – Stadial'naja tipologija* (Leningrad, Gosudarstvennoe social'no-ekonomičeskoe izdatel'stvo, Leningradskoe otdelenie, 1936) and *Obščee jazykoznanie* (Leningrad, 1936).

See also: Herbert Rubenstein, "The Recent Conflict in Soviet Linguistics", *Lg*, 27, No 3 (1951), pp. 281-287; Lawrence L. Thomas, *The Linguistic Theories of N. J. Marr* (Berkeley and Los Angeles, 1957).

The discussion which led to the overthrow of Marrism as a scientific theory was conducted in the columns of the Moscow newspaper *Pravda* in 1950 in May, June and July (Stalin's articles: 20. VI and 4. VII).

EXPERIMENTAL PHONETICS

214. Phonetics was the first linguistic discipline to establish an exact method of analysis, thanks to the help of technical instruments. Its development was made possible by the development of physics; once physicists provided the technical means for experiments, phonetics made a significant advance.

215. Men have investigated sounds from ancient times onwards.[27]

[27] While the Greeks were primarily interested in the acoustic aspect of sounds (see above § 14), the Indian grammarians have left us an excellent classification of sounds according to their articulatory characteristics. Among the tasks undertaken in the field of phonetics before the nineteenth century, the most important were the attempts to make "music machines" = machines which

However it was not until the beginning of the nineteenth century that phonetics became a serious discipline, owing to the research of the famous French mathematician B. J. Fourier (1768-1830). Fourier was the first to measure sound waves. He advanced the theory of *formants* (i.e. the specific resonances of a sound wave which depend on its localization in the speech organs).

216. The science of sounds is divided into *acoustic* phonetics (which study the nature of sound waves) and *articulatory* (or *motor*) phonetics (which study the speech processes on which the formation of sounds depends). The first important work in the field of acoustic phonetics (a description of consonants) was that of Wolfgang de Kempelen, the inventor of a musical machine.[28] The first systematic work on articulatory phonetics was by the psychologist H. von Helmholtz.[29]

217. The Frenchman P. J. Rousselot was the first experimental (or instrumental – both terms are used though the first is more frequent) phonetician among specialists in language problems. He introduced into the study of phonetics the *kymograph* (used for measuring articulatory energy, though somewhat imperfectly) and the *palatogramme* (which shows the impression made by the articulation of the tongue on an artificial palate introduced for this purpose into the mouth of a person pronouncing specially chosen sounds or words). The tradition of phonetic research was established mainly under the influence of his description[30] of his own phonetic investigations performed by means of these instruments.

218. During the nineteenth century considerable attention was devoted to the study of phonetics. Among the scholars who have left notable works in this field (Brücke, Grammont, Meyer and others), two are specially outstanding by reason of their influence on their contemporaries: Sievers (*Grundzüge der Lautphysiologie*,

---

could "talk". As early as the seventeenth century (1681) the English physicist Robert Hooke made such a machine which produced sounds. Similar attempts were made in France and Germany during the eighteenth century.

[28] W. de Kempelen, *Mechanismus der menschlichen Stimme nebst der Beschreibung einer sprechender Maschine* (Vienna, 1791).

[29] *Die Lehre von den Tonempfindungen* (1862).

[30] Published in *Principes de phonétique expérimentale* (Paris, 1897-1905).

1876) and Sweet (*Handbook of Phonetics*, 1877). Sweet and Sievers in fact laid the foundations of motor phonetics.

219. Not all of these nineteenth century phoneticians made equal use of instruments in their phonetic analysis. Some of them were even sceptical as to the value of such assistance (e.g. Sievers), which is understandable in view of the fact that the instruments of that time were somewhat primitive. It was only after the First World War that phoneticians began to acquire technical aids of increasingly good quality. These new instruments finally made it possible to give correct answers to many basic questions in phonetics.[31] They even made it possible to widen the scope of scholarly interests and extend the range of phonetic research in a manner hitherto undreamt of.

220. In the twenties of this century Germany was in the forefront of experimental phonetics in Europe.[32] However at the same time phonetic research with instruments was developing rapidly in the U.S.A.; and it was there, owing to the growth of electronics, that the exact methods in phonetics have been radically improved.

221. Before 1930 American engineers began to investigate sound waves with the help of a new technical instrument known as *vacuum tubes*. Harvey Fletcher introduced vacuum tubes into experimental phonetic analysis. His study *Speech and Hearing* (New York, 1929) soon became familiar to phoneticians.

222. But it was the use of the *spectrograph* which caused a real revolution in phonetics. This is a device which enables a sound to be seen: characteristic formants of sounds are visible in the form of a line. The first linguistic scholar to use a detailed spectrographic analysis in describing phonetic phenomena was the American Martin Joos. His book *Acoustic Phonetics* (1948) remains a classic work of modern phonetics.

---

[31] Thanks to the aid of precise instruments, we have at last learnt that the actual nature of vowels depends on the concentration of energy in the particular frequencies of vibration.

[32] The German Carl Stumpf, for example, had notable success in solving phonetic problems with the help of instruments. His study *Die Sprachlaute* (Berlin, 1926), though at one time highly valued, is now already obsolete owing to the discovery of improved technical methods.

223. In the second half of the twentieth century, phonetics has made a notable advance from every point of view. It is now entirely based on experimental methods which include the wide use of instruments, and may be considered a discipline close to physics as well as to linguistics (and even to physiology when concerned with the study of motor processes). Phonetics has gained in importance, owing to the fact that its help is increasingly necessary for carrying out the large-scale linguistic enterprises of the present day.[33]

224. Today phonemic research is so directly connected with that of phonetics that it is impossible to draw a sharp line between the two disciplines. In the search for the distinctive features of the phoneme, phonetic analysis of sounds made with the most modern technical devices have played a decisive rôle.

225. The development of information theory (see below § 449) has inspired the so-called *perceptual* research in phonetics, the aim of which is to establish which sound features are important for intelligibility. For example tests are organized so that a voice recorded on a tape is damaged to some extent, and the listeners are then asked to say how much they have understood. In this connection spectrographic recordings have also proved useful; when an acoustic phenomenon is changed into a visual one there are greater possibilities of observing what is vital for intelligibility and what can be omitted without impairing understanding.

Today help is also sought in this direction in the task of explaining the complicated phenomenon of individual variations in speech perception.

226. A method of automatically transferring "visible speech" back into sound has recently been perfected in the U.S.A. A way of producing artificial (synthetic) speech by means of electronic devices has also been invented. All this has the aim of enriching our knowledge of perceptual phonetics, the application of which would be extremely useful in practical work.

[33] The eminent German scholar E. Zwirner, stressing the valuable contribution of recent phonetic research to linguistics, called the modern phonetics, of which he is an exponent, *phonometrics* in order to avoid the usual term reminiscent of a time when the study of sounds was a discipline with a quite different scientific status.

Bibliographical references

227. The most important of the old classical works on phonetics are the above-mentioned books by Rousselot (§ 217), Sweet (§ 218), and Sievers (§ 218), to which should be added the well-known manual by the French phonetician M. Grammont: "Traité de phonétique" (see above § 164).

Up to the outbreak of the Second World War the following books were also very popular: R. H. Stetson, "Motor Phonetics", *Archives Néerlandaises de phonétique expérimentale* III (1928), pp. 1-216; A. Sotavalta, *Die Phonetik und ihre Beziehung zu den Grenzwissenschaften* (Helsinki, 1936).

The first classical American works in phonetics include K. L. Pike's book: *Phonetics, A Critical Analysis of Phonetic Theory and a Technique for the Practical Description of Sounds* (Ann Arbor, 1943).

The work of the English scholar D. Jones *The Phoneme, Its Nature and Use* (Cambridge, 1950) is highly esteemed among phoneticians.

The important study by M. Joos, "Acoustic Phonetics" (Suppl. to *Lg*, vol. 24, No. 2, 1948) not only expounds the opportunities offered by the application of the spectrograph in phonetics, but also gives a general indication of the advantages of the use of instruments in linguistic work. It includes certain theories, which were then topical, about the perception of sounds in connection with the problem of intelligibility.

N. I. Žinkin's book *Mehanizmy reči* (Moscow, 1958) has been highly appreciated. The rôle of the diaphragm in the formation of sounds was here indicated for the first time.

The following are among the better-known textbooks on phonetics: R.-M.S. Heffner, *General Phonetics* (Madison, 1949); E. Dieth, *Vademekum der Phonetik* (Berne, 1950); W. Brandenstein, *Einführung in die Phonetik und Phonologie* (Vienna, 1950); L. R. Zinder, *Obščaja fonetika* (Leningrad, 1960).

G. Trager's study: "Phonetics, Glossary and Tables", *SIL*, *Occasional Papers*, 6 (New York, University of Buffalo, 1958), pp.

1-27 gives useful information about the basic terminology of modern phonetics.

The following provide an introduction to modern experimental method: K. Potter, G. A. Kopp, and H. C. Green, *Visible Speech* (New York, 1947); E. Pulgram, *Introduction to the Spectrography of Speech* (= *Janua Linguarum*, 7) (The Hague, 1959) (a significant work for linguistics: gives a clear explanation of the principles of spectrography without going into details); C. G. M. Fant, "On the Predictability of Formant Levels and Spectrum Envelopes from Formant Frequencies", *For Roman Jakobson*, pp. 109-121.

The volume *Manual of Phonetics* (ed. L. Kaiser, Amsterdam, 1957) contains a number of papers by eminent writers (Jakobson, Halle, Panconcelli-Calzia, etc.) which give the main information about the history of phonetics, its place within the framework of linguistic disciplines, its relation to psychology and physiology as well as a survey of the most important achievements in the field of modern phonetic analysis.

An excellent retrospect of the history of phonetics, particularly its experimental aspect, is given in Morris Halle's book *The Sound Pattern of Russian* (The Hague, 1959); especially Chapter IV: "Critical Survey of Acoustical Investigations of Speech Sounds", pp. 91-109.

An account of the development of experimental phonetics in the United States is given by P. Delattre in "Les indices acoustiques de la parole: Premier Rapport", *Phonetica*, 2 (1958), pp. 108-118 and 226-251.

The achievements in the field of experimental phonetics not only in the U.S.A. but in the world as a whole, are expounded in the following two studies published in the *8th Proceedings*: C. G. Fant, "Modern Instruments and Methods for Acoustic Studies of Speech", pp. 282-358 and E. Fischer-Jørgensen, "What can the New Techniques of Acoustic Phonetics contribute to Linguistics?", pp. 433-499.

The latest results in acoustic phonetics so far are best represented in Gunnar Fant's book *Acoustic Theory of Speech Production – With Calculations on X-Ray Studies of Russian Articulations* with a selective bibliography (The Hague, 1960).

15

STRUCTURAL LINGUISTICS

BASIC TENDENCIES OF DEVELOPMENT

228. The epoch of structural linguistics began before 1930 in both Europe and U.S.A.

As in other branches of scholarship, structuralism in linguistics means, first of all, a new approach to facts already known: these facts are reconsidered with regard to their function in the system. In addition the structuralist standpoint implies an insistence on the social (i.e. communicative) function of language, and a clear distinction between historical phenomena and the characteristics of a linguistic system at a given moment.

229. Forerunners of the new epoch had appeared here and there in the past, some as early as the nineteenth century.[1] But these solitary attempts were not heeded by their contemporaries. The first voice which really made itself heard, to such an extent that its echoes still resound today, was that of Ferdinand de Saussure (see below § 242). Because he was the first to inspire his contemporaries so powerfully with new ideas on linguistics, and because even those who were not under his direct influence started from the same theoretical basis which underlay his ideas – De Saussure is now regarded as the founder of structural linguistics.

230. De Saussure's fundamental statements on language, what

[1] Marty, a representative of psychological linguistics (see above § 89) pointed out as early as 1884 that the description of the contemporary state of a language should be the main object of linguistic study; but as his general angle of approach was philosophical rather than linguistic, his views did not receive adequate attention. There were other scholars who had progressive ideas for their day – for example the Scandinavian grammarians (such as Rask and Noreen) and the English (Sweet and his pupils). However it was the outlook of the Slavist Baudouin de Courtenay that proved most challenging (see above §§ 188 and 189).

one might term the alphabet of structural linguistics, is as follows.

Language is a system, and should be studied as such: individual facts should not be taken in isolation, but always as a whole, taking into account that every detail is determined by its place within the system.

Language is primarily a social phenomenon which serves the purpose of mutual understanding, and ought to be studied as such: the correlation of sound and meaning should always be borne in mind, since it is of crucial importance in the process of communication. The evolution of language and its actual state are two fundamentally different phenomena; from the point of view of method it is inadmissable to bring historical criteria into the interpretation of the present state of a language.

231. In linguistics, as in the field of other disciplines, structuralism also implies both the search for invariants (see above § 116), and an effort to set apart *relevant* phenomena from *redundant*.

All the representatives of structural linguistics aspire to find objective standards in analysis (which would exclude the possibility of mentalistic criteria).

232. The beginning of structuralism in linguistics was characterized by a diversity of attitudes with regard to the criteria used for the determination of linguistic units. Today the main differences have been removed, and there is an ever increasing approximation in methods and in the scope and trend of linguistic interests.

233. Structuralism began to develop at the same time in both Europe and the U.S.A., but without much mutual contact.[2] From the beginning the fundamental difference lay in the fact that European structuralism was based on the influence of De Saussure's ideas, whereas in America De Saussure was practically unknown.[3]

[2]   In fact the first actual subjects of interest were the same: Trubetzkoy in Europa and Sapir and Bloomfield in the U.S.A. began to talk about the phoneme at practically the same time. It was then too that the Chinese scholar Yuen Ren Chao (now in the U.S.A.) expounded his views in a now classical study: "The Non-uniqueness of Phonemic Solutions of Phonetic systems", *Bulletin of the Institute of History and Philology, Academia Sinica*, Vol. IV, Part 4, (1934), pp. 363-397.

[3]   Bloomfield, the founder of American linguistic structuralism (see below § 325), agreed with De Saussure only in those basic views which have been men-

234. There are three basic types of European structuralism. The first was the *Geneva school* (see below § 262). This was the classic structuralism of De Saussure which later developed in a specific direction. However the main achievements of this school belong to the past; its contribution to present-day trends in linguistics is of marginal significance. The second type is represented in the works of the *Prague School* (consisting mainly of eminent Slavists) and their adherents (see below § 292). The Prague school is also known under the name of *functional linguistics* (its primary interest is the way in which a sound unit functions as a communicative sign). Nowadays the term most frequently used is the *phonological school* (the proponents of the Prague school were mainly interested in phonological problems). This school has played an exceptionally significant rôle in the development of linguistics. Its ideas and methods as a whole are the most representative of structural linguistics in general. The theoretical outlook of these adherents of structuralism evolved directly from the roots of traditional linguistics. From the very beginning they have been free from extremism and remained primarily interested in concrete linguistic facts: they neither pretend to dematerialize language (as the glossematicians do, see below § 368), nor do they insist on bare, formal description without any reference to meaning (which would conform to the Bloomfieldian standpoint, see below § 329). The Prague school has experienced a consistent upward surge, which has brought it straight from the most progressive attitudes of traditional linguistics to the new outlook of the present day in the field of scholarly method. The third type is represented by the school of glossema-

---

tioned as underlying structural linguistics in general. Otherwise they not only had little in common as regards methodological conceptions, but in some details even held directly opposing opinions. For De Saussure, language was above all a psychological phenomenon – the linguistic sign exists in us as an abstract entity (as the representative of a particular acoustic impression which evokes a particular meaning); hence linguistic research should be primarily directed to surveying the way in which language structure is manifested in the linguistic consciousness of the speech group. For Bloomfield, on the contrary, language was primarily a concrete, empirical fact; hence linguistic research should be concerned only with data actually recorded.

ticians (see below § 371) which is sometimes called *neo-Saussurianism* (because of its pronounced tendency to abstractness which is in harmony with De Saussure's interpretation of the linguistic sign). This school certainly owes much to De Saussure's teaching, but just as much to symbolic logic (see below § 368). Today it is more concerned with constructing a general theory about the language sign than with studying concrete linguistic problems.

235. The structural epoch in American linguistics originated at Yale University. The first structural school, distinguished by the *distributional* method of analysis, was founded by Bloomfield (see below § 330). Hence this school is known under a variety of names: the *Yale school*, the *Bloomfieldians* and the *distributionalists*.

When the Americans finally directed their attention to the achievements of European structuralism, it seemed to them (provided differences in terminology were resolved) that there were most points of contact between their distributionalist school and the glossematicians.[4]

Neither the distributionalists nor the glossematicians share the pivotal interest of the Prague school in the *distinctive features* of linguistic units (see below § 302), but focus their attention on the distribution of these units (i.e. the rules governing the possibility of their co-occurrence in the speech chain). According to the Americans, it is only after stating all the rules of the distribution of linguistic units in the speech chain that we can gather the most objective, exact information about their function within the system. As regards the glossematicians, they have no interest in the material aspect of language, but only in determining all types of relationships existing between the elements which are organized in a system of communication. Thus both schools represent a definitely *formalistic* method;[5] they approach linguistic analysis without taking directly into account the category of meaning. However the American distributionalists and the glossematicians diverge funda-

---

[4] The American scholar Einar Haugen speaks in this sense in his study "Directions in Modern Linguistics", *Lg.*, 27, No. 3 (1951), pp. 211-222.
[5] The terms *form, formal* and *formalistic* are here used with the values given them by modern logic.

mentally in one basic conception: the former are concerned with actual linguistic data, while the latter deliberately neglect the material (sound) aspect of language.

236. One of the most important events in the not so distant history of linguistic structuralism was the arrival of Roman Jakobson, the leading representative of the Prague Circle, in the U.S.A. (during the Second World War). Harvard University soon became the most distinguished centre of the Prague school, and a new generation of modern linguists has been trained there. At first there were sharp clashes of opinion between the Yale and Harvard centres. Jakobson and his followers, although insisting consistently on the theory of distinctive features, did not, however, neglect the use of distributional criteria in analysis. The attitude of the Bloomfieldians in this respect was obviously biassed: they maintained that only the distributional approach to linguistic phenomena should be allowed; they even tried to solve phonological problems exclusively in the light of the theory of distribution. As regards phonology, the representatives of the Prague school emerged victorious; today phonological studies are usually based on the investigation of distinctive features (see below § 302). On the other hand the value of the Bloomfieldian method in the fields of morphological and syntactical research has been proved by machine translation.

The development of the theory of information and the penetration of mathematical criteria into linguistics have helped to remove the most obvious differences between these two schools. Now it is linguistic scholars of the "mixed type" that have the main say in world linguistics: the founder of transformational grammar, Noam Chomsky, for example, is a student of a distributionalist, versed in the procedures of mathematical linguistics, and acquainted with the achievements of the *Harvard school* (i.e. Prague structuralism as modernized by Roman Jakobson); Morris Halle (who was the first to introduce the generative approach into phonology) was trained at Harvard and is conversant with distributionalism, mathematical linguistics and the theory of information; the dialectologist and semantician Uriel Weinreich also has a many-sided outlook, etc.

237. The penetration of structuralism to the U.S.S.R. is undoubt-

edly of paramount importance for the history of modern linguistics. This did not take place until after the collapse of Marrism[6]
(see above §§ 197-212). At first Soviet structuralism was obviously
eclectic.[7] Although it has still not emerged from this phase, today
there is a noticeable tendency toward *psycholinguistics* (see below
§ 352) in connection with information theory and machine translation. New and original scholarly achievements are expected
from the younger generation of Soviet structuralists in the near
future.

238. The basic programme of the structural approach at the
present moment is as follows:

A. *Descriptive linguistics* is the study of linguistic structure by
means of objective criteria. These criteria rest on the process of
distinguishing the relevant from the redundant and revealing oppositions based on the principle of *binarity*.

B. Linguistic descriptions must reflect the hierarchy of phenomena within the system. In defining a phenomenon, the particular
linguistic *level* on which it manifests itself is regularly kept in view:
whether it is of lexical, phonemic, morphological, semantic or
syntactical character (i.e. what type of linguistic organization

[6] Although De Saussure's ideas were expounded at Moscow University by
Sergej Karcevskij between 1917 and 1919, because of the special circumstances
of that time this had no influence on the development of Soviet linguistics.
Marrism practically wiped out traditional linguistics, and any new trend, especially from the West, was received with indignant disapproval. (For instance the
famous American linguistic scholar E. Sapir was known to the Soviet linguistic
public only through the unwarranted criticisms of the Marrists; he was even
called a racist. Sapir was fully rehabilitated in the U.S.S.R. only in 1956, in the
pages of the periodical *Voprosy jazykoznanija*). From the time of the Twentieth
Party Congress in the U.S.S.R. (1956) there has been talk of the need to construct
machines for translation. In connection with this Soviet linguistic scholars have
seen the necessity for becoming acquainted with the structural method and the
achievements of mathematical logic, undertaking work in phonology and
experimental phonetics (hitherto neglected in the U.S.S.R.) and making use of
statistical criteria in linguistic research. In 1956 the periodical *Voprosy jazykoznanija* opened a discussion on the value of the structural method in linguistics – a discussion which ended in a definite victory for structuralism.

[7] S. K. Šaumjan is one of the most prominent and typical representatives of
Soviet structural linguistics. He has a good knowledge of the principles of the
Prague School, but his particular enthusiasm is glossematics (see below his
works, § 385).

should be borne in mind in determining the function of a particular unit within the system).

C. The function of a language element is checked by *substitution* (i.e. a test by which other linguistic forms, whose grammatical function is already known, are placed in the same linguistic environments in which the element under investigation occurs: if they fit into the same frame the function in question is identical with their grammatical function).

D. Definitions of phenomena try to achieve the greatest possible simplicity, exactness and consistency (for this purpose a variety of symbols, formulae, sketches and diagrams are used whenever possible).

239. Structural linguistics has brought new concepts which require new terminology. Inadequate contact between various schools has facilitated the uncontrolled growth and irrational distribution of different terms (sometimes the same terms are used for several phenomena). This has provided arguments for critics and caused misunderstandings among the adherents of different schools. At the present moment efforts are being made to establish an ordered system of terminology.

240. Thanks to the steady development of the structural method, the utility of linguistic achievements is indisputably confirmed every day. The study of foreign languages is advanced by the use of efficient grammatical text-books. Engineers and linguists have successfully co-operated to produce translation machines. The same co-operation has led to greatly improved instruments of communication (such as telephone, radio, gramophone, microphone and others). Today even physicians show increasing willingness to co-operate with linguistic scholars (in investigating mental disturbances, and in the field of correcting speech and hearing defects). As regards psychologists, they have turned their attention to the latest achievements in linguistics in order to work out their theories of the learning process (how facts are remembered and most easily learnt, etc.). Everything would appear to justify the conviction that even more valuable results will be obtained in the future in this respect.

Bibliographical References

241. One of the first works in which the concept of structuralism in linguistics was defined is an article by H. J. Pos, "Perspectives du structuralisme", *TCLP*, VIII, (1939), pp. 71-79. The same theme is treated by V. Brøndal "Linguistique structurale", *Acta Linguistica*, I, 1 (Copenhagen, 1939), pp. 2-10, and E. Cassirer, "Structuralism in Modern Linguistics", *Word*, I, 2 (1945), pp. 99-120.

Hjelmslev's views concerning the basic concepts of structuralism are presented in his article "Metod strukturnogo analiza v lingvistike", *Acta Linguistica*, VI, 2-3 (Copenhagen 1950-51), pp. 57-67.

E. Haugen in "Directions in Modern Linguistics", *Lg*, 27, 3 (1951), pp. 211-222 expounds structural principles in the form of a parallel between the Yale and the glossematic schools.

A. Martinet in "Structural Linguistics", *Anthropology Today* (Chicago, 1953), pp. 574-586, gives a comparative estimate of Yale, Prague and glossematic structuralism, and in "The Unity of Linguistics" *Linguistics Today* (New York, 1954), pp. 1-5 sketches in broad outline the relationship of traditional linguistics to structuralism.

S. K. Šaumjan in "O suščnosti stukturnoj lingvistiki", *V Ja*, V, 5 (1956), pp. 38-54 and "Strukturnaja lingvistika kak immanentnaja teorija jazyka" (Moskva, AN SSSR, Institut slavjanovedenija, 1958) speaks of structuralism, with special emphasis on those views which are most popular with the Soviet structuralists.

An explanation of the terminology and concepts of the Prague school is given by J. Vachek in *Dictionnaire de linguistique de l'école de Prague* (Utrecht – Antwerp, 1960).

The terminology adopted in American linguistics is explained by E. P. Hamp in *A Glossary of American Technical Linguistic Usage 1925-1950* (Utrecht-Antwerp, 1957) and George L. Trager, "Phonetics: Glossary and Tables", *SIL*, *Occasional Papers*, 6 (New York, University of Buffalo, 1958).

An introduction to the structural method is provided by the classic textbooks of American linguistics: H. A. Gleason, *An Intro-*

duction to Descriptive Linguistics (New York, 1955; 2d rev. ed., 1961); John B. Carroll, *The Study of Language* (Cambridge Mass., 1955) (good on the relationship between structural linguistics and other disciplines, particularly modern psychology); Charles F. Hockett, *A Course in Modern Linguistics* (New York, 1958).

A collection published in New York in 1954 (ed. A. Martinet and U. Weinreich) under the title of *Linguistics Today* contains articles in which the challenging views of various eminent linguistic scholars are expounded. A representative choice of works which have exercised a decisive influence on the development of American linguistics is given by M. Joos in a collection entitled: *Readings in Linguistics – the development of descriptive linguistics in America since 1925* (Washington, 1957).

The past and present currents of world linguistics can best be studied in the appropriate periodicals. For example the development of the Geneva school can be traced in the periodical *Cahiers Ferdinand de Saussure* (pub. Société Genevoise de Linguistique, Geneva). The Praguists are represented in works published in *Travaux de Cercle Linguistique de Prague* (1929-1939). *The International Journal of Slavic Linguistics and Poetics* (The Hague), actually one of the most distinguished linguistic publications, is mainly dominated by the adherents of the Harvard (i.e. Jakobson's) school. The favourite forum of the glossematicians is *Travaux du Cercle Linguistique de Copenhague*, and also *Acta Linguistica – Revue internationale de linguistique structurale* (Copenhagen). American linguistics are represented in such periodicals as *Language* (Journal of the Linguistic Society of America, Baltimore), *Word* (published by the Linguistic Circle of New York – New York) and *International Journal of American Linguistics* (Baltimore). The most convenient survey (especially for beginners) of the problems at present being treated in structural linguistics throughout the world can be found in the communications, discussions and reviews published in the Soviet periodical *Voprosy jazykoznanija* (Moscow).

This does not exhaust the list of periodicals dealing with the problems of structural linguistics. A complete bibliography of publications in linguistics from the Second World War to the present day is given in *Bibliographie linguistique* (bibliographical reports published by the Permanent International Committee of Linguists, Utrecht-Antwerp).

FERDINAND DE SAUSSURE

242. The Swiss Ferdinand de Saussure (1857-1913) was one of the greatest linguistic scholars of all times. His powerful personality, original linguistic talent, exceptional flair for the theoretical aspect of research, and the influence he exercised on his students not only made him the founder of an important school (the so-called *Geneva school*) but of a whole epoch of linguistic scholarship: the ideas which he first openly and persuasively expounded were the roots from which modern structural linguistics sprang.

243. De Saussure was professor of linguistics at Geneva and Paris (the Geneva period was particularly important in his work). He taught Sanskrit, Germanic languages, Greek, Latin and Lithuanian. It was only after 1894 that he began to interest himself in general linguistic ideas. He published little. Apart from his first and most important work *Mémoire sur le système primitif des voyelles dans les langues indo-européennes* (see below § 244) De Saussure only published some twenty articles connected with Indo-european languages (on the Baltic, Germanic and Greek languages, and on Phrygian inscriptions). He also left some notes and short articles on etymological problems, and a few reviews.

244. De Saussure received his linguistic training from the most eminent of the neo-grammarians (Brugmann, Osthoff, Leskien, see above § 95). He was also well acquainted with the views of the linguistic naturalist Schleicher (see above §§ 60-63) and the linguistic geographer Gilliéron (see above §§ 149-151). He had a high opinion of the American linguistic scholar W. D. Whitney, especially of his work "The Life and Growth of Language" (see below note to § 317). However his particular enthusiasm was the Kazan school (see above §§ 186-190). There is evidence that he talked to his pupils

about the originality and importance of the ideas of Baudouin de Courtenay and Kruszewski, and insisted that it was to the detriment of Western linguistics that so little was known of their work. De Saussure was also interested in the progress of other, non-linguistic disciplines, especially sociology: Durkheim's theories made a deep impression on him.[8] It might have been expected that De Saussure, as a pupil of the neo-grammarians, would begin his scholarly career by following faithfully the theoretical and methodological conceptions of his teachers. But this did not happen. His very first work[9] showed an exceptional independence in scholarly approach: linguistic phenomena are regarded as a whole, i.e. in a system, which amounted to a revolution in linguistic methodology. The year 1879 when this study by the young De Saussure appeared (*Mémoire sur le système primitif des voyelles dans les langues indoeuropéennes*) has remained a memorable date in the history of linguistic research.

245. This brilliant pupil of the neo-grammarians made a successful attack on the puzzling question of the relationship between long and short Indoeuropean vowels, which had seemed until then insoluble. Taking as his point of departure the idea that everything in language is interconnected, that there is a basic structure uniting the grammatical forms of the same system into a whole, De Saussure expounded his own original explanation of the linguistic riddle. His explanation may be briefly summarized as follows.

As had already been proved, Indoeuropean languages had an alternation of short vowels: $e/o/ø$[10] (in such syllables as *derk/dork/drk*; in Greek *dérkomai, dédorka, édrakon*). De Saussure

---

[8] Emile Durkheim (1858-1917), a famous French sociologist, emphasized among other things that collective opinion, which is impersonal and therefore not subjective, is far more important in building up the general knowledge of mankind than individual opinion. Not only has the collective view a greater value than that of the individual, but the individual opinion is dependent on it and developes directly under its impulses. Echoes of this idea can be noticed in De Saussure's theory about the relationship between the language of the speaking group ("langue") and the individual's speech ("parole"), see below § 259.

[9] Written when De Saussure was 21 and still a student of Leipzig University.

[10] ø denotes the absence of a vowel.

affirmed that it was necessary to presuppose that the Indoeuropean sound system had, in addition to the sounds known to us, a sound of unknown value which was later lost (De Saussure designates this by A), and which by its presence, in similar phonetic contexts, made possible a similar series of alternations: *dheA/*dhoA/*dhA like *derk/dork/drk*. The disappearance of this mysterious A led, according to the laws of Indoeuropean phonetics, to a characteristic lengthening of neighbouring short vowels, and to the appearance of a vowel where it had not previously occurred, i.e. between consonants, instead of ø (in Greek, for example we get the relationship *dhē/dhō/dhe: títhēmi/thōmós/thetós*).

The convincing way in which De Saussure expounded and developed his theory made a deep impression on his contemporaries. The linguistic public was no less excited when in 1941 Hendriksen,[11] in the course of his researches on Hittite,[12] discovered a laryngeal sound in just the positions which De Saussure had connected with the occurrence of the mysterious A. So scholars have had the opportunity to put the correctness of De Saussure's theory beyond all doubt.

246. De Saussure's basic views on language are set out in the book *Cours de linguistique générale* published under his name in 1916. But De Saussure was not actually the author of this book; it was put together after his death from the notes of his pupils, who were deeply devoted to the ideas and memory of their great teacher.[13] As R. Godel has recently shown (see below § 261), the book contains a version of De Saussure's ideas which does not correspond at all points to his views on language as expounded in the course of his university lectures and in conversations with his pupils. For instance he did not insist so strongly on a strict distinction between "langue" and "parole", i.e. between the language of the whole speaking group (which exists in the speech consciousness of every

---

[11] H. Hendriksen, "Untersuchungen über die Bedeutung des Hethitischen für die Laryngal-Theorie", *Det kgl. Danske Vidensk. Selskab. Hist.-filolog. Medd.*, 28, 2 (Copenhagen, 1941).
[12] One of the most archaic Indoeuropean languages, unknown in De Saussure's time.
[13] The book was edited by Ch. Bally and A. Sechehaye.

individual), and the phenomenon of individual speech (which reflects the pattern of the "langue"). Although he pointed to the necessity of making a precise theoretical differentiation here, De Saussure was nevertheless aware that such a strict distinction was untenable in practice. On the other hand, certain ideas on which De Saussure laid greater emphasis are toned down in the book. As Godel competently shows, De Saussure's enthusiasm for a mathematical approach to language is quite insufficiently represented; De Saussure was in fact the first linguist who insisted that an adequate description of the structure of a language could be obtained only by introducing mathematical procedures into analysis. The book also suffers from the fact that, in the absence of instructions from the author, it was impossible to avoid a certain amount of repetition, vagueness and even some contradictory statements.

However, in spite of the uneven character of the text and occasional (and in the circumstances unavoidable) divergences from authenticity (as regards nuances of thought and degree of emphasis, but not in the essence of the ideas) the book *Cours de linguistique générale* played a missionary rôle in linguistics. It gave De Saussure the fame of a man who had inaugurated a new era. Whether or not it spoke with the authentic voice of the master, it proved a powerful inspiration to new generations of linguists and a potent source of new linguistic theories. It frequently gave rise to fruitful discussion, being both highly praised and subject to severe criticism. In the eyes of the world De Saussure is – this book.

247. De Saussure was interested above all in the nature of language as a subject for scientific research, i.e. how language should be comprehended and approached. In order to illustrate his ideas as directly and vividly as possible, De Saussure made an ingenious comparison with a game of chess.

248. The pieces used in a game of chess can be made from very varied materials. The choice of material is quite arbitrary. The only essential thing is the value allotted to the pieces in the game. It is the same with language: whether the word *water* represents a noun, preposition or verb in a particular language, depends on the

meaning linked with the sound sequence "water" in a particular language. But the word form by itself does not determine the actual meaning of a word. Every word is a language unit possessing its own specific position within the system. It is this specific position which determines the word's meaning.

Chessmen are moved according to specific rules which must be observed. It is forbidden to make a sudden arbitrary change in the value of the pieces in the course of a game. It is the same with language. An actual combination of sound, form and meaning occurs arbitrarily, as a result of chance: one language has it and another has not. But once it is fixed, such a combination cannot be changed at will. In this sense, then, every language sign is on the one hand arbitrary and on the other obligatory.

Such phenomena as linguistic *suppletivism* (which concerns two quite different sound forms occurring as the closest grammatical correlates, e.g. Eng. *person* sg/*people* pl) also have a parallel in chess. Let us imagine that a chessman is lost. In its place we can use a thimble, a piece of rubber, whatever we like – only we must remember that this new object, which has its own specific form, will in the game have the value of the lost piece.

249. Every move in the game creates a new situation of the chessboard. But each "new situation" is in accordance with the rules of the game. The passage of time gives rise to a variety of linguistic changes. But the nature of these changes is invariably regulated by the basic rules on which the constitution of linguistic signs depends.

250. Each move in a game of chess is made with one piece only. The results, however, may be of secondary importance for the main course of the game, or they may be decisive. It is the same with language: a linguistic change begins, develops and ends: the completed process may affect only a minute detail, or cause the reshaping of a whole system.

251. Each new situation created by a move on the chessboard has its own rules. The arrangement existing before the move no longer has any significance: only what exists now is important and it is this that must be observed and estimated. The same is valid for language: a survey of the present linguistic situation always shows a

coherence of mutually related facts; this actual state exists independently of the earlier states of the same language, observed
from the evolutionary point of view.

252. Each chessman has its own value according to the rules of
the game, but in the course of the game the pieces occupy different
positions in relation to each other. Their positions give them new
values (for example it makes some difference whether a pawn is in a
position where it can attack an opposing piece, or whether it is outside the lines of battle). So the particular value of language units is
determined by their actual use. (*A* has one communicative value as
the indefinite article and another if it is used as a prefix, e.g. in
amoral.)

253. Modern linguistics had its origin in the same convictions
which De Saussure had stated as the basis of his teaching: language
is an organized system with a specific social function. In elaborating this basic view, the great Swiss master established many
theoretical distinctions, which have exercised a tremendous influence on the linguistic thought of the new generation. The most
prominent may be briefly summarized here.

254. Language is a system of signs correlated in such a way that
the values of each of them are mutually conditioned. A language
system is in fact based on *oppositions*.

255. A language sign is complex in character. It is a combination
consisting of both the sound form by which a meaning is denoted
(*signifiant*) and the meaning itself (*signifié*). The awakening of a
scholarly interest in the relations between *signifiant* and *signifié*
gave rise to a new branch of linguistics – *semiology* (the study of the
language sign, see below § 397). Research in this direction produced
animated discussion among scholars, which still continues, as to
whether the language sign is arbitrary or not (a question first raised
by De Saussure, see below § 411).

256. The use of a language sign is not necessarily implied by its
meaning. For example the French word *redouter* (to be afraid of)
will not occur in all instances where the meaning "to be afraid" has
to be denoted. There are two other synonymous expressions:
"craindre" and "avoir peur" which are required in particular situa-

tions from which the use of *redouter* is ipso facto excluded. The actual capacity of a word to be used in situations basically corresponding to its meaning is called by De Saussure the *value* (*valeur*) of a word.

257. Human speech is linear in the sense that every element of which it consists has to be successively pronounced in a spoken chain. In fact language signs are invariably modified by their environment in the spoken chain: this should be borne in mind in approaching the problem of linguistic units.

258. Such psychological categories as analogy and association have a powerful influence on linguistic development. Linguists should include the problem of the range and form of such influences in their immediate field of scholarly interest.

259. Language (*langue*) is a property of the whole speaking group, but it is actually realized by the speech of the individual (*parole*). The words actually spoken correspond in principle to the norms imposed by the language of the speaking society. Yet the very act of speech allows the possibility of destroying an existing linguistic norm: an individual begins a change which spreads afterwards by the process of imitation, and finally finds a place in the inventory of standard expressions.

260. Language can be investigated in two directions – synchronically and diachronically. The *synchronic* approach takes the linguistic situation at a given moment, while the *diachronic approach* is concerned with a phase of linguistic evolution. Language observed synchronically shows itself to be an organized system which lives in the language consciousness of a given society. A diachronic study, on the other hand, is concerned with successive linguistic phenomena which are not preserved in the linguistic consciousness of the same speakers, and which simply replace each other without necessarily co-occurring in the same system. In linguistic analysis the distinction between a synchronic and a diachronic phenomenon must always be strictly observed. *Diachronic* (or *dynamic*) linguistics is concerned with the history of language; the description of the existing state of a language belongs to *synchronic* (or *static*) linguistics.

Bibliographical References

261. The book *Cours de linguistique générale* (Geneva, 1916) has run through several editions and been translated into a number of languages. An estimate of its authenticity in representing De Saussure's views is given by Robert Godel in "Les sources manuscrites du Cours de linguistique générale de F. de Saussure", *Société de publications romanes et françaises*, LXI (Geneva-Paris, 1957).

R. Godel's study "Cours de linguistique générale (1908-1909). Introduction", *CFS*, 15 (1957), pp. 3-103, throws more light on the development of De Saussure's theory: it reproduces one of his courses in general linguistics (recorded from the notes of three of his students, mostly those of A. Riedlinger).

A critical analysis of the theory expounded in "Cours de linguistique générale" is given by R. Wells in "De Saussure's System of Linguistics", *Word*, vol. 3, No. 1-2 (1947), pp. 1-31.

THE GENEVA SCHOOL

262. The name "Geneva school" is used to describe the school of linguistics which sprang from De Saussure's teaching but gained its final form from the work of his pupils, especially Charles Bally (1865-1947), also a professor of general linguistics at Geneva. Another disciple of De Saussure's, well-known for his work in general linguistics, was Albert Sechehaye (1870-1946); his main interest lay in the relationship between psychological and linguistic factors (in the field of sentence phenomena). Today the most eminent member of this school is Henri Frei, whose work deals with the theory of syntactical relations.

263. This school is characterized: by a strong inclination towards studies of the emotional (affective) element in language, by a consistent devotion to synchronic linguistics (see above § 260), by the conviction that language manifests itself as an organized whole (i.e. a system) which has an important social function.

This school has achieved very good results in the investigation of the emotional (stylistic) element in language. However during the last three decades its development has not kept pace with the mainstream of events in the field of linguistic methodology.

The classic form of the Geneva school can be seen in the linguistic theory of Charles Bally.

264. Bally is best known as the founder of *rational stylistics*, that is, the investigation of emotional linguistic expressions in general, i.e. without laying particular emphasis on the manifestation of aesthetic and individual emotions. Bally took his linguistic material from French and German (he had an excellent knowledge of both languages), and his most inspiring observations were based on comparative stylistic studies.

265. Many people describe Bally's linguistics as *affective*: it proceeds from his conviction that every utterance bears a personal, emotional imprint (so that there is no sentence which is not modal). In this respect Bally was of the same opinion as some representatives of the French school (e.g. Vendryes, see above § 161).

266. Bally adopted De Saussure's principle of the distinction between *language* (*langue*) and the individual speech phenomen (*parole*), and developed from it his theory of *actualization*.

By themselves words designate quite generalized (virtual) concepts. But speech is concerned with concrete phenomena. The transformation of language into speech in fact yields the transference of virtual (abstract) concepts into concepts relating to reality (for example the word *sister* denotes the general idea of a person in a particular relationship to another person, but does not refer to an actual person until somebody begins to speak; only then does it become clear, either from the situation itself, or from the fact that the speaker uses a particular attribute – *my*, *your*, etc., who the person in question is). The process of actualization is thus concerned with the passage of language into speech, that is the transference of the abstract (virtual) to the real (actual). All the means used in language to transfer virtual concepts to the level of reality are called *actualizers* – French *actualisateurs*. (For example possessive pronouns are actualizers; note the difference in the determination of *hair* in the phrases *my hair* and *fair hair*). Bally also attacked the syntactic problem of determination. His promising observations in this field have strikingly influenced the linguistic interest of his followers, who have up till now been involved in elaborating a general theory of determination.

267. In examining the different problems which occur with the realization of speech Bally also established his theory of syntagmatic and functional transposition. This theory concerns the principles by which a linguistic sign has changed its grammatical function without altering its fundamental lexical meaning (the French verb *blanchir* "to show white" is derived from the adjective *blanc* "white", etc.).

268. This interest in syntactic function led Bally to investigate *syntagms* (the combination of words at the syntactic level). In this he was an adherent of the principle of *binarity*: the idea that the relations in syntagms are binary – they invariably consist of a combination of two members. (Bally regarded every pair of related words as a syntagm, including the sentence itself; it is the inclusion of the sentence among syntagms that has given rise to much discussion among scholars.)

Bibliographical References

269. Bally's chief works are: *Précis de stylistique* (Geneva, 1905); *Traité de stylistique française*, 2 vols. (Heidelberg, 1909); *Linguistique générale et linguistique française* (first ed. 1932; the second, thoroughly revised edition published in Berne in 1944 has been used as a basis for later ones).

See also: J. Vendryes, "L'oeuvre linguistique de Charles Bally", *CFS*, 6 (1946-47), pp. 48-62.

See also: A. Sechehaye, *Programme et méthodes de la linguistique théorique* (Paris, 1908); H. Frei, "Critères de délimitation", *Word*, 10 (1954), pp. 136-145, and "Caractérisation, indication, spécification", *For Roman Jakobson*, pp. 161-168.

THE PHONOLOGICAL EPOCH IN LINGUISTICS

The Forerunners

270. Phonology[14] is a linguistic discipline connected with phonemes,[15] that is with sounds functioning as language signs, which make communication possible: the rôle of the phoneme is *distinctive*; its purpose is to signalize differences in meaning.

271. A concept approximately corresponding to the present-day idea of the phoneme appeared a long time ago, among the Indian grammarians (see above § 19). However it had no influence on the development of linguistic thought anywhere else in the world.

272. The Englishman Henry Sweet (1845-1912) and the Frenchman Paul Passy (1859-1939) pointed out the necessity of bringing to light those articulatory characteristics of sounds which directly contribute to the recognition of the meaning of a word. Although the works of these two phoneticians received attention from their contemporaries (Sweet especially had considerable influence on the modernization of linguistic ideas in England and America), the phonological era was merely hinted at in their work, but not actually established.

273. The Swiss dialectologist Jost Winteler (1846-1929) was an exceptional figure in the linguistic world: in a descriptive inventory of dialectal sounds he in fact used phonological criteria as early as

---

[14] The term *phonology* is here used in conformity with the teaching of the Prague School (see below § 292). Today it has the same connotation in practically all European languages except English; the representatives of French linguistics also conceived it differently (see below § 274). The corresponding American term is *phonemics*.

[15] This term is an adaptation of the Greek word *phonēma* (= sound). It was suggested to the French Société de Linguistique by the Phonetician A. Dufriche-Desgenettes (as an alternative to the French expression hitherto used "son du language"). The Romanist L. Havet accepted Dufriche-Desgenette's suggestion and began to use the new term. De Saussure took over the word (*phonème*) from him, which ensured it a wide publicity in linguistic circles. Among the Slavs the expression phoneme (*fonema*) was first used by Kruszewski, a representative of the Kazan school(see above § 186). But none of the above-mentioned scholars gave the term the value it now has in structural linguistics.

1876.[16] But his pioneer work remained almost unnoticed by his contemporaries; it was only much later that he received the recognition he deserved.

274. In 1879 De Saussure (see above § 244) published his work "Mémoire sur le système primitif des voyelles dans les langues indo-européennes" in which he used the term *phoneme* (*phonème*). De Saussure used it to designate the sound element which, whatever its actual articulation, was clearly distinguished from the other elements of the same phonological system. However later De Saussure also introduced psychological criteria into the definition of the phoneme. From this later interpretation the French school (see above § 158) took the idea of the phoneme as a linguistic unit in the sense of an auditory-physiological, psychological and functional complex which may be realized as a sound, but need not be (the important thing is that it should always exist in the consciousness of the speaking society). This is not in conformity with the present-day standard conception of the phoneme.

275. It was the representatives of the Kazan School (see above §§ 186-189), Baudouin de Courtenay and Kruszewski, who played the most important part in preparing the ground for phonology; their views were well-known and highly esteemed by the members of the Prague Circle, the founders of phonology (see below § 292).

As early as the late sixties of the nineteenth century Baudouin de Courtenay clearly stated that sound features were used to differentiate meanings.[17] Kruszewski, about a decade later,[18] developed this idea further and maintained that the phoneme was a phonetic unit with a special function in the process of communication. However by 1894[19] Baudouin de Courtenay had abandoned his former phonetic principle in the identification of the phoneme; under the

---

[16] In his study, *Die Kerenzer Mundart des Kantons Glarus in ihren Grundzügen dargelegt* (Leipzig, 1876).

[17] See "Wechsel des *s* (*š*, *ś*) mit *ch* in der polnischen Sprache," *Beiträge zur vergleichenden Sprachforschung*, VI (1869), pp. 221-222.

[18] In the introduction to his thesis on vocalic alternations in the Rig-Veda, which was separately printed in 1881 under the title of *Über die Lautabwechslung*.

[19] In "Próba teorij alternacji fonetycznych", *Rozprawy Wydziału Filologicznego Polskiej Akademii Umiejętności w Krakowie*, XX, pp. 219-364.

influence of psychologism in the linguistics of his day (see above §§ 79-91) he gradually came to prefer psychological criteria. The final version of Baudouin de Courtenay's idea of the phoneme was a mental picture of a sound which, as an invariant category, opposed a variable one – the actual physiophonic realization of the mental picture, i.e. an actual sound.[20] This view corresponds in the main to the relationship Sprachgebilde/Sprechakt formulated in German scientific circles in the nineteenth century. It diverges from the present-day conception of the phoneme.

276. All these pioneer efforts, although they did not lay the foundations of phonology, nevertheless cleared the ground for reflection on the subject of the phoneme, so that by the twenties of the present century the moment was ripe for the blossoming of a new linguistic discipline which brought with it enormous progress in both the theory and practice of linguistics.

Bibliographical References

277. An excellent survey of the first important ideas on the phoneme before the days of the Prague Circle, with special emphasis on the work of the Kazan school, is given by Roman Jakobson in *Kazańska szkoła polskiej lingwistyki i jej miejsce w światowym rozwoju fonologii* (see above § 191). See also D. Jones, *The History and Meaning of the Term "Phoneme"* (London, 1957).

The Phonological Principles of Trubetzkoy

278. The great Russian linguist Nikolaj Sergeevič Trubetzkoy (1890-1938), a member of the Prague school, has the credit of being the founder of phonology.[21]

---

[20] Baudouin de Courtenay divided phonetics into *physiophonetics* – concerned with the investigation of actual sounds, and *psychophonetics* – the study of the mental picture of sounds.

[21] Trubetzkoy was a man of wide linguistic culture. He began his scholarly career as an ethnologist, but very early became interested in linguistic problems (from 1907 onwards he studied isolated linguistic groups: the Paleo-Siberian

The formation of Trubetzkoy's phonological ideas was fundamentally inspired by the illuminating statements formulated in *Cours de linguistique générale*: language has a social function; it is a system; sound units play the rôle of linguistic units through which communication is carried out (see above §§ 188 and 275). It was however his activity in the Prague Circle which decisively determined his theoretical standpoint: in many stimulating discussions with the linguists of an exceptionally talented generation the first conception of modern linguistic theory came to maturity.

279. In 1929, being already closely connected with the Prague Circle, Trubetzkoy began his work on the historical phonetics of the now extinct Polabian language. His wide acquaintance with various (including some non-Indoeuropean) languages led him to his first significant observations on phonetic systems: in all languages sounds are related to each other as members of an *organized whole*, i.e.

---

and Caucasian languages; while he was still in the high school he wrote a grammar and dictionary of the now extinct Kamchadal language). He studied linguistics under the outstanding Russian scholar Poržezinskij. From 1913 onwards he studied at Leipzig under the neo-grammarians Brugmann, Leskien and Windisch. When in 1915 Šaxmatov published his work *Očerk drevnejšago perioda istorii russkogo jazyka*, in which he interpreted the problem of sound changes in Common Slavic in the spirit of Fortunatov's conceptions, Trubetzkoy subjected this study to searching criticism. (He stressed the fact that Common Slavic refers to a long period of development, which probably lasted about 2,500 years, and therefore included different stages of linguistic evolution; hence not all the linguistic phenomena attributed to Common Slavic belong to the same epoch, which should be constantly borne in mind in the task of reconstruction.) This criticism had lively repercussions among Russian linguists, and Trubetzkoy was at once hailed as a scholar of serious stature and independent ideas. From 1922 Trubetzkoy held the chair of Slavistics at Vienna. This direct contact with Slavic languages by no means weakened his interest in general linguistic problems; on the contrary. He organized and further examined his material on Caucasian languages and at the same time studied with careful attention and enthusiasm the theories of Baudouin de Courtenay and De Saussure. His activity in the Prague Circle was decisive both for the full ripening of his original ideas on phonology and for the development of the Prague school as a whole. More detailed information about Trubetzkoy's life and work can be found in *Principes de phonologie*, in the section dealing with autobiographical notes (ed. Roman Jakobson, pp. XV-XXIX, see below § 291).

system; the actual relations within a sound system can be shown in the form of symmetrical schemes. These observations, illustrated by concrete examples, marked the beginning of phonological studies in linguistics. Thus the theoretical view that language should be conceived as a system (which had already been introduced by De Saussure) acquired its first methodological elaboration.

280. Trubetzkoy founded his phonological theory on the conviction that the phoneme has to be regarded as a language sign: it serves to convey the word meaning; the substitution of one phoneme by another would therefore yield a change of meaning (in English /p/ and /b/ are two phonemes; cf. the result of replacing /p/ by /b/ or vice versa in such examples as *pull* vs. *bull*).

Sounds consist of a complex of articulatory and auditory characteristics (see § 216). However not all of these are relevant for the process of mutual understanding, but only some of them. In fact the phoneme is that minimum of articulatory and auditory features which has to be brought into use in the process of communication.[22] (For example the dental /n_1/ in the Serbo-Croatian word *Ana* = proper name and the velar /n_2/ in *Anka* = proper name are two different phonetic entities; but in the phonological sense it is the same phoneme /n/ with particular realizations conditioned by the immediate phonetic context: the phoneme /n/ simply represents those articulatory-auditory characteristics which are equally represented in both /n_1/ and /n_2/). What is relevant and what is not in a particular case is established by comparing actual phonetic contrasts.

In speech practice phonemic entities are recognized by the automatic selection of the relevant acoustic elements from the redundant,

---

[22] At the same time as Trubetzkoy was elaborating his phonological theory, the eminent English phonetician Daniel Jones gave his own definition of the phoneme. According to him the phoneme should be conceived as a "family of sounds". By investigating all the actual speech variants of a language sound, Jones tried to make a clear distinction between relevant and redundant sound features. He emphasized that the specific nature of a sound unit results from the sum of the relevant features. Indeed his investigations were not very far from the programme of the Prague school, but his methods were not sufficiently rigorous. Jones remained consistently faithful to these views and gave his fullest exposition of them in his book *The Phoneme: Its Nature and Use* (London, 1950).

according to fixed criteria ("automatic" here means subconscious; the criteria of selection are learnt together with language). What is relevant and what is not in a particular case varies from language to language. Since the criteria of selection are learnt according to the norms of a known language, in the sudden contact with a new language, in which a person has not been instructed, the identification of the phonemic entities of the foreign language is not always reliable (a Serbian has difficulty at first in pronouncing the English /θ/ because he has not the habit of selecting those articulatory-auditory features which are relevant here; some Germans do not distinguish voiced and unvoiced sounds in pronouncing Serbo-Croatian words, simply because in their mother tongue such a distinction is redundant).

281. All these and other considerations, which proceeded directly from Trubetzkoy's phonological theories, have been gradually elaborated in the last three decades. New investigations based on these theoretical standpoints have enabled linguists to give a more satisfactory explanation as to how languages are learnt, how they can be best and most quickly mastered, what are speech faults, and in what direction attempts should be made to remove them, etc., which has today an extremely useful practical application.

282. Trubetzkoy was the first to determine the relationship of the invariant linguistic unit, i.e. the phoneme, to its actual (and variable) sound realizations. The following assertions made by him are still regarded as classic in linguistics.

A. If two sounds in the same language cannot be mutually replaced in an identical phonetic context without yielding changes in the word meaning, they have the status of two different language units, i.e. two phonemes (e.g. the opposition p/b in the Serbo-Croatian words *pora* 'pore' *bora* 'wrinkle).

B. If two sounds occur in the same phonetic positions without any consequences for the word meaning, then they are not two different phonemes, but occasional variants of the same phoneme (e.g. the nasal pronunciation of certain sounds due to a cold in the head, the pronunciation of a dorsal instead of the standard apical Serbo-Croatian *r* by some native speakers, etc.).

C. If two sounds which belong to the same language show similarities in articulatory-auditory features, but can never occur in the same phonetic context, then they should be regarded as *combinatory variants*[23] of the same phoneme (cf. the relationship of the above-mentioned $/n_1/$ and $/n_2/$ in *Ana* and *Anka*).

283. As can be seen from the above arguments, the determination of the concept "variant" in relation to the phoneme makes it necessary to resort to distributional criteria, i.e. to state all the positions within the spoken chain in which the phoneme may occur, and to find out in what respect and to what extent they are directly connected with the characteristics of the given phonemic pattern.

284. The phonemes belonging to the same language are in mutual opposition, expressed by particular sound contrasts. These sound contrasts are produced by the presence and absence respectively of particular articulatory-auditory features.

285. Trubetzkoy successfully elaborated the theory of phonemic oppositions. In his fundamental work "Grundzüge der Phonologie" he showed how the classification of these oppositions can be carried out with reference to both the relationship of each pair of oppositional members and to the phonemic system as a whole. Many of his observations were later corrected, expanded or surpassed, but it is beyond question that his basic theory is still firmly upheld, and that future generations will regard it as the valuable foundation of modern linguistics.

286. Trubetzkoy also drew attention to the pivotal rôle played in phonemics by *binary* oppositions. These oppositions manifest themselves in a series of parallel formations conditioned by the same phonological criteria; the identification of these criteria explains the structure of the phonological system in question (e.g. in Serbo-Croatian the relationship voiced/unvoiced proves to be distinctive in many instances: d/t, b/p, g/k, $ž/š$....; the wide application of such a criterion proves its importance for the organization of the Serbo-Croatian consonantal system). The large number of parallel oppositions is today interpreted as a general linguistic

---

[23] Combinatory variants are now more frequently called *allophones*, according to American terminology.

tendency to economy in distinctive factors (i.e. the tendency of a distinction once established to cover an increasing number of examples). Simple binary oppositions, like those referring to the distinction voiced/unvoiced consonants, are very easily reproduced in a language once they are established.

287. In studying these simple binary oppositions Trubetzkoy observed that one member of the opposition functions as a *marked* one in contradistinction to the *unmarked*: for example in the opposition of voiced /b/ to unvoiced /p/ both members have the same phonetic characteristics, but the marked /b/ has one more property (that of being voiced), which the unmarked consonant lacks.

288. Trubetzkoy's idea about the relationship *marked/unmarked* was exceptionally important as a theoretical principle which became the basis of many fruitful ideas in modern linguistic methodology. Another eminent representative of the Prague school, Roman Jakobson (see below § 301), further elaborated the *marked/unmarked* criterion and demonstrated its application at other linguistic levels, higher than the phonological (for the first time in his well-known study *Zur Struktur des russischen Verbums*, see below § 307).[24]

289. Trubetzkoy stated that linguistic oppositions need not be constant; under certain conditions they become neutralized.

Neutralization arises in positions where instead of two members of the opposition, only one phonetic value may appear, which represents the archiphoneme, i.e. the bundle of distinctive features common to both the phonemes in question. E.g. in German, in word final position the opposition *p/b* is neutralized and /p/ appears as the representative of the archiphoneme *p/b*.

290. Phonemic oppositions are expressed by vocalic, consonantal and prosodic elements (prosodic elements are phenomena relating to pitch, stress and relative length of sounds). In Trubetzkoy's opinion the acoustic element is of primary importance as a distinc-

[24] Jakobson illustrated his theory from the Russian language, and pointed to the difference in use between the word *telka* (= a female calf) and *telenok* (calf in general); *telka* is the marked form, because it refers only to the female sex, while *telenok* is unmarked; it refers in the first instance to a male calf but may be used in connection with a female, provided that the identification of the female sex is not of special importance.

tive criterion in establishing such oppositions. Trubetzkoy plunged into phonemic research above all as a phonetician in his efforts to determine the phonetic structure of actual phonemes. Although later a more adequate selection of phonemically relevant articulatory-auditory criteria was made, his basic conception of the need to examine the phonetic structure in order to establish the phonemic pattern remained classic, as well as his basic schemes of oppositional relationships within phonemic systems (his quadrangular and triangular vocalic schemes, for example; Trubetzkoy was particularly famous for his investigations of vocalic systems).

Bibliographical References

291. Trubetzkoy's phonemic theories are most fully expounded in his fundamental work "Grundzüge der Phonologie", *TCLP*, 7 (1939). In the French edition *Principes de phonologie* prepared by J. Cantineau (Paris, 1949) there are a number of useful additions, including the necessary biographical and bibliographical data (the select bibliography of Trubetzkoy's works on phonology given there is mainly based on information from B. Havránek's article "Bibliographie des travaux de N. S. Trubetzkoy", *TCLP*, VIII, 335-342). The periodical *TCLP* is the best source of information for those interested in the period of the foundation of phonological studies.

The later period of the development of phonology can be followed in the works of R. Jakobson, see below § 310. The present state of its development is conveniently illustrated in the work of Morris Halle (Jakobson's disciple and collaborator): *The Sound Pattern of Russian* (The Hague, 1959.)

A typical American theory of the phoneme is set out in § 333; for bibliographical information, see below § 341.

The recent views of the Copenhagen school on phonological problems (which throw light on the relationship between the "Americans" and the "Praguists") are given by Eli Fischer-Jørgensen in "On the Definition of Phoneme Categories on a Distributional Basis", *Acta Linguistica*, VII (Copenhagen, 1962), pp. 8-39; and

"The Phonetic Basis for Identification of Phonemic Elements", *Journal of the Acoustical Society of America*, 24 (1952), pp. 611-617; "The Commutation Test and Its Application to Phonemic Analysis"; *For Roman Jakobson*, pp. 140-151.

The Prague Linguistic Circle

292. In 1926 a linguistic society was founded in Prague under the name of the "Prague Linguistic Circle". It was founded by a generation of people full of enthusiasm for what were then the most modern trends in linguistics: the ideas of De Saussure (see above §§ 248-260), Baudouin de Courtenay (see above §§ 186-189), and the Slavistic school of Fortunatov (see above §§ 192-193). The success of this enterprise was guaranteed by the already established tradition of linguistic thinking in Prague. The central figures in this society were three Russian émigré scholars: R. Jakobson, S. Karcevskij (1884-1955), N. Trubetzkoy (1890-1938), a member of the society from 1928; and the eminent Czech linguists V. Mathesius (1882-1945), B. Trnka and B. Havránek, as well as the theoretician of literature J. Muhařovský. They were joined soon by a younger generation of scholars such as J. Vachek, V. Skalička and A. V. Isačenko.

293. This society developed its fruitful activity in Prague only for some ten years (until the German occupation of Czechoslovakia). With the death of Trubetzkoy and Mathesius, and Jakobson's departure from Czechoslovakia the "Praguists" lost their most eminent leaders in linguistics. The ideas of the Prague Circle continued to flourish in a quite different environment: at Harvard in the U.S.A. which became, through force of circumstances, the home of Roman Jakobson, the greatest living "Praguist". However the name "Prague school" continued to be applied to all those linguistic doctrines which are akin to the programme of the Prague Circle.

294. The Prague Circle had published this programme as early as 1929, in the first number of their publication *Travaux du Cercle Linguistique de Prague*. In essentials they still hold to it today. The

programme specifies the subjects which should be treated, in a manner which plainly indicates particular theoretical views. They comprise, in the main, the following points.

Language is a system of means of expression which serves to promote mutual understanding. Hence linguists should study the actual function of concrete utterances: what is being communicated, how, to whom, and on what occasion.

Language is a reality (i.e. an actual, physical phenomenon) whose type is largely conditioned by external (non-linguistic) factors: social environment, the audience to which the communication is made, and the subject matter it includes. Thus it is essential to make a distinction, in both theory and practice, between the language of culture an general and the language of literary works; between the language of the scientific periodical and that of the newspaper; the language of the street and that of the office, etc.

Language includes both the intellectual and the emotional manifestations of human personality. Thus linguistic research should also embrace the relationship existing between language forms by which ideas and emotions respectively are communicated.

Written and spoken language are not identical; each has its own specific characteristics. The relationship between spoken and written language should be scientifically investigated.

Synchronic investigation (see above § 260) should be of primary interest for linguists, because it has a direct bearing on actual linguistic reality. But that does not mean that history of language should be excluded from the sphere of linguistic interests. History of language acquires its real sense if the evolution of the language is seen as the evolution of the system as a whole, that is, if it is not exclusively concerned with describing separately the development of particular linguistic characteristics. The system must always be kept in view in diachrony, and diachrony in synchrony (every synchrony contains half-finished processes and the initial tendencies towards a new process, which should be brought to light). The repudiation of diachrony would exclude the possibility of explaining such phenomena as archaism in language.

The comparative method in linguistics is justified only insofar as it is not limited to observing isolated phenomena and searching for their genesis without a general view of the correlation of all existing linguistic facts. The comparative method should make possible work on the typology of languages, i.e. the description of particular types of linguistic structure.

Phonological research should be primarily concerned with determining types of phonemic oppositions in particular languages. Morphological phenomena should not be isolated from phonological. Phonemic oppositions are often significant at the morphological level (for example the alternation *k/č* in the Serbo-Croatian forms *jezike/jeziče*, from *jezik* 'tongue', where the relationship *k/č* denotes a difference in case: accusative plural/vocative singular).

From the basic views expounded in this programme have sprung new, far-reaching ideas and valuable scholarly achievements.

295. The development of the view that the particular aspects in which language manifests itself should be distinguished has opened up new paths of research into different linguistic styles, particularly in the investigation of the language of poetry. Finally different phenomena occurring in the language of conversation – intonation, gesture, etc. – have come into the sphere of linguistic study.

296. A correct attitude to the problems of history of language has meant the beginning of a new and important epoch in the development of this discipline (see below §§ 311-315).

297. Linguistic theory has been vitally enriched by the direction of scholarly work to the investigation of linguistic typology. The members of the Prague Circle were the first to work out the problem of *language alliance* (*Sprachbund*) – the phenomenon of neighbouring languages which, although otherwise unrelated, nevertheless share several peculiar common features (the "Balkan language alliance", for example, refers to Balkan languages characterized by a number of common structural properties, although they are descended from different Indoeuropean language groups: Rumanian, Bulgarian, Macedonian, Modern Greek, Albanian).

298. The study of the rôle of the phoneme in the morphological patterns has developed into a special branch of linguistic studies known as *morphophonology* (the corresponding American term:

morphophonemics). Its results are not only important for general linguistic theory but for the practical solution of specific grammatical problems.

299. The entire working programme of the Prague School envisaged the application of new linguistic attitudes towards Slavic linguistic material.[25] Its representatives have remained true to this standpoint as to all others, and it is thanks to their efforts that the firm foundations of modern Slavistics have been laid.

Bibliographical References

300. The works published in *TCLP* (especially the programme published in the first number) should be studied. See the above-mentioned article by Martinet "Structural Linguistics" (§ 241) and Vachek's dictionary of the terminology of the Prague school (§ 241). See "Prague Structural Linguistics" by B. Trnka, J. Vachek and others, published in *Philologica Pragensia*, I (Prague, 1958), 33-40. See also the collection of articles, selected and translated into English from the original Czech by Paul Garvin (ed.), *A Prague School Reader on Esthetics, Literary Structures, and Style* (Washington, 1955).

The Binarism of Roman Jakobson

301. The Slavist Roman Jakobson (b. 1896), at present one of the world's greatest linguists, a member of the Prague Circle, as regards his basic linguistic convictions, was, together with Trubetzkoy, one of the pioneers of phonology while he was still in Prague. After Trubetzkoy's death the development of phonology pursued its steady advance under his distinguished leadership.

302. Jakobson is the great theoretician of the concept widely

---

[25]   The 1929 programme explicitly stressed, in separate items, the necessity of investigating: actual problems connected with Church Slavonic; the problem of the phonetic and phonological transcription of the Slavonic languages; the principles of linguistic geography; the relationship of linguistic geography to ethnographic geography on Slav territory; the problems connected with making atlases of the Slavonic languages (especially lexical atlases); the methods of Slavonic lexicography, etc.

known today in world linguistics under the English term *distinctive features*. This term denotes sound properties distinguishing one phoneme from another (e.g. the tenseness of English /t/ vs. the laxness of English /d/). According to Jakobson's definition, a phoneme is a bundle of such distinctive features. To state them correctly means to determine correctly the very nature of the phoneme.

Distinctive features emerge from the specific articulatory-auditory properties of sounds. They can be demonstrated by phonetic investigations made with the help of suitable instruments. One of Jakobson's great merits undoubtedly lies in his successful introduction of experimental phonetics into phonological research.

303. Jakobson's phonological theory is based on the conviction that distinctive oppositions are established on the principle of *binarism* (or dichotomy).

This principle is manifested in the fact that linguistic units occur as members of twofold oppositions, being marked by the presence vs. absence of a distinctive feature (e.g. English /t/ is tense in contradistinction to its partner /d/ which is not).

304. Jakobson's descriptions of distinctive features, on which depends the establishment of phonemic oppositions according to the principle of binarism, have been carefully elaborated and today are already classic. He usually defines these oppositions by following an acoustic criterion and speaks, for example, about the opposition between acuteness (= high tonality) and graveness (= low tonality), between the compactness and diffuseness of sounds, etc. These facts stand in correlation to the relevant articulatory factors which include differences in both the localization and way of articulation (for example sounds with high tonality are always pronounced in the front part of the mouth cavity). Recent psychological tests on a large number of individuals have shown that distinctive features are not something invented by scholars, but do indeed exist as relevant categories in the process of mutual understanding.[26]

---

[26] The American linguist J. Greenberg read a paper on this subject in January 1961 at one of the regular meetings on linguistics organized by the Department of General Linguistics at Columbia University.

305. The theory of information (see below § 454) has attested most directly the validity of Jakobson's binary method: the adoption of the same method has thrown light on a series of problems connected with sending and receiving information. It has been rightly pointed out that the co-operation of linguistics in the field of information theory could not have been so effective if Jakobson had not worked out his theory of "distinctive features". Today he and his followers are taking a very active part in the further development of information theory.

306. Scholars are now trying to apply the same binary method in their study of other aspects of human culture, e.g. in researches into folklore, the art of dancing, the language of gesture (i.e. *kinesic* phenomena, see below § 350).

307. Jakobson's merits are not limited to phonology; morphological studies also owe much to his work. His researches on the Russian verbal and case systems are particularly important.[27] Jakobson elaborated a method of determining relations within a morphological system which has remained classic in linguistics. According to him morphological categories also range themselves into oppositions following the principle of binarism: a *marked* category (characterized by the presence of a particular feature of meaning which defines the limits of its use) has its corresponding *unmarked* category (characterized by the absence of the same feature of meaning). For example the Slavic perfect tense is a marked verbal category in relation to the present: while the present tense, although it denotes primarily present time, can also be used for the past, the perfect cannot denote the present moment, but only the past.

308. Jakobson's many-sided scholarly activity has, from its beginning until the present day, been in accordance with the programme of the Prague school (see above § 294). He was the first to approach the history of language with the aim of revealing the inner (linguistic) logic of language evolution. He has worked on the problems of linguistic typology and the problem of different styles

---

[27] His studies: *Zur Struktur des Russischen Verbums* and *Beitrag zur allgemeinen Kasuslehre* (see below § 310) have played a historic rôle in the foundation of modern linguistic method.

in the manifestation of language (he is at present engaged on important investigations concerning poetic language). In order to establish the hierarchy of phonological phenomena on a firm basis, Jakobson has studied incomplete language systems, seeking what is always or most frequently present in them and what can be omitted. Thus he devoted a series of works to the language of children and to *aphasia* (various organic deficiencies which make it impossible for the patient to have full mastery of his speech apparatus).

309. It is also Jakobson's great merit that the Harvard school of Slavistics, which he created (see above § 236), is now one of the most distinguished in the world.

Bibliographical References

310. Jakobson's theory of distinctive features and the principle of binarism are worked out in the following studies:

R. Jakobson, "On the Identification of Phonemic Entities", *TCLC*, V (1949), pp. 205-213 (with applications to Serbo-Croatian language material);

R. Jakobson, C. G. Fant, and M. Halle, *Preliminaries to Speech Analysis* (Cambridge, Mass., 1952);

R. Jakobson and M. Halle, *Fundamentals of Language* (The Hague, 1956);

E. C. Cherry, M. Halle, R. Jakobson, "Toward the Logical Description of Languages in their Phonemic Aspect", *Lg*, 29 (1953), pp. 34-46;

M. Halle, "The Strategy of Phonemics" *Word*, 10 (1954), pp. 197-209;

M. Halle, "In Defense of the Number Two", *Studies presented to J. Whatmough* (1957) pp. 65-72.

As has already been mentioned (see above § 291) the present stage of the development of Jakobson's binary theory is best illustrated in the book of his pupil and colleague M. Halle: "*The Sound Pattern of Russian....*"

In addition to the above-mentioned classic works by Jakobson: "Zur Struktur des Russischen Verbums", *Charisteria Guilelmo Mathesio oblata* (Prague, 1932), pp. 74-84, and "Beitrag zur allgemeinen Kasuslehre", *TCLP*, VI (1936), 240-288, see also "Morfologičeskie nabljudenija nad slavjanskim skloneniem" *American Contributions to the Fourth International Congress of Slavicists* (The Hague, 1958), pp. 127-156, and "Russian Conjugation", *Word*, IV (1948), pp. 155-167.

The modern (structural) approach to the history of language had its origin in Jakobson's study: "Remarques sur l'évolution phonologique du russe comparée à celle des autres langues slaves", *TCLP*, II (1929), pp. 1-109. See also "Prinzipien der historischen Phonologie" *TCLP*, IV (1931), pp. 247-267 (a French translation of the same article is published together with Trubetzkoy's classic work: *Principles de phonologie*, the chapter "Appendices", pp. 315-336, – see above § 291).

See also the following works by Jakobson: *Kindersprache, Aphasie und allgemeine Lautgesetze* (Uppsala, 1941); "Typological Studies and their Contributions to Historical Comparative Linguistics", *8th Proceedings*, pp. 17-25; *Linguistics and Poetics, Style in Language*, ed. Thomas Sebeok (1960), pp. 350-377.

A bibliography of Jakobson's works up to 1956 is published in *For Roman Jakobson* (The Hague, 1956).

The Structural Interpretation of Sound Changes

311. Structural linguistics has brought to historical and comparative-historical studies not so much new material as new, revolutionary ideas. The traditional description of sound changes was completed by the study of the significance which the changes have for the phonemic system. This yielded a tremendous improvement in diachronic linguistic research.

312. Today linguistics has at its disposal a fully worked out theory of sound changes: some changes are of secondary importance for the phonemic system, while others are decisive. (An example of

the first type is the change of word final /l/ to /o/ in Middle Serbo-Croatian; since this change occurred only in certain positions in the word, /l/ did not disappear from the pattern, and /o/ had also existed before the change, so that the number and character of its phonemes remained unaltered. But when the Common Slavic /ě/ was replaced in Serbo-Croatian by /i/ or /e/ the number of vocalic phonemes was reduced, i.e. the change affected the structure of the pattern). At the basis of historical studies of language there lies today the following theoretical axiom: the history of language should not be primarily concerned with the evolution of each linguistic detail taken separately, but with the fate of the system. Structural linguistics holds firmly to the view that linguistic evolution cannot be regarded simply as the gradual and constant transition of one linguistic state into another. Most important are those moments in development which bring about a change of structure (for example the moment when two phonemes, whose phonetic realizations had in the course of time come increasingly close, finally fuse into a single phoneme). Changes in language, then, are not gradual (i.e. they do not happen by degrees). On the other hand, the period when new linguistic phenomena emerge completely victorious is immediately preceded by one in which they were optional – that is, when they appeared side by side with the older phenomena, sometimes in the speech of the same individual (as free variants or as dependent on speech style), and sometimes marking a difference in the speech of two generations (the older generation would keep to the more archaic forms, while the younger generation adopted the newer ones).

313. The members of the Prague Circle were among the first to carry out the modernization of the history of language. For example Roman Jakobson in his famous study *Remarques sur l'évolution phonologique du russe comparée a celle des autres langues slaves* (see above § 310) made a number of observations which have remained fundamental in the history of modern diachronic linguistics. A few of them may be mentioned here.

A. In the development of a language the clash of incompatible tendencies plays a decisive rôle. For example at one point in the de-

velopment of the Slavonic languages the tendency towards the principle of opposition between palatalized and non-palatalized sounds
(as in Russian) and the tendency towards word-tone oppositions (as
in Serbo-Croatian) became incompatible. Later both principles were
never realized in a single language, but only one principle or the
other.

B. Systems search for parallel or symmetrical series of phonemes:
if in the process of development the system loses a phoneme and its
place becomes vacant (thereby destroying the symmetrical principle)
the language shows a tendency to fill this gap in the pattern.

C. Sometimes the phonemic system becomes overcrowded: it
has too many phonemes which are not sufficiently distinct as to
articulation or acoustics, and so cannot be differentiated with
adequate precision in the speaking or listening. In this case the language tries to simplify the situation; either it gets rid of some phonemes, or two phonemes merge into one.

314. Slavistics has made particularly notable progress in the
field of the history of language since it began to adopt the structural
method.[28] Not only have various diachronic phenomena been
explained in a quite new and highly satisfying way, but many
hitherto generally accepted interpretations have been successfully
subjected to revision.[29]

[28] Many eminent scholars (N. S. Trubetzkoy, R. Jakobson, N. Van Wijk,
F. Mareš and others) have already made observations on the phonemic system
of Common Slavic. The historical phonemics of individual Slavonic languages
has also been adequately treated: the phonemic problems of Old Slavonic have
been most successfully treated by N. S. Trubetzkoy and H. G. Lunt; R.Jakobson
has done work of fundamental importance on the development of the Russian
sound system; Z. Stieber and S. K. Šaumjan have made important contributions
to Polish phonemic studies; the phenomena of Serbo-Croatian historic phonemes
have been studied by P. Ivić; and the divergent tendencies of development in
different Slavonic languages have been most clearly indicated by A. V. Isačenko
and E. Stankiewicz.
[29] The most valuable revision of the hypotheses so far advanced on Slav (and
Indoeuropean) accentology have come from J. Kuryłowicz (who has done
special service to structural linguistic theory by elaborating the concept of
isomorphism, i.e. parallel manifestations of characteristic system relations at
different levels of linguistic organization – for example the same criterion
marked/unmarked ranges both morphological and phonemic units into oppositional pairs).

315. The most important contribution to the theory of historical phonemic changes in recent years has come from the French structuralist André Martinet (who is very close to the Prague school in his methods of work). He is now considered one of the most eminent theoreticians of diachronic linguistics. His basic ideas may be summarized as follows.

A. There exist in man two mutually opposing tendencies whose parallel influence in principle regulates the development of language: the need to satisfy all the requirements of communication, and the tendency to economize physical and mental energy in the speech process, i.e. inertia.[30] The relationship of these tendencies to each other may actually be manifested in a variety of ways, but under one unvarying condition: communication must be ensured.

B. Sound changes do not occur incidentally. They are always conditioned. Traditional linguistics tries to find an explanation for them in the mutual influence of sounds adjacent to one another in the spoken chain. Although this pressure at the syntagmatical level (i.e. the level concerning co-occurrences of phonemes in the spoken chain) to some extent endangers the phonemic integrity of the phonemes, it is, however, the influence of the neighbours in the system which is much more important.

C. Every unit in a phonemic system takes up specific positions in relation to other units – some are closer to each other as regards their relevant articulatory-auditory features, and some more distant. Every phoneme has a *field of dispersion* (i.e. the field covered by its possible realizations). Between the fields of dispersion of neighbouring phonemes, there usually exist margins of security. Sometimes these margins become too narrow, owing to the development of phoneme A in the direction of phoneme B. But in order to secure communication a merger must be prevented. Then the field of dispersion of phoneme B begins to move away in another direction. Thus a series of reactive changes takes place which finally results in the reshaping of the whole system.

---

[30] Inertia often shows itself, for example, in the reduction of the voicing of consonants at the end of a word, or in the general tendency for sounds in a speech chain to come as close together as possible, in fact to integrate.

Bibliographical References

316. See the above-mentioned classic study by Jakobson *Remarques sur l'évolution phonologique du russe*.... (see above § 310) and the well-known book by A. Martinet: *Economie des changements phonétiques* (Berne, 1955).

See also: A. Martinet, "Function, Structure and Sound Change", *Word*, 8 (1958), pp. 1-32; A. W. de Groot, "Structural Linguistics and Phonetic Law", *Lingua*, I, 2 (1948), pp. 175-208.

THE SCHOOLS OF AMERICAN LINGUISTICS

The Pioneers: Boas, Sapir and Bloomfield

317. A tradition of linguistic research began to develop in the U.S.A. in the second half of the nineteenth century with the work of William Dwight Whitney[31] (1827- 1894), professor of Sanskrit at Yale College. Whitney's views, although highly esteemed by his contemporaries, were usually quite in tune with European linguistic thinking at that time, and did not decisively influence the formation of Franz Boas (1858-1942), professor at Columbia University, a specialist in American Indian languages.

318. A truly American school of linguistics began with the works of Franz Boas (1858-1942), professor at Columbia University, a specialist in American Indian languages.

Indian languages had been investigated before Boas' time,[32] but according to the pattern of classic Indoeuropean grammar which was inappropriate, and at times even misleading. Although Boas was trained in the spirit of traditional grammatical principles, he did not let this hinder his practical work. Having quickly realized that he was dealing with specific grammatical structures which would not fit into the moulds of classical grammar, he advanced the bold opinion that languages have their own inner logic which ex-

---

[31] His linguistic convictions are most adequately expressed in *Language and the Study of Language* (1867); and *"The Life and Growth of Language"* (1874).
[32] As early as 1788 Jonathan Edwards described the language of the Massachusetts Indians, following traditional linguistic methods.

cludes the application of any general methodological principle; a suitable method of analysis is imposed by the material itself. He kept to this principle and made successful descriptions of types of languages hitherto unknown. These descriptions are still of considerable value today.

319. Circumstances favoured this departure from the classical grammatical method: the Indian languages had no written tradition, and therefore no history in the true sense of the word. Hence the historical approach, the mainstay of classical grammar, was excluded at the outset. The entire attention of the investigator had to be concentrated on the correct description of existing linguistic phenomena, i.e. the approach had to be exclusively synchronic (see above § 260).

320. With his serious and systematic approach to the study of the Indian languages, Boas inaugurated a great tradition in American linguistics as regards fields of interest and work. This tradition is still alive today. He was also the first to make synchronic description the central object of attention, and American linguists still accord it this pivotal position.

One of Boas' greatest achievements was the publication of the monumental work *Handbook of the American Indian Languages*. This is not only a collection of admirably assembled and classified material (from nineteen North American Indian languages), but also a fundamental contribution to the theoretical problem of establishing a descriptive method. In the introduction to this work Boas pointed to the possibility of enriching psychological knowledge from the results of linguistic research; this later became an increasingly popular theme in American linguistics. Almost everything which was to be considered specifically American in linguistic development in the first decades of the twentieth century was predicted in *Handbook of American Indian Languages*.

321. The classic representative of American linguistics, the pioneer of structuralism in America and the teacher of many generations of linguistic scholars was Boas' disciple Edward Sapir.[33] A man of exceptionally wide general culture and scientific

[33] Sapir received his first training (he studied Germanic languages) in the

interests,[34] Sapir began, independently of De Saussure, to spread abroad ideas of language as an organized system, and threw himself enthusiastically into descriptive linguistics, the first task of which was to examine types of linguistic structure.

Sapir considerably advanced the study of Indian languages and put his basic theoretical views into practice in this work. His classifications of these languages were of great significance for the further development of typological studies.[35]

"classical" school, but as Boas' pupil he obtained his doctorate in anthropology. From 1925 he was professor of linguistics and anthropology at Chicago; in 1931 he moved to Yale University.

[34] He not only worked on linguistic problems but also made successful contributions in the fields of psychology and anthropology.

[35] Nineteenth century scholarship had divided languages into three groups according to morphological criteria: radical, agglutinative and flectional (see above § 63). Later a fourth group was added, *polysynthetic* (in which the words are joined together in such a way that a whole sentence has the appearance of a single morphological unit; e.g., the language of the Eskimos). Sapir demonstrated that this morphological classification was inadequate, since it was based on an over-simplification of existing facts. He proposed the adoption of a more complex criterion, which he called *conceptual*, based on the conviction that the actual types of morphological structures are conditioned by the specific concepts which the speaking society is particularly anxious to express. The selection of these relevant concepts is in fact optional, so that the structural types of languages vary greatly (e.g. the morphological distinction of nominal genders is maintained in Indoeuropean languages, but not in many other linguistic groups). Hence the classification of languages should rest primarily on the observation of those conceptual factors which determine structural organization. Sapir (in his fundamental work *Language*) indicated those four basic types of concepts which directly influence language structure: 1. concrete concepts (relating to objects, actions and qualities); 2. relational concepts (concerning the relationship of members by which the proposition is constituted, i.e. concepts referring to the organization of the proposition); 3. derivational concepts (including only those ideas which bring an increment of significance to the concrete concepts but are irrelevant to the proposition as a whole – usually expressed by affixes or stem modification); 4. concrete-relational concepts (having both an element of concrete meaning and one which is purely relational; usually expressed by inflectional suffixes or stem modification). Only the first two types are necessarily expressed in all languages. By taking into account whether and to what extent the "non-compulsory" concepts are represented in languages and which devices are used to express the "basic concepts", Sapir gave examples of a new typological classification. This was later further developed by his followers. A worthy contribution in this direction was made by Joseph Greenberg who, considering morphological structures in all their complexity and with the help of statistical

322. Sapir was the founder of the idea of *linguistic patterns*: every man carries within himself the basic schemes of the organization of his language, i.e. patterns of all the actual devices which his language provides to ensure communication; according to these psychological language patterns he then proceeds to express his ideas, and in so doing brings into use actual language material.

323. In order to understand the organization of these patterns which regulate speech practice, a very thorough knowledge of the cultural environment of the language being studied is necessary, since the type of communication in a society is normally conditioned by the cultural atmosphere. This aspect of Sapir's teaching was decisive for the further development of American linguistics: it stimulated the inclusion of "anthropological" investigations of language (see below § 342) in the programme of linguistic studies.

324. Keeping consistently to his theory of patterns, Sapir designated the phoneme as a complex of psychological associations which merge into an "ideal sound", i.e. into a particular concept lying in the subconscious as a pattern according to which concrete examples of a speech sound are created.[36] His psychological (mentalistic) conception of the phoneme remained of quite marginal importance in the history of phonemics. But in defining the phoneme Sapir introduced a very important criterion – the *distributional* criterion. He believed that a decisive factor in determining the nature of the phoneme was the combinational possibilities in the speech chain: i.e. all the positions which a given phoneme can occupy in relation to other phonemes – members of the same linguistic system. The application of the distributional criterion soon

---

methods, gave a survey of linguistic affinities and divergencies (for example Greenberg determined the degree of synthesis in a language by considering the statistical relationship between autonomous words and *morphemes* – for this term, see below § 334). See his study: "A Quantitative Approach to the Morphological Typology of Language", *Method and Perspective in Anthropology, Papers in Honor of Wilson De Wallis* (Minneapolis 1954), pp. 192-220.

[36] Sapir first expounded his views on this subject in 1925 in *Sound Patterns in Language*, and again in 1933 in *La Réalité Psychologique des Phonèmes* – reprinted in *Selected Writings of Edward Sapir* (Berkeley and Los Angeles, 1949), pp. 33-45 and 46-60.

became the basis of American linguistic methodology (see below § 330).

325. Another classic representative of American linguistics was Leonard Bloomfield (1887-1949), also a professor at Yale[37] (the term "the Yale school" is now in fact used to describe those American linguists who have further developed his method of linguistic analysis).

326. Bloomfield also received a classical grammatical training, but he kept to it more faithfully than Sapir. In general Bloomfield's interests were narrower, and he remained above all a linguistic scholar. The difference in the historic rôle of these two great Americans mainly lies in the fact that Sapir determined the scope of interest and type of general culture proper to a typically American linguist, while Bloomfield laid the foundations of typically American linguistic method.

327. Bloomfield was well acquainted with the problems of European linguistics, and closely followed its further development. But although he himself finally opted for structuralism, he did not actually adopt European linguistic theories but sought for paths of his own.

The independence of his scholarly thought increased gradually.[38] European influence was still clearly apparent in his *Introduction to the Study of Language* (New York, 1914), a very popular work at that time, in which, for example, he expounds certain problems on the basis of Wundt's conceptions of language (see above § 84).

His general culture was strongly influenced not only by European linguistic scholars and psychologists, but also by sociologists.[39] However the most decisive factor in the formation of his scientific

[37]   From 1940-1947; before that he lectured in Chicago.
[38]   He never broke completely with the tradition of classical grammar; even the historical approach was not neglected by him. For example he tried to reconstruct some ancient linguistic forms from which the actual forms of the Algonquian Indian languages might be derived. See Charles Hockett, "Implications of Bloomfield's Algonquian studies", *Lg*, 24 (1948), pp. 117-131.
[39]   Bloomfield's disciple Zellig S. Harris notes that Bloomfield, reading Marx's *Capital*, was impressed by the fact that Marx treated problems concerning social phenomena and languages in a similar way (see *Lg.*, 27, No. 3, 1951, p. 297).

outlook was his contact with the doctrine of American behaviourism.

328. Behaviourism[40] is concerned with the idea that differences between human beings are conditioned by the environment in which they live, and that all behaviour is reactive, i.e. comes as an response to a particular external stimulus. One's behaviour reveals one's psychology, which is formed by one's environment. Psychological studies should therefore be concentrated on the investigation of behaviour, since this does admit exact and experimental study, while all other more direct approaches to an intellectual phenomenon automatically carry with them the application of subjective criteria. A person's behaviour includes his communication with his environment, i.e. language. Linguistic investigation also must be strictly objective and exact in order to provide satisfactory data about man and his psychology.

329. In accepting the basic ideas of behaviourism, Bloomfield took up a corresponding stand in linguistics. The physical (i.e. sound) aspect of language was best suited to exact, objective investigation – hence Bloomfield concentrated his scholarly attention exclusively on this topic. The statement that Bloomfield underestimated the meaning aspect of language is not borne out by the facts. On the contrary Bloomfield, acting in the spirit of behaviourism, was strongly interested in clearing paths of scientific research which would lead to the aim of revealing the laws of the human psyche. But he thought that this goal should be approached gradually, by way of objective descriptions of actual phenomena which are accessible to exact examination. Hence he deliberately limited the scope of linguistic analysis because of this general theoretical stand-

[40] The founder of American behaviourism was the psychologist John Broadus Watson. He gave definite form to the general ideas which captured European and American psychologists at the beginning of this century under the influence of the theory of the famous Russian scientist Pavlov. (Pavlov's theory is the theory of conditioned reflexes which are developed by habit as a mechanical response to a particular stimulus.) Watson's works had a paramount influence in the formation of American thought and culture. The programme of behaviourism was first stated by Watson in 1913 in "Psychology as the Behaviourists View It", *Psychological Review*, XX. See also his book *Psychology from the Standpoint of a Behaviourist* (Philadelphia, 1919).

point. He was persuaded that the inclusion of the meaning aspect of language would involve the danger of admitting subjective criteria into analysis. Meaning had to be left aside in the task of establishing an adequate linguistic method. Thus Bloomfield became the apostle of *anti-mentalism* (an opponent of the introduction of mental criteria) in linguistics.[41]

330. Traditional grammar had rested on mentalistic definitions which could no longer give satisfaction.[42] It was necessary to replace them by highly objective, precise definitions based on an exhaustive description of the behaviour of linguistic units. This behaviour is manifested in the concrete possibilities of mutual combinations in the speech chain. Hence the new linguistic method was based on noting and describing all the positions which units of a given language system could occupy – i.e. on determining the *distribution*[43] *of linguistic units.*

The term *distributionalism* means the linguistic trend based on the elaboration of this methodological principle of Bloomfield's.

Bibliographical References

331. See the above-mentioned work by Boas *Handbook of American Indian Languages* (= *Bulletin of the Bureau of American Ethnology*, 40, Parts 1 and 2) (Washington, 1911); Part 3, (New York, 1938) (ed. J. J. Augustin). See also: R. Jakobson, "Franz Boas' Approach to Language", *IJAL*, 10 (1944), pp. 188-195 and "Boas' Views of Grammatical Meaning", *American Anthropologist*, vol. 61, No. 5, Part 2, (1959), pp. 139-145.

The most important of Sapir's works is *Language, An Introduction*

[41]   Although he explicitly stated that he was an opponent of mentalism Bloomfield himself (in contrast to his followers) did not always strictly observe this in practice; later he was reproached for this (see E. Buyssens, "Conception fonctionelle des faits linguistiques", *Grammaire et psychologie*, Paris, 1950, p. 37).
[42]   Bloomfield had in mind such cases as the traditional definition of a verb: a word which denotes an action. This definition automatically excludes from the verbal category such forms as *to be* or *to seem*.
[43]   This term was popularized by Sapir's disciple Morris Swadesh in his exposition of the methodological principle of phonemic research in the spirit of Sapir's conception of distributionalism (see below § 324). See Morris Swadesh, "The Phonemic Principle", *Lg*, 10 (1934), p. 124.

to the Study of Speech (New York, 1921). A selection of his works was published by D. G. Mandelbaum (Berkeley and Los Angeles, 1949) under the title of *Selected Writings of Edward Sapir in Language, Culture and Personality*. See also M. R. Haas: "Sapir and the Training of Anthropological Linguists", *American Anthropologist*, 55 (1954), pp. 447-449.

Bloomfield's famous *Language* (New York, 1933), is still an excellent introduction to modern linguistics. See also Charles C. Fries, "The Bloomfield School", *Trends*, pp. 196-224.

The Epoch of Distributionalism

332. Bloomfield's methods were further elaborated by his pupils who kept strictly to his principles: the category of meaning had to be excluded from analysis; the criteria used had to be rigorously objective and mechanical. The centre of attention was the distribution of linguistic units, which was tested by the method of *substitution*. This method consists of an attempt to replace the unit under investigation by another, known, unit in the same context, and if the substitution can be performed without an essential change in the context, then both units belong to the same class, i.e. they have the same grammatical properties (for example the words *programme* and *man* belong to the same class, namely the class of nouns, since they can both equally well occupy the same place in the following sentence: *that...disappointed me*).

333. From the late thirties to the fifties the distributionalists devoted considerable attention to investigations in the field of phonemics. They did not search for distinctive features (for this term see above § 302) since this would have meant an impingement on the field of psychophysiology, which conflicted with the programme of their school. Instead they carefully worked out the principle of analysis which was based on the theory of distribution and exemplified by substitution tests. This one-sided approach imposed some limitations on the value of their results. However these investigations did bring into the sphere of linguistic interest

certain phenomena which had not so far received adequate attention (for example the rôle of the *juncture*, i.e. boundary between linguistic units, and associated phenomena).

334. The Bloomfieldians had much more success in the field of morphological research. In his book "Language" Bloomfield had already made the basic distinctions between relations occurring at the morphological level, and had introduced appropriate terminology. The morphological unit is the *morpheme*, i.e. the smallest language unit having a meaning (according to this definition a morpheme can be both a whole word or part of a word, e.g. *playing* consists of two morphemes: *play* and *-ing*). In grappling with the complex problem of language units of a higher rank, Bloomfield realized the necessity of distinguishing various levels of linguistic structures (for example /s/ is a phoneme in the word *snow* and a morpheme indicating the plural in *lips*). This strict distinction of structure levels[44] ensured a higher degree of precision in the grammatical descriptions made by the distributionalists.

Grammatical definitions based on this new method were much simpler, more precise and practical than those used in the traditional (classical) European grammar (for example the English adjective category is defined as follows: a word which can stand between the definite article *the* and a noun, and which never takes *-s* in the plural). This not only helps considerably in learning foreign languages, but also ensures the correct preparation of language material for machine translation (see below § 477).

[44] This resulted in a veritable flood of new terms ending in *-eme* for language units hierarchically higher than phonemes: tagmeme, grammeme, semanteme, episememe, etc. These terms are not always used with the same meaning, but terminological confusion is usually prevented by the fact that each author defines the value of the terms in the actual case. For example Bloomfield designated as *tagmeme* the smallest meaningful units of grammatical forms. Not so long ago K. L. Pike, also an eminent American linguist, founded a new grammatical theory which he called *tagmemics*. The theory lays the emphasis on the correlation between *slot* (position of occurrence of language units) and *filler* (class of units which fill that position). At each level of structure a slot and a filler together constitute a unit, called a *tagmeme*. All the units should be viewed in their complex mutual relationships. To show these relationships, Pike introduces into his analysis the concept of linguistic *matrix* which is also an "emic" unit in Pike's system.

335. Modern syntactical studies have in fact sprung directly from this kind of morphological research. In order to establish the distribution of morphemes in a language it is necessary to describe all their combinational possibilities in the speech chain, which means to encroach directly on the field of syntactical phenomena.

336. The most important contribution to the theory of syntax has been the analysis of *immediate constituents* – those parts of the utterance directly connected with each other grammatically (and also semantically). This analysis helped to reveal the principles by which the structure of a message may be linguistically organized. In this connection special technical devices in the form of charts and diagrams have been used.

337. The simple sentence has also acquired a new and more satisfactory definition: a linguistic form which is not in a construction with any other linguistic form.

338. The distributionalist method in its most orthodox phase, that is the end of the forties and the very beginning of the fifties, has been represented in the work of one of the most eminent Bloomfieldians, Zellig Harris: *Methods in Structural Linguistics* (Chicago, 1951).[45] At that time American linguistics still lacked adequate contact with European,[46] and was somewhat narrow and exclusive in its methodological conceptions.

339. After 1950 an essential change took place: the Americans began to get acquainted with the Prague type of structuralism. The most important factor in this was the arrival of Roman Jakobson in the U.S.A. and the creation of the Harvard school (see above § 236). In the fifties Americans also got to know A. Martinet's views on the phoneme. Those views were close to the principles of phonology established by the Prague Circle, and contributed to their popularization (see above § 315). The theory of the phoneme, resting on the search for distinctive features (see above § 302), was more satis-

[45] This book (which has aroused much varied discussion) sets out the method and gives a practical demonstration in the analysis of the phonemic and morphemic units of the African language Swahili and those of modern Hebrew.
[46] This fact was deplored by Einar Haugen, an eminent representative of American linguistics, who spoke of its provincialism in "Directions in Modern Linguistics", *Lg*, 27, pp. 211-222.

factory than the traditional American one which moved exclusively within the framework of distributional criteria. Even the distributionalists themselves began to admit this more or less explicitly.[47] 340. However in the field of morphological and syntactical studies the distributionalists were much more successful. Their elaboration of mechanical procedures in linguistic analysis made it possible to prepare languages for machine translation. In the period between 1950 and 1960 their resources were concentrated on the further development of a complex grammatical theory which would provide the methodological solutions required to advance the work of machine translation.

Bibliographical References

341. See the following works dealing with phonemic problems: W. F. Twaddell, "On Defining the Phoneme", Supplement to *Lg*, 16 (Baltimore, 1935); M. Swadesh, "Phonemic Contrasts", *Lg*, 11 (1936), pp. 298-301; E. Haugen and W. F. Twaddell, "Facts and Phonemics", *Lg*, 18 (1942), pp. 1-22; B. Bloch, "A Set of Postulates for Phonemic Analysis", *Lg*, 24 (1948), pp. 3-46; C. F. Hockett, "Two Fundamental Problems in Phonemics", *SIL*, 7 (1949), pp. 29-51; C. F. Hockett, "A Manual of Phonology", *IJAL*, vol. 21, No. 4, 1955); = *Indiana University Publication in Anthropology, Folklore and Linguistics, Memoir* 11, pp. 1-246.

The most important works dealing with morphological problems: Z. S. Harris, "Morpheme Alternants in Linguistic Analysis", *Lg*, 18 (1942), pp. 169-180; Z. S. Harris, "Discontinuous morphemes", *Lg*, 21 (1945), pp. 121-127; C. F. Hockett, "Problems of Morphemic Analysis", *Lg*, 23 (1947), pp. 321-343; Dwight L. Bolinger, "On Defining the Morpheme", *Word*, 4 (1948), pp. 18-23; E. A. Nida, "The Identification of Morphemes", *Lg*, 24 (1948), pp. 4-41; R. S. Wells, "Automatic Alternation", *Lg*, 25 (1949), pp. 99-116; E. A. Nida, *Morphology*, (Ann Arbor, 1949); C. F. Hockett,

---

[47] See for example, Charles Hockett's review of Martinet's "Phonology as Functional Phonetics", *Lg*, 27, 1951, 333-342.

"Peiping Morphophonemics", *Lg*, 26 (1950), pp. 63-85; C. F. Hockett, "Two Models of Grammatical Description", *Word*, 10 (1954), pp. 210-234; Z. S. Harris, "From Phoneme to Morpheme", *Lg*, 31 (1955), pp. 190-222.

The most important works on "Immediate constituents": R. S. Wells, "Immediate Constituents", *Lg*, 23 (1947), pp. 81-117; C. F. Hockett, "Translation via Immediate Constituents"; *IJAL*, 20 (1954), pp. 313-315; S. Chatman, "Immediate Constituents and Expansion Analysis", *Word*, 11 (1955), pp. 377-385. For a bibliography of works specially important for the development of syntax, see below § 430.

The elaboration of the distributionalistic method is described: in the above-mentioned classic work by Harris *Methods in Structural Linguistics* (Chicago, 1951), in *Outline of Linguistic Analysis* (Baltimore, 1942) by B. Bloch and G. L. Trager, and in "Distributional Structure", *Word*, 10 (1954), pp. 146-162 by Zellig Harris. A clear exemplification of method is given in: G. L. Trager and H. L. Smith Jr., "An Outline of English Structure", *SIL Occasional Papers*, No. 3, (Norman, Okla., 1951).

For Pike's theory see *Language in Relation to a Unified Theory of the Structure of Human Behavior*, Part I (Glendale, Calif., 1954), Part II (1955), Part III (1960).

See also above § 241 for the works there cited which give an insight into typically American points of view in linguistics; and see Eric P. Hamp, "General Linguistics – the United States in the Fifties", *Trends*, pp. 165-195 (and the bibliography there appended).

See above § 241 for the works which throw light on the relationship of the distributionalists to other linguistic schools.

Anthropological Linguistics

342. Anthropological linguistics[48] is concerned with the problem of

---

[48] The term *anthropological* is used with the meaning given to it by the Americans. It embraces the study of everything connected with man, but above all his culture. In addition to the expression *anthropological linguistics*, which is most frequently used today, there are also others, such as *ethnolinguistics, metalin-*

the relationship between language and culture: whether, and to what extent a particular language type is conditioned by the cultural patterns of the speaking society.

343. The twentieth century saw a pronounced development of scientific interest in phenomena relating to culture: in such questions as what its particular forms depend on, the nature of its relationship to individual psychology, whether it is possible to construct a general theory of culture, etc. Taking behaviourism as their theoretical point of departure (see above § 328), American scholars have made linguistic phenomena the centre of attention, maintaining that "language behaviour" (i.e. the concrete form of communication) directly reveals the individual as the bearer of a specific type of culture, and is moreover most suited to direct and objective scientific observation. Thus the representatives of other, non-linguistic disciplines, particularly ethnologists and psychologists, have also begun to concern themselves with linguistic phenomena. During the thirties in the U.S.A. the ideas of philosophical semanticians (see below § 401) acquired considerable prominence. The philosophical semanticians were also interested in the problem of the interrelation between language and culture which provided

---

guistics, and macrolinguistics, but all scholars do not use them in the same way. For the majority macrolinguistics stands in contrast to microlinguistics (linguistics in the narrower sense of the term): microlinguistics is strictly interested in the phenomenon of language, while macrolinguistics embraces all research connected with language which also serves to increase our knowledge of other phenomena outside the domain of purely linguistic facts, yet directly connected with the process of communication. For example dialectology belongs in itself to microlinguistics; but if a dialectologist begins to interest himself in those speech manifestations of his informant which are conditioned by his cultural level – e.g. if the dialectologist begins to take into account the individual sayings of his informant – then the investigation becomes different in quality: it passes into the realm of macrolinguistics). Some scholars use the term macrolinguistics for linguistic research based on the use of methods taken from other, non-linguistic disciplines (Mandelbrot regards the statistical investigation of language as macrolinguistics, see below § 438). Some authors (such as the American linguist G. L. Trager) make the following terminological distinction: macrolinguistics is the science of language in its widest sense, and includes both microlinguistics (= linguistics in the narrower sense) and metalinguistics (= a scholarly approach to language facts interpreted in the light of anthropology).

further impetus for "anthropological" investigations of language in interdisciplinary co-operation.

344. The very conditions for linguistic work in America favoured the orientation of American linguists towards anthropological studies. The problem of a heterogeneous population speaking different languages aroused interest in the technique of translation. Great efforts were made in this direction at the beginning of the present century. Through the practical work of translation contact was ensured with problems of wider significance for general linguistic theory: how to explain the nature of idioms, why the comparisons of one ethnic group differ from the metaphorical expressions found in another society, etc. The need for knowledge of cultural traditions in order to understand linguistic categories became urgent. However the most important factor which stimulated the interest of American linguists in the direction of anthropological phenomena was their contact with American Indian languages.

345. The first step in investigating these languages was the accumulation of lexical material, which in its turn revealed the cultural type of the ethnic group (for example a rich vocabulary of concepts dealing with hunting and fishing gives an extremely reliable indication of the economic system of the population). In order to carry out the work of collecting and explaining lexical material as effectively as possible, some previous knowledge of the life and customs of the ethnic community in question was necessary. Because of this American linguists had from the very beginning shared in the anthropological interests of the representatives of other disciplines. However it was not until more penetrating studies into the structure of Indian languages were made that linguistics seriously began to turn its attention to anthropological problems.

346. The structures of these other languages differ fundamentally from everything that is known about the Indoeuropean linguistic families. They disclose a specific psychology. For example the language of the Hopi tribe does not distinguish the time of an action in the sense that we do, but it possesses grammatical means for classifying phenomena according to duration: a step, a wave, the

action of going – these are temporary phenomena; a stone, a tree,. a man, are lasting, while a cloud is not typical of either category. The Idaho Indians have developed in their language a specific system of differentiating the possession of a certain property: for example a plum is sweet in itself, while coffee is not, since it receives sweetness from sugar; cakes with syrup are still more "indirectly" sweet, since their sweetness comes from syrup which is itself sweet "at second hand" having received its sweetness from sugar, etc. Specialists engaged in translating from English into Indian languages began to complain of the unexpected difficulties which arose in the course of their work. For example it was impossible to translate the New Testament satisfactorily into Zapotec (the language of the Indians of southern Mexico). This language does not differentiate verbal actions according to point of time, but according to whether the action in a particular situation was then performed for the first time or not. When they came to the episode of Christ's descent to Capurnaum the translators had to stop their work for fear of impairing the authenticity of the text, since there was no evidence as to whether or not Christ was then visiting Capurnaum for the first time. All these and other such cases made for the stirring up of anthropological interests in American linguistics.

347. Anthropological linguistics began with the works of Boas (see above § 318) and Sapir (see above § 321). Sapir's influence in particular was of crucial importance in establishing traditions in methods and forms of linguistic work. He also influenced the formation of a special American type of linguist (that is a diligent investigator of Indian languages who lays the emphasis on typological studies, and who is well versed in accumulating information relating to folklore, national psychology, etc. as well as in explaining linguistic facts; he is expected to be a man of wide culture with a special training in anthropology and psychology).

348. Sapir's pupil Benjamin Lee Whorf (1897-1941) had considerable influence on the development of anthropological ideas in linguistics. Whorf studied Indian languages (he made significant contributions to our knowledge of the languages of the Aztecs of Mexico and the Hopi tribe of Arizona). However while working on

this hitherto unknown linguistic material, he expressed himself strongly in favour of the view that one's psychological and intellectual world is very closely linked with the structure of one's language.[49] Whorf insisted that there were no primitive languages; all languages are equally perfect in their own direction. Everything could be expressed in every language. Yet each particular linguistic structure favours a particular way of expressing concepts about the world, and at the same time neglects other possible ways of looking at the same phenomena. Man's psychological scope, which embraces his impressions of the external world, is in fact shaped by his language. This scope can embrace more at some points than at others, depending on the linguistic structure, which in one case permits an extremely precise delimitation of relationships between phenomena while in another it leaves an idea inadequately formulated.

No one would dispute the view that language is affected by culture. But Whorf's theory also stressed the opposite: that the type of culture was conditioned by the type of the language which directly influenced the process of acquiring knowledge. This second point was not capable of proof.

349. Once the tradition was established among linguists that problems not exclusively concerned with the nature of language phenomena should be included in the sphere of their interests, the repertoire of subjects treated in linguistics was considerably enriched. For example the Americans introduced the idea (and the name) of *prelinguistic* and *paralinguistic* research. The first is con-

---

[49]   Whorf in fact supported the "Weltanschauung" theory which had been well-known in European linguistics from the time of Humboldt (see above § 72). But American linguistics did not continue in the European tradition in this respect; Whorf's ideas were not inspired by "Humboldtism". In this, as in many other things, the American linguistic public was inadequately informed about the achievements of European linguistics. Ideas similar to Whorf's views are advocated today in Europe by the "neo-Humboldtians" (see above § 77) and the English school of ethnographic linguistic scholars founded by Malinowski and Firth. (Firth was, for example, a theoretician of *phonoaesthetics* – the idea that all languages incline towards the choice of a particular type of sounds in order to form particular words, and that this choice is conditioned by the mentality of the speaking society).

cerned with accumulating information on all the biological factors preceding the act of speech, and the second with studying the significance of those phenomena which cannot be regarded as linguistic facts in the true sense of the word, but which accompany the speech process, giving it a particular flavour (whispers, shouts, laughter, etc.).[50]

350. This widening of linguistic interests has fostered the growth of another new discipline – kinesics, or the study of gestures, positions of the body and facial expression as a means of promoting understanding.[51] The main task of this new discipline is to solve the problem of how far gesticulation by itself is an adequate means of communication, and how far it simply assists and accompanies the most important means – language.

Bibliographical References

351. For the purpose and tasks of anthropological studies in linguistics see: A. L. Kroeber, "Some Relations of Linguistics and Ethnology", *Lg*, 17 (1941), pp. 287-291; E. Nida, "Linguistics and Ethnology in Translation Problems", *Word*, 1 (1945), pp. 194-208; C. F. Voegelin and Z. S. Harris, "The Scope of Linguistics", *American Anthropologist*, 49 (1947), pp. 588-600; G. L. Trager, "The Field of Linguistics", *SIL, Occasional Papers*, No. 1 (Norman, Okla., 1949); D. L. Olmsted, "Ethnolinguistics so far", *SIL, Occasional Papers*, No. 2 (Norman, Okla., 1950).

The value of linguistic studies as an aid to more penetrating

---

[50] Paralinguistic investigations have developed intensively in recent years because of the importance attached to the analysis of the whole "speech behaviour" of a patient in modern psychiatry.

[51] The adherents of behaviourist psychology were the first to interest themselves in the communicative function of movement (the psychologist Woodworth spoke of this as early as 1938 in *Experimental Psychology*). But kinesics was founded much later, when Ray L. Birdwhistell began to study gesticulation systematically, using the method established in phonology (he introduced the notion of the *kineme*, which is the unit of *kinesics* just as the phoneme is the unit of phonemics, i.e. he formulated the rules governing the selection of the relevant from the irrelevant gest-features in the process of communication).

studies of culture is stressed by E. T. Hall and G. L. Trager in *The Analysis of Culture* (Washington, 1953).

See also the collections: *Language in Culture*, ed. H. Hoijer (= *American Anthropological Association, Memoir* 79) (Chicago, 1954); Results of the Conference of Anthropologists and Linguists, by Claude Lévi-Strauss, Roman Jakobson, C. F. Voegelin, Thomas A. Sebeok (= *Memoir* 8, Suppl. to *IJAL*; = *Indiana Univ. Public. in Anthr., Folklore and Ling.*, vol. 19, No. 2) (1953).

Harry Hoijer speaks of the development of anthropological studies in the U.S.A. in "Anthropological Linguistics", *Trends*, pp. 110-127.

Bibliographical information relating to anthropological linguistics is given by D. H. Hymes: "Bibliography of Field Work in Linguistics and Anthropology", *SIL*, 14 (1959), pp. 82-91.

Whorf's most interesting studies have been published by J. B. Carroll: *Selected Writings of Benjamin L. Whorf* (Cambridge and New York, 1956). V. A. Zvegincev in the collection *Novoe v lingvistike* (Moscow, 1960) gives a Russian translation of three of Whorf's most important articles (pp. 135-199). The same collection also contains Zvegincev's study *Teoretiko-lingvističeskie predposylki gipotezy Sepira – Uorfa* (pp. 111-134).

On paralinguistic phenomena see: G. L. Trager, "Paralanguage: A First Approximation", *SIL*, 13 (1958), pp. 1-12 and "Taos III: Paralanguage", *Anthropological Linguistics*, 2 (1960), pp. 24-30; H. L. Smith Jr., "An Outline of Metalinguistic Analysis", *Report of the Third Annual Round Table Meeting on Linguistics and Language Teaching* (Washington, 1952), pp. 59-66. On the value of the investigation of paralinguistic phenomena for psychiatry, see:R. E. Pittenger and H. L. Smith Jr., "A Basis for some Contribution of Linguistics to Psychiatry", *Psychiatry*, 20 (1957), pp. 61-78.

See Birdwhistell's book which laid the foundation of kinesics: *Introduction to Kinesics. An Annotation System for Analysis of Body Motion and Gesture* (Washington, 1952). See also G. W. Hewes, "World Distribution of Certain Postural Habits", *American Anthropologist*, 57 (1955), pp. 231-244.

Psycholinguistics

352. Psycholinguistics is one of the newest linguistic disciplines in U.S.A. The year 1953 is regarded as the date of its foundation.[52] It is concerned with man in the process of communication. Hence the immediate sphere of interest of this science includes: the psychological and physiological phenomena of producing and perceiving speech, the intellectual and emotional attitude towards a given communication, and the cultural and social background against which the individual psychology has been formed.

353. Psycholinguistics interests psychologists just as much as it does linguistic scholars, if not more. Psychologists have long devoted their attention to linguistic phenomena,[53] since they consider them a reliable source of information on various subjects of paramount importance for psychological studies: differences in individual capacity, the processes of learning, perception, etc. During the epoch of behaviourism this conviction grew so strong that some scholars began to insist that the problem of "verbal behaviour" should be placed at the very centre of psychological research. The establishment of psycholinguistics brought together the interests and experience of linguists and psychologists, though the lead in the methodological procedures of testing was in the hands of the psychologists.

[52] A meeting of a group of linguists, psychologists and ethnologists was held that year in Bloomington, at which the limits of psycholinguistic studies were laid down. This event was marked by the publication of the collection "Psycholinguistics" (see below § 360).

[53] A marked interest in language on the part of psychologists first appeared at the beginning of the nineteenth century, with the works of the representatives of the British empiricists (James Mill and his son John Stuart Mill). The first psychologist to write serious studies on language from a psychological point of view was W. Wundt (see above § 83). In the twenties of the present century the ideas of the German school of psychologists (M. Weitheimer, K. Koffka, W. Köhler) gained a wide hearing; they were based on the structural principle of bringing to light psychological phenomena: everything which comprises a part of a larger whole derives its character from the structure of the whole ("Gestalt Psychologie"). This had a strong reverberation in America where the related ideas of behaviourism had already developed (see above § 328). It was at this time that psychologists began to be most actively interested in the problem of language.

354. The psycholinguists are interested in the organization of man's nervous system: what network of nerves corresponds to a particular level of linguistic organization (i.e. how language units function as signals of particular meanings through the co-ordination of the psychological and physiological processes which make possible the integration of all the various relations existing at the different linguistic levels: phonological, morphological, syntactic and semantic). This requires, in addition to psychological knowledge, direct contact with physiological and neurological problems. At the centre of interest are associative processes, which are examined by means of special tests. For example the informant is given a word (often made up without lexical meaning, but one which calls to mind through its grammatical structure the existing vocabulary of a particular language), and asked to reply quickly, with the first word that comes into his head (in this, strict account is taken of the social and cultural level of the informant, since associative reflexes are largely conditioned by this). The results of these tests are carefully classified by statistical methods, and on the basis of these results an attempt is made to reach the laws of the associative processes.

355. Similar tests are used to check the results of linguistic research in the narrower sense, expecially in phonemics. For instance tests have shown that phonemic theory was correct in placing the phoneme /i/ nearer to the phoneme /u/ than to the phoneme /a/: the spontaneous reaction of the informant has shown that the opposition *i/a* is more important in the process of communication than the opposition *i/u*. A table of consonants arranged according to affinity has also been drawn up by this method. Experiments are now in progress which should make an important contribution towards establishing a hierarchical system of the distinctive features (see above § 302) of the phoneme.

356. Psycholinguistics must also take into consideration the problems which interest anthropological linguistics (see above § 342): the phenomena of culture in connection with communication. The act of communication is performed according to a certain code. Basically this code is determined by the cultural habits of the

speaking community, although, of course, it acquires a specific stylization depending on the psychic characteristics of the person involved in the act of communication. Hence it is above all necessary to penetrate to the basic type of social code in order to follow correctly the process of mutual understanding.

357. In many circumstances people will not understand each other completely if their personalities have been formed by different cultural patterns (expressions which in some languages or social classes really denote approval are in others simply an empty formula of politeness which do not indicate anything; what may be an outpouring of sympathy in a simple peasant community may sometimes appear coarse to a sophisticated townsman, etc.).[54] Further, understanding is impossible when, at the very moment of communication, one's mind is possessed by something entirely different from the subject being spoken about.[55] Thus one of the most important tasks of psycholinguistics is to find what factors constitute psychological obstructions to mutual understanding, and how far they can be removed.

358. Psycholinguists strive to penetrate the individual characteristics of personality which give a communication its specific flavour. Hence they devote careful attention to paralinguistic studies (see above § 349). They also assist psychiatric observations of the verbal behaviour of individuals by placing their linguistic knowledge at the disposal of psychiatrists.

359. An important field of psycholinguistic investigation is concerned with the mechanism of memory and the process of learning in general. Here the attempt to establish a theory about learning

[54] Humboldt spoke of the relativity of mutual understanding (see above §74), but this, like many other of his ideas, remained inadequately known in American linguistics.
[55] Psycholinguists illustrate this with examples such as the story about applause . A young priest attended a sermon by a bishop. He did not like the sermon at all. When he read it the next day in the local paper he noticed at the end a remark by a journalist, which he read several times as "apple sauce". However the remark was really "applause". But this positive comment could not penetrate the mind of the man who was pre-occupied by his unfavourable impressions, and though privately agreeing with the impression suggested by "applesauce", he accused the journalist of insulting the bishop.

foreign languages is in the forefront: i.e. how languages may be most easily, quickly and effectively learnt (the problem of immigrants, which still exists, long ago forced the Americans to consider this problem very seriously). In this work also the conclusions of linguistic scholars are checked by psychological tests.

Bibliographical References

360. The programme of psycholinguistics is laid down in the above-mentioned collection: "Psycholinguistics. A Survey of Theory and Research Problems", ed. Charles E. Osgood and Thomas A. Sebeok (= *Indiana University Publications in Anthropology and Linguistics*; *Memoir* 10 of *IJAL*, 1954).

See also: O. S. Axmanova, *O psiholingvistike, Materialy k kursam jazykoznanija* (Moscow University, 1957); A. A. Leont'ev, *Psixolingvistika i problema funkcional'nyx edinic reči*, The collection *Voprosy teorii jazyka v sovremennoj zarubežnoj lingvistike* (Moscow, AN SSSR, 1961), pp. 163-190.

Themes common to linguistics and psychology in the fifties of the present century are given in John Caroll's book, *The Study of Language* (Cambridge, Mass., 1953). The book by George Miller; *Language and Communication* (New York-Toronto-London, 1951) serves as a good introduction to modern psychological studies of language.

THE COPENHAGEN SCHOOL

The Foundation of the School – Viggo Brøndal

361. The term "Copenhagen school" refers in the first instance to the structural linguistics built on the ideas of the Danish scholars Hjelmslev and Brøndal at the end of the thirties of the present century. Many people think that insofar as this term refers to the initial phase of Danish structuralism, it only has a geographical value: Hjelmslev and Brøndal were in agreement as regards their basic structural conceptions, but not in the further elaboration of

their theories and methods. However all adherents of this school, including Hjelmslev and Brøndal, were distinguished from the beginning (which is quite exceptional) by a pronounced interest in the possibilities of applying logistic (see below § 390) procedures to the explanation of linguistic data. Because of this they deserve a special place, under a common name, in the history of modern linguistics.

362. The Copenhagen school had its roots in the "Copenhagen Circle of Linguists" founded in 1934 under the leadership of Hjelmslev and Brøndal. This school acquired an international importance in the development of modern linguistics with the foundation in 1939 of the periodical *Acta linguistica*, which had the explanatory subtitle *International review of structural linguistics*. During the last two decades many works have been published there which have contributed not only to the reputation of the Copenhagen school, but to the development of structural linguistics in general.

At the beginning the prominent figure in this school was the original and persuasive Viggo Brøndal (1887-1942). But he died before his work on structural theory had acquired its definitive form. The leadership of the school finally passed to Hjelmslev, who remains its head today.

363. Viggo Brøndal's[56] pioneer work in introducing the structural method into linguistics began with an article entitled "Linguistique structurale" published in the first number of *Acta linguistica* (1939);

[56] Brøndal was a scholar of high culture (he knew many languages; he was a specialist in Romance linguistics, the history of Nordic languages and in Scandinavian toponomastics). His linguistic orientation was determined by the influence of Danish linguists (Thomsen, Jespersen, Pedersen and others) and the French school (Meillet and Grammont). He had a very high opinion of the ideas of De Saussure. His acquaintance with Trubetzkoy (in 1928) was also of decisive significance, since after that he began to interest himself in phonology. However Brøndal's favourite teachers were not linguistic scholars but philosophers (Aristotle, Spinoza, Leibniz, Kant, Bergson and others). He was most influenced by the Danish philosopher Harald Høffding who gave him the desire to study the theory of relativity and in general to turn towards philosophy, the theories of physics and mathematics. Thus Brøndal developed as a strong proponent of structural, logical-philosophical linguistics. This spirit permeates his writings.

here he expounded the programme of the structural approach to language. His later works contributed primarily to the further development of the theory of oppositions. Thus he maintained that the criteria of opposition, already well established in phonemic research, should also be applied in the analysis of morphological and semantic phenomena.

364. However Brøndal's main scientific interest was centred on noting the ways in which the basic categories of logic manifest themselves through linguistic facts. For him linguistic problems were essentially philosophical, and he solved them as such. For example his investigation of prepositions (expounded in his book *Théorie des prépositions*, see below § 366) was completed with the aim of "determining those logical notions which should be recognized as fundamental and establishing the principle of their application to all possible systems of prepositions (and words in general)".

365. Standing half-way between linguistic scholars and philosophers as regards his scientific conceptions, Brøndal did not entirely succeed in keeping pace with either. The philosophers reproached him for being an idealist who unsuccessfully tried to reconcile modern logic with the ideas of Aristotle. For present-day glossematicians his structuralism did not go far enough, and he was too conciliatory towards traditional linguistics. But they all recognize him as one of the first pioneers of structuralism in linguistics, and a man who rendered outstanding services in modernizing the Danish linguistic school. When Brøndal's work is estimated in retrospect, from the standpoint of present trends in world linguistics, it should be emphasized that he was one of the first linguists who tried to approach language according to the methods of symbolic logic (see below § 395 for the penetration of these methods into present-day linguistics).

Bibliographical References

366. See Brøndal's book *Théorie des prépositions* (Copenhagen, 1950) (this is a French translation of the original Danish text

which was published in 1940), and also the book *Essais de linguistique générale* (Copenhagen, 1943) which includes Brøndal's most important studies and an exhaustive bibliography of his works.

Hjelmslev's Glossematics

367. Louis Hjelmslev (b. 1899) is one of the most interesting personalities among the linguistic scholars of our days. A passionate theoretician, his tireless search after new trends of linguistic thought inspires wonder. However not all his theoretical attempts have been fortunate; he has frequently strayed too far from the main stream of linguistic development, but he has always been ready to accept defeat and to set off again in search of new discoveries. This has had some unfavourable consequences: he has often been reproached for his lack of consistency, for repudiating to-day what he firmly believed in yesterday, for the fact that his theory is not complete in all its details, and even contains contradictory views.[57] People easily become enthusiastic about him, and easily reject him. But one fact is beyond dispute: he has always been original, always eager to seek after new forms of scholarly work. And no one can contest the fact that Hjelmslev was the first linguist to see and to point out that one of the great tasks of linguistics in the future will be the creation of a "metalanguage", a logical instrument for scientific definition (see below § 388).

In their present-day work on machine translation, linguists have seen how prophetic was Hjelmslev's enthusiasm for mathematical abstraction about the time of the Second World War. Even if nothing concrete should remain from his theorizing, he would have a place in the history of linguistics as one who saw new, hitherto undreamt–of scholarly horizons awaiting conquest.

368. No school has so strongly insisted that its roots are in De Saussure's teaching as Hjelmslev's. Hjelmslev more than any

[57]   Berta Siertsema in her dissertation: *A Study of Glossematics. Critical Survey of Its Fundamental Concepts* (see below § 386) criticizes Hjelmslev's inconsistencies in a pedantic manner.

one else has the merit of acclaiming De Saussure as the founder of linguistic structuralism. Because of this many scholars have given Hjelmslev's theories the name *neo-Saussurianism*.

Hjelmslev's linguistics clearly rests on that of De Saussure only in two respects. De Saussure pointed to the rôle of sounds in representing psychological entities in the process of mutual understanding, and Hjelmslev has consistently investigated language sounds as abstract entities, while completely neglecting their material, concrete aspect. De Saussure indicated that language sounds are communicative signs, and that they should be studied in the light of this fact; Hjelmslev has reduced his linguistic teaching to the theory of the communicative sign (which need not even be linguistic in character; it can equally well be a traffic signal or anything else which conveys information). Otherwise Hjelmslev's ideas have much more in common with the logical empiricism of the twentieth century than with De Saussure's views. In fact his linguistic interest is by no means directed towards advancing typical Saussurian viewpoints.

369. From the beginning Hjelmslev strove after "logical grammar", i.e. a scientific treatment of language which would be to the highest degree precise and scientific, clear and logical, "like algebra". This brought him into direct contact with mathematical methods of analysis.

370. His point of departure was that human language is not indispensible in order to secure mutual understanding (deaf-mutes communicate by means of gestures and mimicry; traffic lights "speak": green means – the way is clear; red – stop, don't go forward, etc.). In his scholarly views Hjelmslev stands closest to the adherents of logical empiricism, since they were chiefly interested in creating a general theory of communicative signs – *semiotics* (or *semiology*, a name derived from the Greek word *sēmeion* = a sign). Carnap's works exercised a particularly strong influence on Hjelmslev – both those (from the thirties) in which Carnap considers the phenomena of language within the scope of general semiotics, that is side by side with other means of communication (such as military, railway and traffic signals, the Morse code, the deaf and dumb alphabet, etc.), and the later studies in which he worked out

the application of mathematical methods in linguistic analysis (see below § 396).

371. Hjelmslev called his linguistic theory *glossematics* (from the Greek *glōssa* = tongue). His school is known today under this name.

Glossematics is concerned with the systematic comparison of the structures of existing languages with the basic structures of all semiotic systems, i.e. all means (including non-linguistic) by which communication is made. These basic structures are established by logical analysis carried out by mathematical methods. Hjelmslev's linguistics, then, has a pronounced pragmatic character: its purpose is to help in the creation of a general theory of communicative signs – i.e. a general theory of semiotics. The results of linguistic research conceived in this way are also practical in another sense: they help towards the establishment of a "metalanguage" for machine translation, i.e. a system of formulae to which human language is transferred in the process of machine translation (see below § 468).

372. One of Hjelmslev's most important achievements was to introduce the following new distinctions into linguistic research: the distinction between *expression* and *content*, and between *form* and *substance*.

Expression and content are two basic categories without which there can be no mutual understanding. Content is the living reality itself which is communicated. Expression includes all the means by which information about content is conveyed; transferred to linguistic terms – language.

In the process of mutual understanding it is necessary to distinguish two aspects of content: substance and form. The same two aspects of expression must also be distinguished.

The substance of the content means the living reality in itself (objects, people – the entire world around us).

The form of the content means our psychic representation of the substance of the content, that is, how we receive and conceive the living reality around us.

The substance of expression is the physical sound aspect of language.

The form of expression is the psychic representation of the substance of expression, that is, how we receive and conceive the language sign in the process of communication.

Form can be separated from substance and studied separately. In fact the task of the glossematician is to study the form of expression in relation to the form of the content. As they use the term *form* in this way, the glossematicians frequently call themselves "formalists".

373. In Hjelmslev's opinion the most important thing is to investigate relations.

For instance the glossematician must take into consideration content in itself because a particular expression is conditioned by the relationship between the substance and the form of the content. It is well-known that some African languages have two separate words for a white cow and a black cow, but no word for the general representative of the animal species which would correspond to the English word "cow". This must be explained by the specific relationship between the form and substance of the content among those who speak this particular African language (i.e. by the fact that they, contrary to most other peoples, in this case attach most importance to the distinction between white and black animals, without feeling any need to distinguish separately the representative of the species).

374. The relationship between content and expression is much more complex than it appears at first sight, Hjelmslev asserts. For example how are we to explain that one German word *blau* corresponds to two Russian words: *goluboj* and *sinij*? Do the Russians in this case see more than the Germans while looking at the same thing? In Latin two grammatical concepts – ablative case and plural number – may be designated in nouns by four language signs: /i/, /b/, /u/, /s/ (in the ending *-ibus*) but neither of these taken alone corresponds separately to either of the grammatical conceptions under consideration (/i/ and /b/ are not signs of the ablative case, nor /u/ and /s/ of plural number, nor vice versa; only *-ibus* in its entirety denotes both these grammatical categories).

375. No one has questioned the theoretical justification of

Hjelmslev's separation of content from expression and form from substance in scientific analysis. But many have doubted whether answering questions such as those put above is the proper task of a linguist. However work on machine translation has shown today that a linguistic scholar engaged in this work cannot indeed by-pass these complicated problems.

376. Hjelmslev's distinctions are of indisputable value in lexicological theory.

Scholars have long tried to give a precise definition of the difference between the phenomena of *homonymy* and *polysemy*. Hjelmslev's analysis has at last made this precision possible: if one word embraces two contents between which there is no connection, then it is a homonym, i.e. this one word form includes two different lexical units (e.g. *sound* adj. and *sound* n.); if one word embraces two contents which are mutually connected in some way, then we have to deal with polysemy, that is, the word represents a single lexical unit with two meanings (e.g. *head* = part of the body and *head* as used in the phrase "head of department").

377. In investigating phenomena connected with the utterance, Hjelmslev, faithful to his theoretical convictions, intentionally neglects all the data belonging to the category of substance. In his opinion substance is a variable phenomenon – the sound aspect of language is continually changing from generation to generation – and Hjelmslev is searching for the "ultimate invariants", that is, for those entities which are immutable as long as the given linguistic structure exists. He pointed out, for instance, how much the vocal aspect of the French language had changed in the course of centuries, yet as regards its basic structure it is still the same language. Particular sound values have changed, but the relations between them have remained in the same sense typical of what we understand by the term "the French language". In general we form an idea of the rôle of a language sign primarily on the basis of its relationship with other language signs, that is, on the basis of its place in the system. Outside the sphere of linguistic problems, too, phenomena acquire their true value only in their relationship to other, related phenomena. Let us imagine that a street we know well in our native

town completely changes in the course of a few years. All the houses have been destroyed by bombs, and new, unfamiliar buildings have sprung up in the place of the old ones. Even the name of the street has been changed. But in spite of everything it is always for us the same street, and we can always find it without any difficulty. Its place in the network of other streets remains the same, and this is always the most decisive factor in our recognition of phenomena.

378. This basic theoretical conception gave a very characteristic orientation to the linguistic interests of all the glossematicians. They remained quite unmoved by the classic dilemma which troubled other linguists: whether to decide in favour of synchronic or diachronic linguistic research. Such a decision is quite irrelevant for them. They look for what is fundamental in linguistic structure, without which there can be no mutual understanding, – namely the relations between language signs, present now as they have been in the past and will be in the future. Their linguistics, then, is neither synchronic nor diachronic (see above § 260); the time factor is of no interest.

379. The glossematicians do not treat separately either phonology or morphology, syntax or semantics. For this would inevitably mean to work on substance (i.e. with concrete sounds, words an sentences). For them language is an "immanent phenomenon, inaccessible to the experience of the senses" (according to the brief definition of the Soviet scholar Šaumjan, who is closest to them as regards this conception).

380. In their study of language they make use of abstractions, that is, every language unit is identified by conventional symbols (for example, every vowel may be designated by V, every consonant by C, every relationship by R, every sentence by S, etc.). They describe the entire structure of a language by means of such symbols. The use of such abstractions in methodological procedure does not, however, preclude the study of problems connected with very concrete linguistic phenomena (Hjelmslev himself also worked on such problems as syntactical determination or congruency).

381. The glossematicians call the units of their abstract linguistic system *forms*. Form is an abstract quantity too. It designates the

totality of possible combinations of a particular language sign with other language signs. The range of the actual possibilities of combination is found out by *commutation*: the systematic placing of each language sign in a certain context with the aim of seeing which sign can stand there and which cannot; this provides information as to which signs are mutually related and which are not. For instance the relationship between the verbal forms *sees, looks at, likes* and *lives* can be shown by putting them into the same context: *the man sees the dog | the man looks at the dog | the man likes the dog | the man lives the dog* (the first three combinations are possible, the fourth is not).

382. By their use of the commutation test the glossematicians have necessarily come to observe substance (i.e. concrete linguistic facts). This is at variance with their basic theoretical announcement that they would limit themselves exclusively to form. The unavoidable recourse to such a test in analysis is therefore generally considered to reveal the weakest point in glossematic theory.

383. In studying the structure of language relations Hjelmslev made a variety of theoretical observations which deserve attention. Those connected with his distinction between paradigmatics and syntagmatics are now regarded as notable and widely accepted achievements in linguistic theory.

Paradigmatics is concerned with the investigation of the mutual relations of language units in the whole of a language system, while *syntagmatics* is concerned with immediate relationships of language units in the speech chain.[58] Paradigmatic and syntagmatic relationships are mutually connected, as has been established by the use of commutation tests. The main aim of linguistic analysis should be the revealing of all the principles by which such a connection occurs. Indeed linguistic investigation should be primarily concerned with linguistic phenomena, which mean neither the sound nor the mean-

---

[58] Cf. De Saussure's distinction: syntagmatic relationships ("rapports syntagmatiques") vs. associative relationships ("rapports associatifs"). According to him, the first are concerned with the relationships of language signs in a given context, while the second refer to the associative connection of a language sign with those formed according to the same pattern (cf. *speechless, shameless, useless*, etc.).

ing aspect of language, but the relationship between them. Each individual language has its own particular relationships. The establishment of paradigmatic and syntagmatic relationships by means of the commutation test should determine the very nature of linguistic phenomena, i.e. show in each particular case what is a basic, general characteristic, and what is an individual feature.

384. The twentieth century has seen a flood of new terms. New concepts have required new names (see above § 239). Hjelmslev's glossematics was no exception to the general rule: therefore the beginner in glossematic studies is held up at every step by terminological difficulties. An enthusiastic supporter of modern logicians, Hjelmslev approached the definition of phenomena *epistemologically* (i.e. from the point of view of *epistemology*, the theory of knowledge), which implied an effort to secure the maximum degree of precision in expression. The use of adequate terminology was absolutely necessary, and in many cases it had to be created for the purpose. In this respect Hjelmslev is most open to criticism for failing to make use of existing terminology which was not always unsuitable; on the contrary. There was another weakness which he shared with other structuralists: lack of closer contact, especially in the early years of structuralism in linguistics, between the main schools (see above § 232). This led directly to an inconvenient confusion in the establishment of modern linguistic terminology. The beginner in linguistics must spend considerable time, for instance, in order to realize that Hjelmslev's distinction between *intensive* and *extensive categories* corresponds to the phenomenon designated as the opposition marked vs. unmarked in Jakobson's terminology (see above § 288); that what Hjelmslev understands by the words *deductive method in grammar* corresponds to what the Yale school call the *search for immediate constituents* (see above § 336); that what this same Yale school calls the technique of *substitution* corresponds to *commutation* in glossematicist terminology, etc. But once the initial terminological alphabet of modern linguistics has been mastered by means of patient study, the doors are easily opened on to a view of new horizons.

385. The theoretical conceptions of the glossematicians, which

from the first had a pronounced logistic tendency, distinguished their work from that of other structural schools, especially in the early phases of linguistic structuralism. Accused of excessive love for abstractness and formalism,[59] and not always successful in applying their logical criteria to actual language material (which was immediately greeted with shouts of abuse from critics), the glossematicians have only in recent years ceased to be considered some kind of exotic plant in the field of linguistic structuralism, since work on machine translation has begun to come into its own.

The general acknowledgement and recognition in our day of the value of mathematical methods in linguistics has brought all the structural schools closer together (see above §§ 232 and 236). The adherents of the Yale school were among the first to notice that failure to understand the glossematicians was more the result of lack of mutual contact than of differences in basic theoretical conceptions (see above § 235).

Glossematics is particularly popular among the Soviet structuralists.[60]

Bibliographical References

386. An exhaustive study of Hjelmslev's works up to and including 1954 is given by B. Siertsema in the above-mentioned book *A Study of Glossematics. Critical Survey of Its Fundamental Concepts* (The Hague, 1955).

The complete theory of glossematics was first published in 1943 in Danish (L. Hjelmslev, *Omkring sprogteoriens grundlæggelse*) and in English (translated by F. J. Whitfield) in 1953: L. Hjelmslev, "Prolegomena to a Theory of Language", Suppl. to *IJAL*, vol. 19; = *Memoir* 7, *Indiana Univ. Publ. in Anthropology and Linguistics.* The English version contributed considerably to the popularization

[59] This term, which was often misunderstood by people incorrectly informed as to its actual value here, discouraged many linguists from taking up glossematic studies.
[60] This can be seen, for example, from the linguistic standpoint taken by S. K. Šaumjan as expounded in *Strukturnaja lingvistika kak immanentnaja teorija jazyka* (Moscow, AN SSSR, Institut slavjanovedenija, 1958).

of Hjelmslev's ideas (a list of glossematicist terms, with explanations, was added at the end of the book). A Russian translation of "Prolegomena...." was published in the collection *Novoe v lingvistike* (Moscow, 1960) pp. 264-389. H. I. Uldall speaks about glossematic theory (obviously under the inspiration of Hjelmslev himself) in *Outline of Glossematics* (Copenhage, 1957; there is a Russian translation of this work in the collection *Novoe v lingvistike*, pp. 390-436).

Hjelmslev's general views on structuralism are set out in the study "Metod strukturnogo analiza v lingvistike", *Acta linguistica*, VI, fasc. 2-3 (Copenhagen, 1950-51), pp. 57-67. The first practical demonstration of his method was given in his work: L. Hjelmslev "La catégorie des cas. Étude de grammaire générale" Part I: *Acta Jutlandica*, VII, 1, (1935); Part II: *Acta Jutlandica*, IX, 2, (1937).

The achievements of this school are best illustrated in the contributions published in the jubilee collection (*TCLC*, vol. V) on the occasion of Hjelmslev's fiftieth birthday (1949) under the title of "Recherches structurales". See also the study by Knud Togeby, "Structure immanente de la langue française", *TCLC*, VI, pp. 7-282.

See also: André Martinet, "Au sujet des Fondements de la théorie linguistique de Louis Hjelmslev", *Bulletin de la Société de Linguistique de Paris*, 42 (1946), pp. 19-43 (Russian translation in the collection *Novoe v lingvistike*, pp. 437-462); Carl Hj. Borgström, "The Technique of Linguistic Description", *Acta Linguistica*, 5 (1945-49), pp. 1-14; Eli Fischer-Jørgensen, "Danish Linguistic Activity 1940 to 1948", *Lingua*, II, 1, (1949), pp. 95-109; L. L. Hammerich, "Les glossématistes danois et leurs méthodes", *Acta Philologica Scandinavica*, 21, 1 (1950), pp. 1-21; Svand Johansen, "Glossematics and Logistics", *Acta Linguistica*, VI, 1 (1950), pp. 17-30; G. Ungeheuer, *Logischer Positivismus und moderne Linguistik* (*Glossematik*) (Uppsala, 1959); V. A. Zvegincev, "Glossematika i lingvistika", the collection *Novoe v lingvistike* (Moscow, 1960), pp. 215-243; Henning Spang-Hanssen, "Glossematics", *Trends 8*, pp. 128-164.

16

LOGICAL SYMBOLISM IN LINGUISTICS

LOGISTICS

387. The introduction of the abstract method (i.e. the use of symbols) into scientific analysis has been of revolutionary importance for the development of twentieth-century scholarship. Mathematics and physics experienced a tremendous upward surge as a result of this method. Both the representatives of the exact sciences, and those of modern philosophy – the logicians – have contributed to the perfecting of this methodological procedure.

388. The co-operation between mathematics and logic has been primarily directed to the discovery of a *metalanguage*, an abstract, maximally logical language for the purposes of scientific definition. Human language cannot be the actual language of science because it is not strictly logical. Mathematicians and logicians have agreed that the needs of scientific work would best be served by a system of communication based on abstract units (symbols) so organized as to secure the maximum degree of precision in communication.

389. A *symbol* is a conventional sign by means of which actual phenomena are identified in order to facilitate the process of logical analysis (in mathematics symbols are used even in children's examples: an unknown figure is represented by x and a known one by a, b or c). The way of introducing logical symbols into grammatical analysis, which is based on the substitution test (see § 332) may be exemplified as follows.[1]

1. Let L be the language under investigation; let A and B be two particular signs in the relationship of which we are interested; let X and Y be any other two signs from the language L.

[1] This is a simplified illustration of Carnap's methodological procedure.

2. A and B must belong to the same grammatical category if they are mutually interchangeable in the same grammatical context, and their interchangibility can be logically demonstrated by either of the two following formulae:

a. A and B are mutually interchangeable in L if XAY and XBY are sentences in L;

b. A and B are mutually interchangeable in L if XBY can function as a sentence of L anywhere where XAY can so function, and vice versa.

Since the use of symbols in scientific analysis is so widespread, many people call the present phase of scholarship the era of the *algorithm*.[2]

390. At first the efforts of mathematicians and logicians in the search for metalanguage were not properly co-ordinated. They worked independently, each trying to test the methods of applying symbols in analysis within the scope of their own discipline. Thus there arose both *metamathematics* (first elaborated by the German mathematician Hilbert) and *metalogic* (founded by the Polish school of logicians, mainly by Ajdukiewicz, Leśniewski, Łukasiewicz and Tarski). The final fusion of these efforts came about as a result of the acknowledgment of their common aim – the discovery of metalanguage. This also meant the foundation of a new discipline – *logistics*.

391. The representatives of logistics support the hypothesis that mathematics is in fact based on logic; and that all the methodological experience so far acquired by both disciplines should therefore be combined.[3] They stressed the fact that some mathematicians (Frege, Hilbert, Peano and others) had given brilliant examples of the modern logical method of analysis in their work.

The logisticians soon began to direct their attention to the problem of human language.

[2]   A mathematical term referring to a procedure of calculation by means of symbols.

[3]   This hypothesis was strongly advocated, among others, by Bertrand Russell, one of the greatest logicians of our times (in the famous book which Russell wrote in collaboration with Whitehead: *Principia Mathematica*, Cambridge, 1925).

392. Philosophers have long occupied themselves with such questions as: in what does the essence of language lie? how can it be precisely defined? how is the phenomenon of mutual understanding accomplished? what would be the nature of the perfect language from the logical point of view? etc. This age-old interest has only been more powerfully stimulated in the epoch when people have been searching for metalanguage; in order to organize as effectively as possible the logical structure of the language of science, there was no other course but to look more closely at the structure of the most perfect tool of communication so far devised – human language. But there were also other stimulating factors. First of all the widely held conviction that modern philosophy should be mainly concerned with scientific logic which relies on the study of the phenomenon of communication. Then the fairly frequent opinion (held, for example, by Russell himself) that the differences in the basic aspects of philosophy are directly caused by fundamental differences in the organization of the languages by which philosophical ideas are conveyed.[4] Finally in the twentieth century the attention of scholars has been intensively directed to the problem of the relationship between man and his culture (see above § 343), and the form through which this relationship is most directly expressed is human language.

393. The credit for establishing the logistic approach to linguistic phenomena belongs in the first place to the representatives of the "Vienna Circle of Logicians"[5] (known under the name of "logical empiricists"), especially R. Carnap (who elaborated the application of the symbolic method in syntax), and H. Reichenbach. The logical empiricists have placed scholarship as a whole in their debt by their work on a methodology based on the use of symbols. A considerable contribution to the elaboration and popularization of the new method has also been made by the philosopher E. Cassirer,

---

[4] It is here, for instance, that an explanation should be sought for the striking differences between Chinese philosophy and that of peoples speaking Indoeuropean languages.

[5] A school of philosophy founded in Vienna in 1924, which advocated the view that logical investigation should occupy a central place in modern philosophy.

who stands close to the logical empiricists as regards his linguistic interests. Today the strongest centres of symbolic logic are in the U.S.A.

394. The study of human language by means of metalanguage is called *logistic grammar*. This is regarded nowadays as a special scientific discipline.

395. The representatives of modern philosophy have approached linguistic research primarily from the starting point of their philosophical interests (their first important theoretical discoveries connected with the application of the new, logical method to human language, were concerned with their efforts to solve one of the basic age-old problems of philosophy: what is truth?). It was only later that the symbolic logicians began to interest themselves in such phenomena as language signs and the principle of their organization, synonyms, polysemy (see above § 376), etc. In this way they came upon those scientific fields (semiotics, semantics and syntax) which are of immediate interest to linguistic scholars. During this phase of the development of logistics, linguistic scholars began to take an active interest in its achievements and to transfer its experience to their own methodological practice. The new method acquired its true value in linguistics only after language specialists had mastered it.[6]

Bibliographical References

396. For the first contact with the methods of symbolic logic Ernest Cassirer's study is to be recommended: *Philosophie der Symbolischen Formen*, I (subtitled *Die Sprache*), (Berlin, 1923) (an English translation was published in 1953). See also Carnap's

---

[6] The philosophers have for the most part kept to their own beaten tracks and do not as a rule undertake investigations which would be directly useful to scholars with a strictly linguistic orientation. For example the composition of a grammatical text-book on principles of pure logic appears a Utopian project in linguistics, while some symbolic logicians take the idea quite seriously (see H. Reichenbach, *Elements of Symbolic Logic*, New York, 1948, p. 255 and passim).

works: *Die logische Syntax der Sprache* (Vienna, 1934); The English edition *The Logical Syntax of Language* (New York, 1937), is more widely known; "Foundations of Logic and Mathematics", *International Encyclopedia of Unified Science*, vol. I, No. 3 (Univ. of Chicago Press, 1939); *Introduction to Semantics* (Cambridge, Mass., 1942); *Meaning and Necessity* (Chicago, 1947, expanded edition, 1956).

In his book *Elements of Symbolic Logic* (New York, 1948) H. Reichenbach makes a variety of observations about language in general, with factual references to a number of languages, mainly Indoeuropean. It also contains a survey of the results of work on symbolic-logical grammar (especially on pp. 251-354). His book *Essentials of Symbolic Logic* (New York, 1952), is also quite popular among linguists.

P. Ziff's book *Semantic Analysis* (Ithaca, 1960) is one of the newest and most notable works containing an exposition of the application of logical analysis to language.

The works of Noam Chomsky, written primarily for a linguistic public, are specially recommended: *The Logical Structure of Linguistic Theory* (mimeographed, Cambridge, Mass., 1956); *Syntactic Structures* (The Hague, 1957).

SEMIOTICS (SEMIOLOGY)

397. *Semiotics* or *semiology*[7] is the study of the signs used for mutual understanding.[8] In linguistics the sign of communication is first and foremost the language sign. For philosophers semiotic studies include all communicative signals. In this (philosophical)

[7]   From the Greek *sēmiōtikē*.
[8]   This should not be confused with *semology* which has come to be used with increasing frequency by some American linguists to denote a new discipline inspired by the principles of anthropological linguistics (see above § 342). Both the term and the concepts relating to the new discipline are expounded by Martin Joos in his study: "Semology: a Linguistic Theory of Meaning", *SIL*, 13 (1958), 53-70. Semology would be concerned with investigating the problems of polysemy (see above § 376), relying on substitution (see above § 332) as a methodological procedure.

sense semiotics has developed during the twentieth century as a new branch of science, the scope of which is at the present moment accepted by many linguistic scholars (above all the glossematicians, see above § 370).

398. The first great semiotician among linguists was De Saussure:[9] his theory of language was largely based on an examination of the nature of the language sign. This new problem, placed by him in the centre of linguistic interests, is still topical today.

399. The semiotic phenomenon attracted the attention of philosophers much earlier.[10] But the foundations of modern semiotic studies were only laid in the first half of the twentieth century, beginning with the work of the American logician Charles Pierce.[11] The actual scope of the new science was established by another American, C. W. Morris.

400. For Morris semiotics was not only a basic philosophical discipline, but also occupied a central place in scholarship in general, since it had the task of discovering the common language of scientific theory (many people consider that this is overestimating the significance of semiotics, but all agree that its rôle in the development of scholarship as a whole is certainly important). Morris divided semiotics into three branches: pragmatics, semantics and syntax. This division is still generally accepted by scholars today.

Pragmatics embraces the study of means of communication in

[9] People had reflected on the communicative function of linguistic elements before De Saussure, but unsystematically and without penetrating far into the problem. Most worthy of mention is the original attempt (as early as 1885) of the German Wegener to produce a semiotic stratification of human language based on German, Greek and Latin (i.e. to determine the fundamental, logical organization of the phenomenon of language).

[10] As early as 1690 John Locke, in his classification of fields of scholarship, stressed the fact that logic was simply a branch of a wider discipline, semiotics, which embraced the study of the signs used for "understanding and communication".

[11] Pierce's point of departure was the belief that logical investigations should be primarily directed to the study of the communicative sign, since it is the means by which the transmitting of man's ideas about the external world is achieved. His theory is expounded in the work *Collected Papers of Charles Sanders Pierce* (Cambridge Mass., 1932).

relation to man: what happens in man when he sends and receives a message; on what the way in which communication is carried on (in general and in each particular case) depends; to what extent the form of the communication is conditioned by the type of culture.

Semantic and syntactical research are concerned with the phenomenon of communication without taking into account its relationship with man. The aim of *semantics* is to explain the relations between communicative signs and the concepts to which they refer. *Syntax* studies the correlations of signs in a given communicative system, keeping strictly to formal analysis (i.e. without taking account of the meaning).

401. Those who occupy themselves with semiotic problems are called (in philosophy) *semanticians*.[12] They are divided into two groups, according to the trend of their scholarly interests and the form of their work: *general semanticians* and *academic semanticians* (*symbolic logicians*).

General semanticians acknowledge the value of the method of symbolic logic but are not chiefly concerned with its elaboration. They have set themselves the task of discovering a general theory about the human intellect which would contribute to epistemology. Their "linguistic" attention is therefore concentrated on clarifying the relationship between language and culture (i.e. on pragmatic investigations).[13] General semantics is, then, primarily a philosophical doctrine which at first sight appears to be of little interest to the linguistic scholar. However anthropological linguistics (see above § 343) has found plenty of inspiration for its attitudes towards the problem of language in the work of general semanticians.

---

[12] The term *semantics* has long been known in philosophy, ever since Aristotle's times. The term *semantic philosophy* began to be used in the seventeenth century (it first appeared in a work by John Spencer: *A Discourse Concerning Prodigies*, 1665, 2nd ed.).

[13] They have pointed out that language retains traces of primitive psychology (for example many languages have the expressions *the sun sets, the sun rises*, because for many centuries men really believed that the sun disappeared from the sky and appeared again the next morning); and that it reveals a subjective attitude in the estimation of reality (we say: *The water is cold* or *the water is warm*; in fact it is neither cold nor warm in itself, but extimated as cold or warm according to the warmth of our bodies).

Academic semanticians are concerned with logistic grammar (see above § 394), i.e. with semantic and syntactic studies. Rudolf Carnap is specially prominent in this field of scholarship.

402. In Carnap's opinion semantic research may take two basic forms. *Descriptive semantics* is concerned with the description of phenomena which condition the nature of actual, existing signs of communication. Hence it is a discipline pursued primarily by linguistic scholars. It is also of interest to philosophers since it gives them suggestions for their abstract, logical constructions of communicative systems. *Theoretical semantics* embraces the elaboration of the method of logical operations by means of symbols introduced into the construction of abstract semantic systems. It is mainly studied by logicians. Carnap sees the relationship of theoretical to descriptive semantics as similar to that between abstract and applied mathematics, or theoretical and empirical physics.

The task of syntax, according to Carnap, was the construction of a theory of formal relations by the use of logical analysis (in the spirit of Morris's conception, see above § 400). In such an analysis language is regarded as a *calculus*, i.e. a system of conventions or rules expressed by symbols. Syntactical research, then, would relate to such a definition of the communicative system.

Carnap's views on semantics and syntax have had considerable repercussions in modern linguistics and have strongly influenced the development of its methodology.

Bibliographical References

403. Morris's fundamental works are: *Foundation of the Theory of Signs* (Chicago, 1938) and *Signs, Language and Behavior* (New York, 1946).

Carnap's chief works are cited in § 396 above. See also W. Quine, *Word and Object* (New York, 1960) and the collection *Semantics and the Philosophy of Language*, ed. L. Linsky (Urbana, 1952) which presents approved extracts from the works of the following authors: L. Linsky, A. Tarski, C. I. Lewis, Nelson Goodman, Willard V. Quine, Bertrand Russell, Benson Mates, Paul Marhenke, Carl G. Hempel, Rudolf Carnap, Arne Neass and Morton G. White. The philosophical conceptions of the general semanticians and their type of interest in language are described in detail in a book by the Polish mathematician Alfred Korzybski (the publication of which marked the foundation of the philosophical school itself): *Science and Sanity, An Introduction to Non-Aristotelian Systems and General Semantics* (Lancaster, Science Press XX, 1933). A book by S. J. Hayakawa (also a proponent of general semantics) *Language in Thought and Action* (New York, 1949) is popular, especially among the representatives of anthropological linguistics.

Linguists usually get their first acquaintance with the variety of semiotic problems by reading the following two books: C. K. Ogden and I. A. Richards, *The Meaning of Meaning. A Study of the Influence of Language upon Thought and the Science of Symbolism* (London, 1954) and H. Spang-Hanssen, *Recent Theories on the Nature of the Language Sign* (Copenhagen, 1954).

Slavists may find reliable information in Adam Schaff's book: *Wstęp do semantyki* (Warsaw, 1960). For the Yugoslav linguistic public the most accessible source of information is the book by Mihajlo Marković: *Dijalektička teorija značenja* (Beograd, 1961).

LINGUISTIC SEMANTICS

404. Semantics, the science of the meaning of words (and their grammatical forms), was founded at the end of the nineteenth century, mainly as a result of the work of the French linguist Michel Bréal.[14] However it is only in the twentieth century that it has begun to develop seriously as a separate branch of linguistics.

---

[14] The term itself (*sémantique*) was first popularized in linguistic circles by Bréal (he introduced it for the first time in his study: "Les lois intellectuelles du language, fragments de sémantique", *Annuaire de l'Association pour l'encouragement des études grecques en France*, vol. XVII, 1883). English linguistics produced another term: *semasiology*. Today both expressions are used. There are, moreover, some attempts to introduce yet more terms (such as *sematology, glossology, rhematics, rhematology*) but these have no general significance.

In recent years especially its development has been more successful, owing to the increasing number of people interested in its problems, the acquisition of wider theoretical horizons, and the use of more efficient methodological procedures.

405. Bréal and his contemporaries[15] placed semantic studies within limits which suited the general linguistic orientation at the end of the nineteenth century: insofar as attention was focussed on the actual meanings of words, it was primarily in order to throw light on the psychological background of the phenomenon of language; otherwise it remained for the most part in the domain of history of language – the examination of semantic changes which had arisen in the course of linguistic evolution.

406. At the beginning of the twentieth century the methodology of historical semantics improved considerably, most of all thanks to the efforts of French scholars: the classic achievements of linguistic geography were concerned, for example, with the theory of "homonymic conflicts" (see above § 150) and the part played by social and historical factors in the development of vocabulary. The working out of this latter theoretical view owed much to the successful activities of both the representatives of sociological linguistics (see above § 162) and the Italian neolinguists (see above § 180).

407. As early as the first decades of the present century a very important and still topical theme was introduced into linguistic discussions: what are the general principles governing semantic changes, and how can they be established?[16] In this field of research the challenging works of the proponents of *structural semantics* deserve special mention.

408. It has long been noticed that certain words are grouped according to their meaning to form a co-ordinated whole, a system.

---

[15]   Many linguists, e.g. A. Darmesteter, H. Paul (see above § 98), W. Wundt (see above § 83), H. Shuchardt (and other contributors to the periodical *Wörter und Sachen*, see above § 111) were actively interested in the problems of meaning.

[16]   G. Stern's book, *Meaning and Change of Meaning, With Special Reference to English Language* (Göteborg, 1931), was specially important in drawing the attention of linguists in this direction.

The term *semantic system* (*system of meaning*) was explicitly used as early as 1910 by R. M. Meyer, who showed[17] that the names of military ranks, for example, acquire their real meaning only within the framework of the whole terminology of ranks used by an army; this terminology in its entirety comprises a "system of meanings" ("Bedeutungs-system"). It has also been pointed out in a number of instances that semantic systems have changed in the course of time according to the evolution of men's conceptions of reality (for example the system of names for colours was different in the ancient world from what it is today, nor do the present-day names cover all the shades of the solar spectrum).[18] However the first really thorough investigation of the theory of semantic systems took shape only with J. Trier's famous study: *Der deutsche Wortschatz im Sinnbezirk des Verstandes* (Heidelberg, 1931) in which a convincing case was first made for the theory that all words behave as units of a complete lexical system belonging to a particular language at a particular moment of history.

409. Approaching the problem of semantics from a structural standpoint, Trier elaborated a theory concerning *semantic fields*: words which signify related conceptions are connected with specific sectors of human consciousness and form a system (a semantic field) of connected semantic units; if one of the concepts changes in the course of time, the others from the same sector are also modified, which automatically means a change in the meanings of the corresponding words.[19]

410. The well-known linguistic theoretician Karl Bühler (see above § 91) also declared himself in favour of the structural approach

---

[17] In the study "Bedeutungssystem", *Kuhns Zeitschrift*, XLIII (1910), pp. 352-368.

[18] Most work on this problem was done by L. Weisgerber (an adherent of the Neo-Humboldtians), even earlier than 1930.

[19] Trier illustrated his ideas with examples from German lexical history. He showed how in the course of centuries, and depending on changes in the conceptions of particular phenomena concerning social ranks, knowledge and culture, there was a change in meaning, and together with it a change in the mutual relations of words which denote general concepts referring to wisdom and skill (he explained historically the relationship between the expressions: *Wisheit, Wizzen, Kunst* and *List*).

to semantic problems (in 1934 in his book *Sprachtheorie*). His great authority with his contemporaries in determining fields of general linguistic interest made a vital contribution towards focussing attention on the theory of semantic systems in general, and thus on Trier's exposition of "semantic fields". This theory was later developed further by the adherents of French sociological linguistics (see above § 163), with the emphasis on the rôle of social factors in determining the fate of words (most work on this was done by G. Matoré). The subject of fields of meaning does not belong only to linguistics; it is also studied by the proponents of modern psychology.

411. Semantic studies also embrace semiotic problems: the investigation of the nature of the language sign. As has been mentioned above (see above § 255) discussion still continues as to how far the connections of a particular sound chain are arbitrarily linked with a particular meaning (this problem has been treated, since De Saussure's time, by such eminent writers as Bühler, Buyssens, Ullman, Zvegincev, Regnéll and many others). At the centre of attention is the phenomenon of *nomination* (the giving of names to phenomena): to what extent the name is given simply because of the needs of communication, i.e. to make conversation about a phenomenon possible, and how far the process includes a subjective estimate of the phenomenon to which the name refers (this last problem has been discussed by a large number of writers, some of whom do not in fact belong to the immediate circle of semanticians, but who are interested in the problem of the psychological element in language – e.g. Wundt, see above § 83, and Bally, see above § 265).

412. The question of what a word is and how it should be defined is a very important and ever topical subject of discussion. Then there is the problem of how to separate polysemy (see above § 376) from homonymy. This second problem in itself poses the need to make a theoretical differentiation between what could be potentially included in one meaning and what is in fact included in it (the Serbo-Croatian word *meso* embraces the concepts expressed both by the English words *meat* and *flesh*). The effective analysis of

meaning would seem to require the delimitation of the logical and psychological fields in language: in what way and to what extent logical and psychological categories are apparent in the phenomenon of language.[20]

413. A much discussed subject in linguistics (especially today in connection with the needs of machine translation)[21] is the relationship between "lexical" and "grammatical" meaning (e.g. the Serbo-Croatian morpheme -ić has a lexical meaning denoting a diminutive: cvetić = little flower; but the form se used as a sign of intransitiveness with the Serbo-Croatian verb peći 'bake' peći se 'be baked' has a grammatical meaning).

414. A useful contribution to the progress of practical semantic analysis was the indication of the value of the context in throwing light on particular shades of meaning.[22] However this has not yielded a decisive improvement in this field of linguistic studies, which still suffers from the lack of an adequately elaborated methodological approach. The well-known imperfections of one-language dictionaries lie in the ineffectiveness of their means of definition: there is no possibility of replacing synonyms by other methods of description, nor is homonymy adequately differentiated from polysemy.

415. In 1957 a group of American psychologists[23] tried to improve lexicological methods by using special tests, the purpose of which was to find the "semantic profile" of a word. A scale was made, consisting of seven empty fields and two opposite poles; on one of these poles an adjective was inscribed, and on the other another adjective, the semantic opposite (antonym) of the first

---

[20]   In present-day linguistics there is an increasing tendency to adopt the distinctions introduced by logicians (for example the pronoun it or the conjunction or are called formators – they express primarily concepts from the field of logical thought, while the words house and run belong to the category of designators and refer directly to actual phenomena).

[21]   See below § 475.

[22]   The greatest emphasis on this trend has come from the (English, Oxford) school of ethnographic linguistics (also known under the name of the contextual school) founded by Malinowski and Firth (see above note to § 348).

[23]   C. E. Osgood, G. J. Souci, P. H. Tannenbaum, The Measurement of Meaning (Urbana, 1957).

(e.g., beautiful – ugly, wise – foolish, useful – harmful). Plus or minus signs were to be distributed over the seven fields. Selected words were then given to various people who would, by putting the appropriate signs in the empty fields, describe towards which pole the characteristics of the given word moved: e.g. whether the word *mother* was characterized by the property "beautiful" or "ugly", "stupid" or "wise", etc. After the conclusion of the tests, the "semantic profile" of the words under examination (i.e. the numerical index of their properties) was obtained by the application of statistical methods. In the opinion of the authors this made it possible to measure the distance between one word and another as regards meaning. This method was, however, very critically received on the part of linguistic scholars.[24]

416. The most recent discussions among semanticians (particularly in the U.S.A.) have been concerned with discovering an objective method of analyzing semantic categories. There is an increasingly firm conviction that this objective method lies in applying the metalanguage criteria which are being elaborated by the adherents of symbolic logic (see above § 388). By accepting such a method, linguistics would at last begin to move towards its great but so far unachieved aims: 1. exact lexicography; 2. the discovery of universal semantic categories (i.e. the establishment of those semantic structures, and the laws governing them, which are always present in a language without regard to its concrete realization). The achievement of these aims would also be of paramount assistance to the progress of machine translation.

Bibliographical References

417. Classic semantic studies are represented by: Bréal, *Essai de sémantique* (Paris, 1897) and A. Darmesteter, *La vie des mots* (Paris, 1893). The recent methodological orientation of the French

---

[24] See Weinreich's criticism in the periodical *Word*, XIV, 2-3 (1958), pp. 346-366, Osgood's reply and a further statement by Weinreich in No. XV, 1 (1959), pp. 192-200 and 200-201.

semanticians is well illustrated in G. Matoré's book: *La méthode en lexicologie, Domaine français* (Paris, 1953).

A criticism of traditional semantics with an explanation of lexical terminology is given by Leo Weisgerber in "Die Bedeutungslehre – ein Irrweg der Sprachwissenschaft", *Germanisch- Romanische Monatschrift*, XV, (1927), pp. 161-183.

A theory of the semantic system is shown in: R. Hallig – W. von Wartburg, *Begriffssystem als Grundlage für die Lexicographie* (Berlin, 1952).

The lexicological method of the school of aesthetic idealism is illustrated in Leo Spitzer's book: *Essays in Historical Semantics* (New York, 1948).

The fundamental sources for the study of modern semantics are the following books: S. Ullmann, *Principles of Semantics* (Glasgow, 1957) (this is the second edition, more important than the first, published in 1951, because of the additional chapter: "Supplements to the Second Edition: Recent Developments in Semantics", pp. 300-321); A. V. Zvegincev, *Semasiologija* (Moscow, 1957); H. Regnéll, *Semantik* (Stockholm, 1958).

See also the following works by Ullmann: the book *Précis de sémantique française* (Berne, 1952) – an excellent practical demonstration of the more recent semantic methods; the study "Desciiptive Semantics and Linguistic Typology" *Word*, 9 (1953), pp. 225-240, important because it raises the question of bringing to light universal semantic categories in languages.

A clearly written general survey of the development of semantic studies and of basic semantic problems is given by P. Guiraud in *La Sémantique* (= *Que sais-je?*) (Paris, 1955).

The collection *O točnyx metodax issledovanija jazyka* (authors: O. S. Axmanova, I. A. Mel'čuk, E. V. Padučeva, R. M. Frumkina) (Moscow University, 1961) in Chapter II ("Nekotorye voprosy semantiki v sovremennom jazykoznanii", pp. 20-32) contains a short but competent exposition of the most topical semantic problems in modern linguistics. See also the collection *Voprosy teorii jazyka v sovremennoj zarubežnoj linguistike* (Moscow, AN SSSR, 1961) where many interesting studies are published, for example:

R. A. Budagov, *K kritike reljativističeskix teorij*, pp. 5-29; A. A. Ufimceva, *Teorii 'semantičeskogo polja' i vozmožnosti ix primenenija pri izučenii slovarnogo sostava jazyka*, pp. 30-63; K. A. Levkovskaja, *Nekotorye zarubežnye jazykovedčeskie teorii i ponjatie slova*, pp. 64-89.

E. A. Nida in "A System for the Description of Semantic Elements", *Word*, 7 (1951), pp. 1-14, demonstrates the application of the traditional American way of analysing semantic problems. His study "Analysis of Meaning and Dictionary Making", *IJAL*, 24 (1958), pp. 279-292 is of special interest to lexicographers.

The approach to the problem of meaning according to the ideas of anthropological linguistics has in recent years found expression in a variety of works, of which the following may be mentioned: D. L. Olmsted, "Towards a Cultural Theory of Lexical Innovation", *Report of the Fifth Annual Round Table Meeting on Linguistics and Language Studies* (1954), pp. 105-117; U. Weinreich, "Travels in Semantic Space", *Word*, 14 (1958), pp. 346-366; D. H. Hymes, "On Typology of Cognitive Styles in Language", *Anthrop. Linguistics*, 3, No. 1 (1961), pp. 22-54.

On the attempt to secure an objective analysis of meaning by the use of psychological tests, see: the above-mentioned study *The Measurement of Meaning* and Weinreich's criticism (see above § 415 footn.).

The contribution of information theory to the perfecting of semantic analysis is discussed by D. M. Mackay in "The Place of 'Meaning' in the Theory of Information", *Information Theory*, ed. by C. Cherry (= Basic Books) (New York, 1956).

Among studies which treat the problem of the analysis of thought through the analysis of language the following may be mentioned: R. Wells: "Meaning and Use", *Word*, 10 (1954), pp. 235-250; "Is a Structural Treatment of Meaning Possible?", *8th Proceedings*, pp. 654-666, "A Mathematical Approach to Meaning", *CFS*, XV (1957), pp. 117-136; Charles C. Fries, "Meaning and Linguistic Analysis", *Lg*, 30, No. 1 (1954), pp. 57-68; Shirô Hattori, "The Analysis of Meaning", *For Roman Jakobson*, pp. 207-212.

The interesting approach of the Soviet lexicologists has been exemplified in Zvegincev's book mentioned above. See also: O. S. Axmanova *Očerki po obščej i russkoj leksikologii* (Moscow, 1957) and the studies presented in the periodical *Leksikografičeskij sbornik*, which has been published since 1957 (the contributors include such writers as Ožegov, Vinogradov, Axmanova, Avrorin, Zvegincev, Kotelova and others). A. I. Smirnickij's book *Leksikologija anglijskogo jazyka* (Moscow, 1956) was particularly important for the development of modern conceptions regarding semantic problems in the U.S.S.R. It can still today serve as a good introductory textbook for those interested in lexicology.

The use of symbolic-logical criteria in analysis is conveniently illustrated in the following works: J. Bar-Hillel, "Logical Syntax and Semantics", *Lg*, 30 (1954), pp. 230-237; N. Chomsky, "Logical Syntax and Semantics: their Linguistic Relevance", *Lg*, 31 (1955), pp. 36-45.

17

LINGUISTIC SYNTAX AND THE
GENERATIVE APPROACH

418. Syntax is a linguistic discipline which did not begin to develop intensively until the twentieth century. The slow progress of syntactical studies (both then and in the first decades of the twentieth century) was conditioned by serious weaknesses in methodology, which was in general elaborated less thoroughly and with much less sophistication than the methodology relating to phonemics and morphology. A syntactic phenomenon was usually approached from the point of view of meaning and analysed on a basis of subjective criteria, according to the "linguistic feeling" of the investigator; this deprived syntactical definitions a priori of their most necessary element – a strict scientific precision[1] (in fact it was mainly on account of syntax that traditional linguistics acquired its bad reputation as a "mentalistic discipline").

419. The first important innovations in syntax did not appear until the thirties of the present century. Then the field of syntactic studies began to widen: for example there was a growing conviction that in order to understand the sentence and the relations of its members, it was necessary to examine the actual relationship existing between the partners involved in the act of communication (K. Bühler and A. Gardiner in particular called attention to this point). Attempts were made to throw light on the sentence from a quite different angle. The "mentalistic" definition was replaced by a "physical" one: the sentence was designated as a linguistic unit whose component parts – words – were united by intonation into a single speech whole (this conception was upheld, for example, by the Dutch syntacticist A. de Groot).

[1] It is typical of this situation that at the beginning of the thirties of the present century, there were over over 160 definitions of the sentence.

420. A decisive step forward in the development of syntax was taken only when the structural method elaborated according to the principles of the Yale school (see above § 335) began to be applied.

421. The adherents of traditional linguistics had taken no account of syntactical problems if they were working on morphology, and vice versa. They believed that morphological and syntactical problems should be sharply divided, both in theory and in practice, and that the investigation of the use of forms should be assigned to syntax. The attitude of the proponents of structural linguistics is quite different. They do not draw a sharp dividing line between the two disciplines, and stress that the problem of the use of forms is primarily morphological in character. The eminent morphologists of the Yale school were at the same time the pioneers of modern syntax (see above § 335). Their study of sentence structure rested on the abstraction of "immediate constituents" types in sentences (see above § 336) by observing the rules of distribution.

The American linguist Paul Garvin, who in the fifties expounded the most original non-generative ideas on syntactical problems, also belongs to the generation well-trained in the distributional approach to syntax.

422. Just before 1960 modern syntax entered the most significant period of its development: it was then that *generative grammar* was founded.

The term was coined in order to underline the fact that such a grammar intends to discover the rules governing the structure and composition of sentences. The type of generative grammar which is based on a particular method of analysis introduced by Chomsky (see below § 426) is usually called *transformational grammar* (Chomsky uses the term *transformation* to identify the variety of rules which come into operation after the establishment of the "phrase-structure" component which produces the basic sentence structure, see below § 426).

423. Some intimations of generative grammar were already present in the works of Zellig Harris, an eminent representative of the Yale school (see above § 340). In elaborating the theory of

distribution, Harris became convinced that an effective morphemic analysis could be carried out only by the successive introduction of symbols into the methodological procedure. This procedure would be characterized by a gradual penetration towards the underlying structure of the utterance: first each morphemic unit must be identified, then their mutual relationships, which would yield information about the immediate constituents (see above § 336), and finally the basic structure of the utterance as a whole must be stated.

Starting from the smaller linguistic units, the analysis would proceed to the larger ones. Harris expounded his first ideas on this subject as early as 1946, in his study "From Morpheme to Utterance" (see below § 430).

However it was Harris' pupil Noam Chomsky who finally established transformational theory and introduced the new method into syntactical studies. The publication of his book *Syntactic Structures* (1957), which laid the foundation of transformationalism and gave it wide publicity in the linguistic world, is considered one of the most important events in linguistics in recent years.

424. Chomsky too opted for both the gradual approach in analysing linguistic facts and the introduction of symbols into analysis. But his procedure went in the reverse order: starting from larger linguistic units, the grammatical description should move towards smaller ones, i.e. first the basic structure of the utterance is established (determination of the immediate constituents), while the descriptions of the basic morphemic units come last. Harris' analysis was morphological as regards its point of departure, while Chomsky's was primarily concerned with the syntactic level. Moreover these two scholars differ in the scope of their theoretical ambitions. Harris was interested in throwing light on the actual sentence structures belonging to concrete languages (i.e. as a grammarian), while Chomsky directed his interest also towards detecting the laws which govern the correlation between the grammatical and logical organization of an utterance.

425. Chomsky's scholarly approach was basically influenced by the theory of distributionalism (see above § 322) and the logistic conception of syntax (see above § 402). He believed that it was

necessary to discover a general theory of grammatical structure, and he introduced the use of symbols into analysis, convinced that such a methodological procedure would ensure the maximum degree of precision in scientific description.

426. Transformational grammar is founded on the belief that an adequate grammar should always provide a basis for explaining how sentences are used and understood. The transformationalists seek to state as a synchronic fact the processes which take place during speech and listening. In contradistinction to the Bloomfieldian approach, they propound a theory which presents the description of the processes of sentence formation.

The grammar of a language is a system of rules. The transformationalists insist upon the fact that those rules should be ordered one after the other. Thus, a transformational grammar is made of ordered rules consisting entirely of symbols.

There are two levels for representing the structure of sentences in transformational grammar: the *phrase structure level* and the *transformational level*. There are consequently two different kinds of rules: *phrase rules* (or *constituent structure rules*, or *P-rules*) and *transformational rules*. In constructing a grammar for any given language, one should use both the phrase structure and transformational levels of description.

A phrase structure grammar operates with rules of the form X → Y (where → means "rewrite as"); they are rules for rewriting individual symbols, one symbol at a time.

Any sentence (S) should be developed first of all as follows: S→ NP + VP (where NP means "noun phrase" and VP "verb phrase"). Then follows a further derivation which consists in the rewriting of NP and VP, one symbol at a time. The sentence *John likes Bill* may be described as follows:

S   → NP + VP
NP → John
VP → V + N
V   → likes
N   → Bill

Such a derivation can be represented as a diagram in the form of a tree:

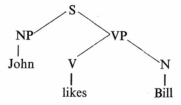

On the phrase structure level we would always have "trees".

The transformational level provides formulae of sentence generation. The derivation on this level begins after the establishment of the "tree". It is based on the application of transformational rules. They operate on the tree effecting particular changes (reordering, addition or deletion of elements, etc.) the result of which is a new string of symbols with a new structural description. For example, one such transformation will convert the active structure *John saw Bill* into the corresponding passive sentence *Bill was seen by John* in the following manner:

(a) Structural description: NP, Aux, V, NP
(b) Structural change: $X_1 - X_2 - X_3 - X_4$ is transformed to
$X_4 - X_2 + be + en - X_3 - by + X_1$
input: *John — past — see — Bill*
result: *Bill — past + be + en — see — by + John*

Transformations are of two different kinds: optional and obligatory.

Optional transformations may or may not be applied in constructing a derivation; the result is still a sentence. As for the *obligatory transformations*, if they are not applied, the result is not a sentence at all.

In contradistinction to a *derived sentence*, a *kernel sentence* means a sentence to which no optional transformations have been applied.

427. Sentences differ in their grammatical well-formedness. Some are less well-formed than the others, which means that they possess a lower degree of grammaticality. The evaluation of sentences according to the criterion of grammaticality belongs to the linguistic competence of the native speaker.

This competence involves the ability to understand new sentences, to detect deviant sentences, and even to interpret them. Since the transformationalists intend to find a device for generating permitted sentences, without including sentences the native speaker would not accept, the study of linguistic intuitions and judgements seems to be of pivotal interest for them. Chomsky even explicitly states that he would like to find a theory which will predict such intuitions.

428. Generative grammar (although, so to speak, only born yesterday) has become one of the central disciplines of modern linguistics. Even many people who do not share the conviction that Chomsky's theory possesses an omnipotent explanatory power in linguistics accept his method of analysis in the field of syntax. The transformation method has already been introduced in dialectology, in semantic studies, in the studies of word formation and language history. Its achievements have begun to be used also in phonological research. M. Halle was the first to introduce the generative approach into phonological description (see his book *The Sound Pattern of Russian* quoted in § 291). He too applies ordered rules which operate not on sound segments as units but on the distinctive features of which they are composed. His phonological underlying forms are more abstract than traditional phonemic transcription, just as Chomsky's syntactic underlying forms are more abstract than an immediate constituent analysis. These underlying forms are similar to what is frequently called the morphophonemic level, since they include information about the grammatical structure of the sentence. A great saving in efficiency results from omitting the "phonemic" level of representation.

429. Generative grammar, although it arose in the U.S.A., has been enthusiastically received in the Soviet Union, primarily because of its possible applications in machine translation. At present American and Soviet linguistics are competing to achieve results in this field of research.

BIBLIOGRAPHICAL REFERENCES

430. Traditional syntax is best represented in J. T. Ries' works:

Was ist Syntax? (Marburg, 1894; Prague 1927) and *Was ist ein Satz?* (Prague, 1931).

Handbuch der erklärenden Syntax (Heidelberg, 1931) by W. Havers provides an introduction to a wider repertoire of syntactic problems.

Classic works on syntax include: K. Bühler, *Sprachtheorie, Die Darstellungfunktion der Sprache* (Jena, 1934); O. Jespersen, *The Philosophy of Grammar* (London, 1924, new ed. 1948) and *Analytic Syntax* (Copenhagen, 1937).

The general climate of syntactic interests in the period from the thirties to the fifties is well illustrated in the following books: A. Gardiner, *The Theory of Speech and Language* (Oxford, 1932; second ed. 1951) and J. R. Firth, *General Linguistics and Descriptive Grammar* (London, 1951).

L. Tesnière introduces the reader to the structural conception of syntactic problems in his book *Éléments de syntaxe structurale* (Paris, 1959).

The views of the eminent structuralist-syntactist A. W. de Groot are best expounded in a booklet, written in Dutch: *Structurele Syntaxis* (The Hague, 1949). De Groot also speaks of the structural approach to syntax in his study "Structural Linguistics and Syntactic Laws", *Word*, 5, I (1949), pp. 1-12.

Hockett's *A Course in Modern Linguistics* (New York, 1958) expounds the principles of syntactic analysis in harmony with the methodological conceptions of pre-generative American linguistics. E. Nida's work *Outline of Descriptive Syntax* (Glendale-California, 1951) is regarded as the classic American textbook of syntax. Nida is also the author of a book on English syntax once very popular: *A Synopsis of English Syntax* (1943; new edition 1960).

Pickett's book *An Introduction to the Study of Grammatical Structure* (Glendale-California, 1956) gives an analytical survey of both morphological and syntactic problems; for this reason many people consider it a particularly useful textbook for beginners in syntactic studies.

The anthropological approach to syntax is illustrated in a study by George L. Trager and Henry Lee Smith Jr.: "An Outline of

English Structure", *SIL, Occasional Papers*, 3 (1951), pp. 1-91. The collection *Report of the Seventh Annual Round Table Meeting on Linguistics and Language Study* (= *Georgetown University Monograph Series on Languages and Linguistics*, No. 9) (Washington, 1957) contains two challenging articles: P. L. Garvin, *Operations in Syntactic Analysis* (pp. 59-72), which champions modern methodological procedures in syntax, and H. L. Smith Jr., *Superfixes and Syntactic Makers* (pp. 7-24), in which the author speaks of suprasegmental phenomena (i.e. phenomena connected with intonation and accentuation, including pauses) used as a means of organizing sentence structures. For Garvin's approach to syntax see also: Paul Garvin, "Syntactic Units and Operations", *8th Proceedings*, pp. 626-632.

See also the article by V. N. Jarceva, "Problema formy i soderžanija sintaksičeskix edinic v traktirovke deskriptivistov i mentalistov" in the collection, *Voprosy teorii jazyka v sovremennoj zarubežnoj lingistike* (Moscow, AN SSSR, 1961), pp. 90-105.

The first introduction to the transformationalist method can be found in Harris' works: "From Morpheme to Utterance", *Lg*, 22 (1946), pp. 161-183; "Discourse Analysis", *Lg*, 28 (1952), pp. 1-30; "Discourse Analysis: a Sample Text", *Lg*, 28 (1952), pp. 474-494; "Transfer Grammar", *IJAL*, 20 (1954), pp. 259-270. The first study of his which is strikingly transformationalist in ideas and exposition: "Co-occurence and Transformation in Linguistic Structure", *Lg*, 33 (1957), pp. 283-340.

The central and already classic work of transformationalism is Noam Chomsky's book *Syntactic Structures* (The Hague, 1957). The following studies by the same author are also important: "System of Syntactic Analysis", *Journal of Symbolic Logic* (1953), pp. 242-256; *The Logical Structure of Linguistic Theory* (Cambridge, Mass., mimeographed, M.I.T. edition, 1956), and "Some Methodological Remarks on Generative Grammar", *Word*, 17 (1961) No. 2, pp. 219-239.

R. B. Lees gives a thorough review of Chomsky's "Syntactic Structures" in *Lg*, 33 (1957), pp. 375-408. This writer also gives a very convenient account of transformationalism in general in the

Soviet periodical *Voprosy jazykoznanija*, X (1961) fasc. 3, pp. 69-77, under the title "Čto takoe transformacija".

The new method in syntax is briefly expounded by T. M. Nikolaeva in "Čto takoe transformacionnyj analiz?", *V Ja*, IX (1960), fasc. 1, pp. 111-115.

Illustrations of the application of the transformationalist method to actual language material are given in the following works: Robert B. Lees, "The Grammar of English Nominalization", *IJAL*, Part II, vol. 26, No. 3, (July, 1960), pp. 1-XV + 1-205, and Dean Stoddard Worth, "Transform Analysis of Russian Instrumental Constructions", *Word*, vol. 14, No. 2-3 (1958), pp. 247-290. Worth's study was an important event in the recent history of Slavistics: there for the first time Slavonic language problems are treated according to the transformationalist method.

The application of logical operations following the conceptions of symbolic logic to syntactic analysis is demonstrated in Carnap's book: *The Logical Syntax of Language* (New York, 1937) and in the works of J. Bar-Hillel: "On Syntactic Categories", *Journal of Symbolic Logic*, XV (1950), pp. 1-16 and "Logical Syntax and Semantics", *Lg*, 30 (1954), pp. 230-237.

Information about many problems of syntactic analysis in connection with machine translation is given in the book *O točnyx metodax issledovanija jazyka* the section entitled "Sintaktičeskij analiz pri mašinnom perevode" (joint authors: O. S. Axmanova, I. A. Mel'čuk, E. V. Padučeva, R. M. Frumkina) (Moscow University, 1961). There is a very well-informed and ably written exposition of modern methods in syntax by Warren Plath in his article "Mathematical Linguistics" in the chapters: "Models for sentence synthesis and syntactic description" and "Models for syntactic analysis", *Trends*, pp. 41-51.

18

MATHEMATICAL LINGUISTICS

INTRODUCTORY REMARKS

431. The linguistics of the second half of the twentieth century is characterized by the widespread application of methodological procedures from the mathematical sciences.

At the beginning of the twentieth century statistical methods penetrated to all branches of science, including linguistics. The usefulness of these methods had in fact been known to some of those interested in language studies for a long time (the old Indian grammarians – see above § 20 – had minutely counted the lines, words and syllables of the Rig Veda). But it was only in the twentieth century that statistics really became an indispensible aid for all those who were seriously concerned with the description of linguistic facts.

But it is not only statistics which has given modern linguistics its mathematical character. The whole system of linguistic research has in a certain sense been given a mathematical orientation. The strictly logical character of mathematical analysis proceeds from the legitimate desire of linguistic scholars to make their definitions as exact, clear and brief as possible; to ensure the most precise knowledge of the actual structure of language by introducing abstract concepts into methodological procedure; to facilitate their own work of analysis by approaching the precision of mathematical formulae.

432. The interest of linguistic scholars in mathematics sprang up at exactly the same time as the interest of mathematicians in linguistics. Actually it had long been noticed on both sides that these two disciplines could find identical fields of interest.[1]

[1] As early as 1847 the Russian mathematician V. Ja. Bunjakovskij indicated

The first serious step towards such co-operation was taken at the beginning of the twentieth century by the mathematicians. The year 1913 saw the publication of a famous study by the Russian mathematician A. A. Markov: "Primer statističeskogo issledovanija nad tekstom 'Evgenija Onegina' illjustrirujuščij svjaz' 'ispytanij v cep' ", *Izvestija Imper. Akademii nauk*, series VI, t. VII, No. 3 (1913). Markov examined the laws governing the co-occurrences of Russian vowels and consonants by applying statistical methods to the study of Pushkin's *"Evgenij Onegin"*. His results showed that, under particular conditions, it was possible to predict the actual forms of these co-occurrences with reasonable accuracy. This marked the beginning of a new mathematical era based on the elaboration of the "theory of probability". These same results provided linguistics with evidence as to the usefulness of applying mathematical methods in the study of linguistic problems. Hence this work of Markov's is considered a very important landmark in the history of both mathematics and linguistics.

433. The transplantation of methodological experiences from the mathematical to the linguistic field of research only attained large proportions after the Second World War, just when considerable attention was being devoted to the further development of the so-called *information theory* (see below § 449).

The twentieth century has been an age concerned with the discovery of devices for conveying information. First came the telephone and radio, and then the still more complicated instruments such as radar and the translation machine. This would not have been possible if the working out of the theory of information as a whole had not been going on at the same time.

In order that information may be conveyed, the first requirement is a transmitter of the message on the one hand, and a receiver on the other. Whether machines or people are in question, one thing is essential: there must be a fixed system of signals, known to both the transmitter and the receiver, which are in a position to carry

---

the possibility of using mathematical methods in linguistics, while in 1904 the eminent linguist Baudouin de Courtenay expressed the conviction that linguistics could be helped by higher as well as elementary mathematics.

and transfer a particular meaning. Thus the basic principle governing the transmission of information is always the same, regardless
of whether it concerns a man or a machine. This fact has become
crucial for the development of present-day linguistics: weighty
resources of scholarship have begun to concentrate on the linguistic aspect of the problem. No one can escape the perfectly
justified view that a detailed knowledge of the process of communication among human beings, in which language plays a decisive
rôle, will equip science with new experience in the task of constructing the appropriate machines.

434. In the U.S.A. and Europe, and even in Asia (mainly in Japan
but now in China also) mathematical linguistics is a commonly
used term among the scholars of today, which denotes scientific
operations in the sphere of linguistic problems carried out by
mathematical methods. Periodicals are being founded devoted to
subjects from mathematical linguistics, and also learned societies of
"mathematical linguists".

In the U.S.A. particularly mathematical linguistics made considerable progress in the years immediately following the last war. Now
it is thriving in the Soviet Union. Since 1958 courses in mathematical linguistics and machine translation for students of both mathematics and linguistics have been introduced into many Russian
universities (first of all in Moscow and Leningrad, and then at
Gorki, Saratov and Tomsk). The whole trend of development in
both mathematical and linguistic studies at the present moment
promises an increase of co-ordinated collaboration in the future.

Bibliographical References

435. An excellent and very thorough survey of mathematical linguistics (the fields it embraces, an introduction into its methods,
an account of the main problems on which it is working now and
of its achievements so far) is given by Warren Plath in the
study "Mathematical Linguistics", *Trends*, pp. 21-57. Plath also
appends a useful bibliography of works in mathematical linguistics.

The book *O točnyx metodax issledovanija jazyka* (Moscow University, 1961) by O. S. Axmanova, I. A. Mel'čuk, E. V. Padučeva and R. M. Frumkina is very informative; it has four separate sections, in which the following problems are surveyed: 1. in what sense can the phenomenon of language be subjected to investigation carried out by mathematical methods; 2. in what way does work on machine translation enrich linguistic theory; 3. where does the value of the statistical method in linguistics lie (with examples of the use of this method); 4. in what way can the achievement of information theory advance the development of linguistics.

Gustav Herdan's book *Type-Token Mathematics: A Textbook of Mathematical Linguistics* (*Janua Linguarum*, Series maior, 4) (The Hague, 1960) has recently been popular among linguistic scholars as a convenient source of information concerning the most important procedures of mathematical methods in linguistics.

A general view of the significance of the use of mathematical methods in linguistics is given in the following studies: A. G. Oettinger, "Linguistics and Mathematics", *Studies Presented to Joshua Whatmough* (The Hague, 1957), pp. 179-186; and J. Whatmough, "Mathematical Linguistics", *8th Proceedings*, pp. 62-73; the discussion arising from this exposition: pp. 74-91. A more general guide to the penetration of mathematical methods into twentieth century scholarship is given by E. Koschmieder in: "Die Mathematisierung der Sprachwissenschaft", *Forschungen und Fortschritte*, vol. 30 (1956), pp. 210-216.

A collection of articles (entitled "Strojno prevođenje i statistika u jeziku") published in 1959 in the Zagreb periodical *Naše teme*, III, 6, pp. 106-298 provides information about a series of problems of mathematical linguistics, particularly machine translation. Detailed bibliographical data are appended.

QUANTITATIVE (STATISTICAL) LINGUISTICS

436. It was only after the Second World War that the statistical method began to be widely used by linguists, though its value in the

study of language had been the subject of serious discussion as early as the beginning of the present century. Stenographers were among the first to point out the practical value of statistics in investigating languages.[2] It was, however, mathematicians who actually opened up the way to the widespread use of the statistical method in linguistics. In this respect the contribution of the Russian mathematician Markov was of decisive significance.

437. In *"Primer statističeskogo issledovanija nad tekstom 'Evgenija Onegina' ..."* (see above § 432) Markov had showed that the mutual dependence of language units in the speech chain could be measured if the measurement was approached in the spirit of what is in scholarly circles today called the Markov process. This process is concerned with bringing to light the different stages through which an utterance passes from the first spoken (or written) language unit until the moment of its conclusion. These stages are conditioned by the ranging of the language units in the spoken chain, which is accomplished according to the rules of the given language: each newly added unit marks a new phase in the formation of the utterance. Markov showed that it could be mathematically established on the basis of statistical probability what chance there was that the addition of a particular new unit would be followed by this or that further unit.

438. As we approach our own days the results achieved by the representatives of statistical mathematics become more important for both mathematics and linguistics. For example such names as Zipf, Yule, Ross and Mandelbrot are today equally well-known to both linguistic scholars and mathematicians. In recent years Mandelbrot has been specially popular with linguists (particularly in the U.S.A.) because of his idea, expounded in 1957, that the time was ripe for a new classification of linguistic studies into two basic groups: *macrolinguistic studies* = all linguistic research carried out by means of exact, statistical methods; and *microlinguistic studies* = linguistic research carried out without the application of statistics (see also below note to § 342). However it is the works of George

[2]   The stenographer Estoup (in his study *Gammes sténographiques*[4] Paris, 1916) stated that the arrangement of words in a text follows specific statistical rules.

Kingsley Zipf that have exercised the greatest influence on linguists involved in the statistical investigation of language.

439. Zipf was especially interested in the frequencies of linguistic units,[3] and worked on that problem with success. He considered that the establishment of the laws governing these frequencies would ensure the possibility of understanding the principles according to which human speech activity develops. He was interested above all in the theory of *psychobiology* (his term), i.e. the discovery of those psychological-physiological factors which most directly determine the specific type of one's engagement in the performance of a given action. In Zipf's opinion this type of engagement rests primarily on the tendency to make the least possible effort. Speech activity is, then, dominated by the principle of economy in means of expression, and this, so Zipf insisted, can be demonstrated by statistical methods. Zipf even suggested that a special branch of linguistics, called *biolinguistics*, should be formed; it would embrace the study of the language phenomenon in connection with man's behaviour in the process of communication, which is biologically conditioned (this would in fact mean the inclusion of specific neurophysiological studies within the scope of linguistic research).

However Zipf's popularity in linguistic circles was primarily the result of a series of fundamental statements concerning the correlation existing between the nature of the language units and their frequency in the spoken chain. Many views on this problem which are already classic in linguistics certainly originated with Zipf, although in the course of time some of his ideas have been modified or even rejected.

440. The following statements concerning the frequency of language units viewed from a statistical standpoint were of paramount importance for linguistics.

A. The complexity of sounds as regards pronunciation is in inverse proportion to their frequency in words[4] (for example un-

---

[3] As early as 1928 the physicist E. U. Condon pointed out the regularity of word frequencies in his study *Statistics of vocabulary*.
[4] This idea was expounded by Zipf in his *Psychobiology of Language, An Introduction to Dynamic Philology* (Boston, 1935), pp. 68-81.

voiced sounds, which are easier to pronounce than voiced, occur more frequently than the corresponding voiced sounds in all languages). This assertion was of particular interest to phonologists and psychologists.

B. If the relation between the sounds in any reasonably long text of a language is calculated as a percentage, the ratio obtained will be repeated in the majority of other texts belonging to the same language, with small deviations. This means that there is a constant ratio in the distribution of sounds within the spoken chain. This statement is of the highest significance for both stenography and *cryptography* (the science of deciphering ciphered messages).[5]

C. The length of words is in inverse proportion to their frequency: the most frequently used words are as a rule the shortest (this explains the shortening of long names, and indeed the process of abbreviation in general – for instance the frequent use of initial letter combinations in English, e.g. JCR, GPO, TV, etc.). By this same rule the most frequently used words are also the oldest. All these assertions are important for the history of language – they provide new elements by which particular changes in a language may be explained.

The establishment of the relationship of polysemy (see above § 376) to word frequency was important for the elaboration of lexicological studies. Zipf expressed this relationship in the following formula: the number of the contextual meanings of a word corresponds to the square root of its frequency.[6]

441. The penetration of the statistical method into the field of lexicology has initiated a new epoch in the learning of foreign languages. Statistics has settled the problem of what are the most frequently used words in a language, i.e. shown which words are

---

[5] Thanks to the efforts of people well-trained in cryptography our knowledge of extinct languages is now much wider. After the decipherment of Hittite (carried out by the Czech linguist B. Hrozný in 1916) the greatest event in this field took place in 1952 when the Englishman M. Ventris succeeded in proving that the Linear B Tablets from Crete (dating from 1,450 to 1,200 B.C.) were written in a hitherto unknown archaic variety of Greek.

[6] See *Human Behavior and the Principle of Least Effort, An Introduction to Human Ecology* (Cambridge, Mass., 1949).

really indispensible for the elementary needs of social life. It is only on the basis of statistical selection that people have begun to compile the so-called *basic dictionaries* – dictionaries containing a stock of standard vocabulary usually sufficient to ensure the communication necessary for everyday life in a foreign society.

442. Right up to the "statistical epoch" in linguistics, stylistics was in some senses a vague linguistic discipline – at the mercy of subjective criteria in the definition of style and the various aspects of its manifestation. It is only the use of the statistical method of analysis which has made the observation of stylistic phenomena completely objective and exact. The banality of an expression stands in direct relation to the high degree of its frequency. This is a dictum of modern stylistics, the result of its acquaintance with statistical rules. Comprehensive investigations of this objective type are now in progress; they are expected to answer with the greatest possible scientific precision the old, challenging question: what is original and poetic in a linguistic expression, as distinct from what is commonplace and standard.

443. The principle governing the distribution of words by means of statistics has been established; this opened up the possibility of elucidating such problems as the authorship or even the chronology of a text (which is of interest not only to linguistic scholars but more particularly to historians and specialists in the history of literature).

444. Statistics has provided dialectology with a new means of exactly determining the amount of similarity and difference between dialects (see also above § 156).

445. In recent years many linguists have become convinced that the application of statistics will be specially useful in comparative and historical linguistic studies. In this connection a new linguistic discipline has been founded: *glottochronology*.

In 1950 the American linguist Morris Swadesh proposed a new methodology with the aim of establishing the degree of relationship among languages, as well as the (approximate) chronology of their splitting off from a common ancestor. Some people adopted a special term, *glottochronology*, for this new linguistic discipline, while others call it *lexicostatistics* (the name generally used for all statistical investigations of vocabulary). In fact such statistical studies of language rest on the study of the lexical stock. As has already been stated by the representatives of anthropological doctrines (see above § 342), all languages contain a basic stock of words referring to fundamental categories of general human culture. These are usually words connected with everyday life, which are most resistant to historical changes and external influences. Scholars set apart a definite number of such words[7] and then proceeded to compare languages, looking for the percentage of basic words common to each pair of languages under consideration. The results achieved are interesting (some people even consider them revolutionary) but do not fully justify the initial hopes as to the reliability of the conclusions reached, which has led some linguists to express doubts regarding glottochronological studies in general. Investigations are now in progress, combined with efforts to improve the methodology, which should certainly determine more excatly in the near future the real value of this new trend in comparative and historical linguistic studies.

446. One of the most important scientific theories of our time – the theory of information (see below § 449) has actually grown out of statistical studies. Even the practical achievement which the elaboration of this theory has produced – the translating machine – would not have been possible without the application of statistics. Beginning with *approximate methods* in machine translation (concerned with predicting the amount of work necessary in order to make translation possible), proceeding via the working out of a *thesaurus*, or of a system of *coding* (i.e. transforming a particular language into a system of mathematical formulae), right up to calculating the most economical way of working with the machine (what would be its most convenient size, how much time must be allowed to work out actual programmes of translation, etc.) – statistical estimates have proved to be indispensible tools.

447. All linguistic researches which rely on the statistical method

---

[7] First 200, then a smaller number, so that today there are only about 100 such words.

are called statistical or quantitative; even linguistics in general is qualified as *statistical* or *quantitative*[8] in so far as language investigators make use of statistics. Statistical research was undertaken much earlier in linguistics,[9] but sporadically and inconsistently. It is only in our time, when the idea that linguistic structure can be studied as a logical calculus (see above § 402) has thoroughly permeated linguistic circles, that statistics has become an indispensible methodological aid in linguistic work, just as the symbolic representation of language relations in analysis has become indispensible for the precise determination of language data. Linguistics is still in the first phase of making use of such modern methodological aids, but the extent of their usefulness has been irrefutably demonstrated. The prospects for the future in this respect are more than encouraging.

Bibliographical References

448. See Plath's study on mathematical linguistics mentioned above, and the collection *O točnyx metodax issledovanija jazyka* (see above § 435) which give a very good general introduction to mathematical methods.

A closer acquaintance with the value of statistics in linguistic studies can be gained particularly from Pierre Guiraud's book: *Problèmes et méthodes de la statistique linguistique* (Dordrecht, 1959). This is a book written by a linguist for linguists and therefore worth consulting. The same author has prepared a bibliography of statistical linguistics: P. Guiraud, *Bibliographie Critique de la Statistique Linguistique* (Utrecht, 1954) (this bibliography has been revised and completed by T. D. Houchin, J. Puhvel, and C. W. Watkins, under the direction of J. Whatmough).

[8] This term was adopted at the Sixth International Congress of Linguists (at Paris) in 1948.
[9] For example as early as 1874 W. D. Whitney examined the frequency of English sounds; in 1905 Arnold published his study *Vedic Metre in Its Historical Development* in which he used the statistical criterion of frequency in order to establish the relative age of the various parts of the Rig Veda.

J. Caroll gives a brief but comprehensive history of the origin and development of statistical linguistics in *The Study of Language* (Cambridge Mass., 1955), in the chapter "The Statistical Study of Language" (pp. 61-64).

The collection *Voprosy statistiki reči* (*materialy soveščanija*) (Leningrad University, 1958) contains a considerable number of instructive articles. See also D. W. Reed's study: "A Statistical Approach to Quantitative Linguistic Analysis", *Word*, vol. 5, No. 3 (1949), pp. 235-247.

Infoimation about the possibilities of applying the statistical method to phonemic problems is given in: J. Lotz, "The Structure of Human Speech", *Transactions of the New York Academy of Sciences*, Ser. II, 16 (1954), pp. 373-384; F. Harary and H. H. Paper, "Towards a General Calculus of Phonemic Distribution", *Lg*, 33 (1957), pp. 143-169. The assistance which statistics may render to our knowledge of the morphological structure of language can be seen in the following studies: E. P. Hamp, "The Calculation of Parameters of Morphological Complexity", *8th Proceedings*, pp. 134-142; and Joseph Greenberg, "A Quantitative Approach to the Morphological Typology of Languages" in the collection *Method and Perspective in Anthropology*, ed. Robert F. Spencer (Minneapolis, 1954), pp. 192-220.

The usefulness of statistics in dealing with lexicological problems is best demonstrated by the prominent British statistician G. V. Yule in *The Statistical Study of Literary Vocabulary* (Cambridge-London, 1944). P. Guiraud's book *Les caractères statistiques du vocabulaire* (Paris, 1954) also gives useful information on this subject.

The above-mentioned book by G. Herdan: *Type-Token Mathematics* (see above § 435) is concerned with various interesting problems, for example the use of statistics in investigating literary style. W. Fucks' book *Mathematische Analyse von Sprachelementen, Sprachstil und Sprachen* (= *Arbeitsgemeinschaft für Forschung des Landes Nordrhein-Westfalen*) (Cologne, 1955) treats the same subject too; the numerical characteristics of various texts are stated there (these texts belong mainly to the German and Latin languages).

An attempt to apply statistical criteria in the genetical classification of languages can be found in the studies: Douglas Chrétien and A. L. Kroeber, "Quantitative Classification of Indo-European Languages", *Lg*, 13, (1937), pp. 83-105; and A. L. Kroeber "Statistics, Indo-European, and Taxonomy", *Lg*, 36 (1960), pp. 1-21.

A closer insight into the scope and method of glottochronology, and also into the criticism it has received, may be gained from the following bookes: R. B. Lees, "The Basis of Glottochronology", *Lg*, 29 (1953), pp. 113-127; M. Swadesh "Toward Greater Accuracy in Lexicostatistic Dating", *IJAL*, 21 (1955), pp. 121-137; H. Hoijer, "Lexicostatistics: A Critique", *Lg*, 32 (1956), pp. 49-60; J. A. Rea, "Concerning the Validity of Lexicostatistics", *IJAL*, 24 (1958), pp. 145-150; W. W. Arndt, "The Performance of Glottochronology in Germanic", *Lg*, 35 (1959), pp. 180-192; H. A. Gleason, "Counting and Calculating for Historical Reconstruction", *Anthropological Linguistics*, vol. I, No. 2 (1959), pp. 22-33. An exhausting survey of works from the field of glottochronology can be found in: D. H. Hymes and others, "Lexicostatistics so Far", *Current Anthropology*, 1 (1960), pp. 3-44 and D. H. Hymes and others, "More on Lexicostatistics", *Current Anthropology*, 1 (1960), pp. 338-345. The collection *Novoe v lingvistike* contains a Russian translation of two of Swadesh's works (pp. 23-87) and one of Hoijer's (pp. 88-107) on lexicostatistics. See in the same collection an article by V. A. Zvegincev: "Lingvističeskoe datirovanie metodom glottoxronologii (leksikostatistiki)", pp. 19-22. See also an article by G. A. Klimov in the collection *Voprosy teorii jazyka v sovremennoj zarubežnoj lingvistike* (Moscow, AN SSSR, 1961): "O lexicostatističeskoj teorii M. Svodeša", pp. 239-253.

A concise and informative survey of the basic uses of statistics in machine translation is given by A. F. Parker-Rhodes, "The Use of Statistics in Language Research", *Machine Translation*, Vol. 5, No. 2 (1958), pp. 67-73.

See the above-mentioned works by Zipf, § 440. Linguists will also be interested in his book *Studies of the Principle of Relative Fre-*

quency in Language (Harvard University Press, 1932), since the author there approaches in a new way the problem of establishing a hierarchy of shades of meaning within the semantic field of a word.

INFORMATION THEORY

449. The theory of information is concerned with scientific investigations which throw light on the processes of transmitting and receiving information, including everything by which these processes are conditioned. It is a comparatively new discipline which has come to maturity since the end of the Second World War.

450. It was engineers who first took a serious interest in the problems of communication, in order to ensure a *transmission* channel in their communication devices, i.e. uninterrupted transmission and reception of information. However the foundations of a new scientific discipline which should concern itself systematically with the problems of communication were not laid until the appearance of the works of the American mathematician Norbert Wiener.

451. Wiener was the creator of cybernetics,[10] the science of the functioning of automata and their controlled reaction to a specific stimulus.[11] His basic scholarly views corresponded to the general behaviouristic conceptions which characterized the intellectual atmosphere in the U.S.A. before the Second World War (see above § 328): the behaviour shown by a person in a particular situation is always the result of an automatic reaction, learnt earlier, to a particular external stimulus. Starting from the conviction that this principle is true not only of human behaviour but could also be valid for machines, Wiener began his important work on machines which could receive a particular message, "remember" it and react in an appropriate way.

During the Second World War Wiener worked on projectiles

---

[10] The term cybernetics comes from the Greek word *kybernētikē*, meaning the skill of steering.
[11] See his classic work *Cybernetics* (New York, 1948).

which could hit their target precisely at a distance. He divided all automata into two basic types, possible in principle: a) machines which should achieve a known aim; b) machines which should find the right answer to a given question. In both cases the same thing was essential for the work of the machine: it must be capable of receiving a message from outside and behaving in an appropriate way in accordance with this message.

The basic model for such machines was man. The human brain and nervous system react in both ways. For example when we automatically take a book from a table the following processes take place. The brain selects the aim – the book, gives the aim an order to make a movement, and the movement is carried out automatically, i.e. without conscious reflection, under the control of our eyes directed to the aim. We are also in a position to give answers to questions only if we have previously learnt the answers. Wiener, taking all these things into consideration, constructed (during the war) the first weapons to achieve their intended aim under particular control (radar, heat perceptors, etc.). Later he concentrated his attention on machines which would be capable of "remembering" specific replies to specific questions.

452. It is, then, quite natural that the theory of information was placed at the centre of cybernetic studies. Its basic propositions were expounded in 1948 by the mathematician Claude Shannon, while another mathematician, Warren Weaver, interpreted its general significance for the development of scholarship in 1949. A book which was the joint work of these two scholars: Claude E. Shannon and Warren Weaver, *The Mathematical Theory of Communication* (Urbana, 1949), is regarded as the classic work on the theory of information and cybernetic studies in general. This book was intended for mathematicians, and linguists who lack a firm foundation in mathematics cannot use it. But there is a review by the linguist C. F. Hockett (*Lg*, 9, 1953, 69-92), also accessible to those who are not mathematicians, which has played an important rôle in popularizing the theory of information among linguists.

453. For mathematicians and physicists engaged in constructing machines it was extremely important to establish the most econom-

ical way in which messages could be sent, and how they could most easily be remembered and most exactly understood. The Linguistic scholars too were interested in all these things, especially structuralists, whose method of linguistic analysis was based on setting apart language phenomena which are relevant in the process of communication from those which are not. This led to the development of one of the most fruitful fields of interdisciplinary co-operation in the history of modern science, the immediate result of which was the translating machine.

454. The linguistic theories of Roman Jakobson acquired their most valuable recognition in the light of information theory. Jakobson had insisted on the need to identify the distinctive features in phonemes (see above § 302), that is, what is invariant, ultimate and elemental in a language unit. It was seen that such a conception of invariant units was of crucial importance for the development of the theory of information. Jakobson also insisted on the principle of binarity in language (see above § 303), and in fact all information theory rests on the application of this principle.

455. Thus linguistic scholars were theoretically prepared to understand and follow the train of ideas of the mathematicians in this field of scientific work. They themselves also had something to contribute, on the basis of their experience with linguistic phenomena, to the general fund of knowledge relating to problems of communication. At the same time linguistics received a new series of terms and concepts hitherto limited to the mathematical and physical sciences.

456. The following two basic problems confront the theory of information: 1. to establish the means by which communication is achieved; 2. what happens in the minds of the speech partners – the one who speaks and the one who receives information – during the process of communication (i.e. what are the immediate psychological and physiological conditions for realizing the process of communication).

457. Every item of information is sent off according to a definite *code*. The term *code* had its origin within the scope of the theory of

information. It concerns the entire system of signals (including their relations) by means of which a particular item of information is conveyed.

Signals used for communication can vary considerably: human languages, Morse signs, signal lights, etc. Whatever their origin, signals used for communication convey messages according to some kind of code. The transformation of every idea into an item of information is a process of *encoding* (i.e. the transference of the idea into a system of communication signals). The reception of every message, i.e. its penetration into our consciousness, originates in the process of *decoding* (i.e. the transformation of the communication signals into our knowledge of the message).

458. The transference of information always occurs between two partners who carry out two different communicative processes – the speaker who encodes an item of information and the listener who receives and decodes it. Encoding, when human language is in question, comprises a complicated process from thinking to sounds (from the lexicogrammatical to the phonemic level), while decoding is the exact opposite: it comprises a process which proceeds from sounds to thinking.

The item of information dispatched is known to the speaker, and his sole task is to transmit it to the listener as intelligibly as possible. Hence his attention is primarily directed to the arrangement of the immediate constituents (see above § 336) according to the code of the given language. The person who receives the information has a much harder task. He must recognize the actual value of every word, excluding, if necessary, a possible misunderstanding due to homonymity. Moreover for him the whole perception of speech lies in what the theory of probability terms the *stochastic* process: the deciphering of the message takes place in his consciousness bit by bit, according to the order of the language units in the speech chain; with each newly-received speech unit he has at his disposal a new element for the elucidation of the message, makes a new effort, each time with greater prospects of success (then he guesses the next element, then the one after that, so that when the speech act is completed, the perception of the message will also be brought to an end).[12] The bringing to light of the differences in the rôles of the speaker and the listener has opened up new horizons of linguistic research. Our fields of knowledge relating to the most effective ways of learning foreign languages have been particularly enriched. The distinction between passive and active grammar (which corresponds to the difference between simply understanding a language and being able to speak it) is becoming increasingly fertile soil for useful linguistic studies. Today it is mainly the representatives of American and Soviet linguistics who have turned their attention in this direction.[13]

459. The amount of information contained in one communicative sign is called *entropy*. The entropy varies in size according to whether the information is more or less predictable. In the theory of information *predictability* is a very important concept, and therefore also important for those modern linguistic studies which take processes of communication into account.

The amount of information is a relative concept: the extent to which an item of news will be new to someone depends on the actual conditions under which it is conveyed. For example if a person has been in Cambridge when there was a hailstorm, the announcement of this in the newspaper the following day will not be specially informative. But if he is a native of the city who was away that day, and strongly interested in everything that happened during his absence, the news of the hailstorm will be much more important for him. Thus the theory of information also acquaints us with the concept of the relative importance of information.

The quantity of information in a language sign can be measured by putting other language signs in its place: the greater the possibilities of substitution, the more information is conveyed by the particular sign whose informativeness is being measured

---

[12] The process of receiving a message by way of a written text is similar: each new word and syllable leads us nearer to the full meaning of the information, which will be grasped in its entirety when the reading is finished.
[13] In this respect the activity of Ščerba's pupils in Russia is particularly significant; even earlier, in the epoch of traditional grammar, Ščerba was able to discern and approach this field.

(i.e. the predictability of the information is small). When a person comes up in a state of excitement and begins: "Just think, John has..." everybody waits impatiently to hear the next word (got married? fallen ill? killed someone?). Clearly the entropy is great in such a situation. It is quite the opposite, for example, when the letter u is used with q in English or Italian: q must always be followed by u in writing, according to the spelling rules of these languages; hence u after q is here to the highest degree predictable, which at the same time means that the informative power of the sign u in such a combination is zero.

460. The principle of dichotomy (binarity) is consistently applied in studying the amount of entropy: the unit of this measurement is a *bit* (an abbreviation of *binary digit*), and its value is based on the application of the *simple alternative* in recognizing the concrete specification given by a communicative sign (i.e. each specification of an event or phenomenon which is the subject of the message means the exclusion of another specification, correlative by contrast). The number of binary decisions required (i.e. the number of times we exclude one of two alternative possibilities) in comperhending a message is equal to the number of binary units contained in the entropy of the language symbols being used on that occasion.

461. It is well known that in the process of communication the person who hears a message actually hears far more than he makes use of. In this process the attention of the listener is concentrated on abstracting from the utterance of the speaker only the elements essential for the stimulation of those binary decisions without which the message cannot be comprehended. As to the speaker, he nearly always says much more than this necessary minimum, because he tries to ensure the transfer capacity of the *communicative channel* (this term refers to everything which makes a communication possible, beginning with the speaker as the source of information to the goal, i.e. the person who comprehends the message). In this effort the speaker uses very varied means, for example special expressions intended to attract the attention of the listener, or the repetition of the same information in different

variations. Indeed human language is loaded with elements which seem redundant for the essence of the information. However redundancy has its function in the process of mutual understanding. The greater the number of redundant elements, the greater the certainty that the message will be received and comprehended to the highest degree. *Metalanguage*, the ideally logical language of science (see above § 388) lacks redundancy and is therefore impracticable for the daily communicative contact of human beings.[14]

462. The fundamental task of the proponents of the theory of information in fact lies in discovering the essential, invariable characteristics in messages, so as to construct a firm theory regarding their invariant structures, which would make possible the further progress of cybernetic studies, work on machine translation, psychological investigations of the process of knowledge, the metalinguistic research of logicians, and the search of structural linguistics for the "ultimate invariants" in language.

463. The theory of information could not have attained the significance which it has in present day scholarship if it had not the achievements of structural linguistics behind it. It is the special merit of structural linguistics to have shown that language is a system of precisely determined, mutually connected units whose number is finite (and not large), but whose combinations stretch to infinity. Relying on this assertion, mathematicians have succeeded in applying their method of analysis to language. The value of statistics has been particularly notable. As to linguistics, it profited from the flourishing state of studies connected with communication in many respects; for example new light has been thrown on such problems as the relationship between written and spoken language, between what is *explicit* (i.e. clearly expressed in language) and what is *implicit* (i.e. what can be understood but is not stated). The comprehension of the decoding process has initiated a new era in the linguistic study of poetry. And the investigation of the process of *transcoding* (i.e. changing from one code to another) has given fresh life to linguistic interest in the history of language, which is

---

[14] For example telegrams are as concise as possible. Therefore the smallest verbal mistake is enough to bring the intelligibility of the text into question.

now once more being intensively studied in the light of new experience and knowledge.

Bibliographical References

464. Linguists looking for a sure and gradual introduction to the theory of information are not recommended to begin by reading the basic sources, i.e. the works of mathematicians, but to read first the reviews of those works written by linguists for their own public. The following reviews deserve special mention.

Hockett's review of the classic work by Shannon and Weaver, "The Mathematical Theory of Communication", *Lg*, 29 (1953), pp. 69-93;

The review of Zipf's "Human Behaviour and the Principle of Least Effort: An Introduction to Human Ecology" written by Y. R. Chao in *Lg*, 26 (1950), pp. 394-401;

The review of Belevitch's "Language des machines et language humain", by N. Chomsky (who explains, for example, the relationship of the theory of information to linguistics with the aim of bringing closer to the linguistic public certain fundamental mathematical laws of information), *Lg*, 34 (1958), pp. 99-105;

Lees' review in *Lg*, 35 (1959), pp. 271-303 of the work by L. Apostel, B. Mandelbrot and A. Morf, *Logique, language et théorie de l'information*.

Roman Jakobson's "Linguistics and Communication Theory", *Proceedings of Symposia in Applied Mathematics, Structure of Language and its Mathematical Aspects*, vol. XXI (1961), pp. 245-252; illuminates in an interesting, convincing and thoroughly linguistic way the significance of language studies within the scope of information theory.

The variety of problems included within a broadly based programme of studies concerning the process of communication is accurately illustrated by the works published in the collection "Psycholinguistics – A Survey of Theory and Research Problems", Supplement to *IJAL*, vol. 20, No. 4 (1954), *Memoir* 10, I-IX + 1-203.

A good, elementary textbook for the theory of information, above all from the point of view of the psychological problems which intrude upon the communicative process, can be found in G. A. Miller's work: *Language and Communication* (New York-Toronto-London, 1951) (this book includes useful bibliographical data). Another inspiring study by the same author is "What is information measurement?" *American Psychologist*, 8 (1953), pp. 3-11. See also Miller's article "The Perception of Speech" published in *For Roman Jakobson*, pp. 353-360.

Linguists can acquaint themselves with the mathematical methods of treating linguistic problems, particularly within the field of phonemics, through a book by C. Cherry: *On human communication* (Cambridge, Mass.-New York – London, 1957).

A book notable for the modernity of its methods and the range of problems connected with speech and the communicative process which it embraces is *Word and Object* (Cambridge, Mass., 1960) by Willard Van Orman Quine.

See also O. H. Strauss's study "The Relation of Phonemics and Linguistics to Communication Theory", *Journal of the American Acoustic Society*, 22 (1950), pp. 709-711; and the following studies (published in *Vosprosy jazykoznanija*): L. R. Zinder, "O lingvistićeskoj verojatnosti" (VII, 1958, fasc. 2, pp. 121-125) and V. N. Toporov, "O vvedenii verojatnosti v jazykoznanie" (VIII, 1959, fasc. 6, pp. 28-35).

Precise insight into general theoretical problems is given in the classic work of the Soviet scholar A. A. Harkevič: *Očerki obščej teorii svjazi* (Moscow, 1955).

For a closer acquaintance with the contribution made to the development of the theory of transformation by Soviet scholars, see also: Ju. S. Bukov, *Sovetskie raboty po teorii razborčivosti reči* (= *Izvestija Akademii Nauk SSSR*, serija fizičeskaja 13, 6) (1949), pp. 728-739 and the collection of works published in Moscow in 1956 under the title of *Vosprijatije zvukovyx signalov v različnyx akustičeskix uslovijax*.

The works of H. Fletcher and B. Mandelbrot, both representative of the exact sciences, are also popular with linguistic scholars. See, for example, H. Fletcher, *Speech and Hearing in Communication* (New York, 1953) and B. Mandelbrot, "Structure formelle des textes et communication", *Word*, 10 (1954), pp. 1-27.

MACHINE TRANSLATION

465. During the last decade an entirely new discipline, machine translation, has been the focus of extremely lively linguistic interest. People expected exceptional results in this field. Machine translation would bring about a revolution in the activity of translating, making the translation of scientific, technical, political and other information incomparably easier and faster. For instance, scholars could be able to give an account of their most important achievements simultaneously in many languages, which would contribute to the universalization of human culture. Moreover many linguists have expressed the belief that even general linguistic theory could derive great profit from such an enterprise.

466. The work on machine translation could not have been undertaken if the method of language description had not been properly elaborated by the structural linguists. But even more important was the high standard of development achieved by the technical sciences and in particular the invention of electronic computers.

467. The "translation machine" is a program for an electronic computer. The adaptation of the language data to the purpose of machine translation has been, of course, achieved by linguists. Today work on machine translation has already advanced a long way, although the solution of many important problems is still awaited.

468. The process of machine translation includes a number of basic tasks, the technical aspect of which has had to be carefully worked out. Translation begins with the reception of the text. What is registered is automatically transferred into the mathematical language of formulae. The resulting mathematical formulae correspond in every respect to the structure of the language from which the translation is being made: the order of words, the type of

their function in the utterance, the number of morphemes used to express various grammatical relationships – all these things are precisely designated in mathematical language. After this a new phase of translation begins: the *mathematical code* (see above § 457), which corresponds to the source text, is transformed into the mathematical code of the language into which the translation is being made. In other words, new formulae are introduced which transfer the thoughts expressed according to the structure characteristic of the target language. Only then, after this process has been completed, work is begun on changing the mathematical signs into human language once more, but this time into the target language. When this last phase of the work of the machine has been carried out, the translation itself is finished.

469. The encoding and decoding (see above § 457) of texts, inherent parts of the process of machine translation, require the highest possible precision of linguistic criteria and methods. Difficulties of various kinds, which are being solved by the combined efforts of linguists and engineers, are encountered at every step. But even with all the improvements that might be achieved in the distant future, machines will not be able to translate adequately literary texts. Only texts written without any pretensions to originality of style (scientific, technical and political works etc.) can be entrusted to machines. Many factors contribute to this, among other things the fact that the machines must store the entire vocabulary of the languages to be translated, and it would be technically impracticable to equip them with all the unusual expressions and turns of phrase which can be found, for instance, in present-day poetry.

470. One of the main problems facing machine translation is that of carrying out the principle of economy in the "memory" of the machine. In principle, the machine can "remember" everything. As many words and grammatical concepts as may be required are stamped on its "memory". However, efforts are made to ensure a satisfactory translation with as small a material outlay and as little complication as possible, though not, of course, at the cost of the greatest possible effectiveness. The lexical stock is therefore care-

fully selected in accordance with the type of texts to be translated. In addition to lexical material of a general character, so-called *micro-glossaries* are made – i.e. vocabularies of expressions peculiar to particular branches of study (chemistry, medicine, physics etc.).

471. However carefully the words are registered in the machine, it is not always certain that they will be adequately selected for the given text, in view of the fact that all languages contain synonyms which express particular shades of a basic word meaning. Hence in making the selection, the theory of probability is applied. Words are statistically classified according to the frequency of their use as common, less usual, and rare, and priority is given to the usual word, since it is most probable that it will include the semantic shade of meaning required, or that it will at least designate it approximately. This is certainly a justifiable methodological procedure in this particular case, though it cannot ensure a completely satisfactory translation. There is another solution, which results in a less elegant translation, but which has certain advantages: all the possible variants are placed side by side (with a sign indicating that they are alternatives), and the reader is left to choose the most suitable expression according to his own criteria, and, of course, to the context.

472. Idioms cause particular difficulties in translation. Compound words are not easy to deal with either. Geographical names, being almost infinite in number, also present a problem. Moreover, all languages contain redundant elements (see above § 461). To decide what is redundant in a particular instance and remove it in the translation – this is a serious task, the technical solution of which is by no means easy.

473. In order to avoid the possible confusion arising from polysemy (see above § 376) there must be mechanical operations which can correctly identify meanings with the help of the context. Moreover, even apart from the polysemic categories, it is necessary to establish special technical processes which will make it possible continually to take account of particular contextual situations. This is a problem which must be correctly solved in order to ensure that the full sense is kept in the translation to be achieved.

474. Every language has its own specific structure. Machine translation is impossible without precise information about linguistic structures. Machine translation cannot be applied to many languages, since they have not been appropriately studied.

Linguistic structures are first compared in order to determine their *degree of congruency* (a term adopted in the technique of machine translation) – i.e. their typological affinity or difference. This work is done by linguists. They consider the lexical, morphological and syntactic factors which condition the specific nature of linguistic units in particular languages. This is done by making an inventory of linguistic units and bringing to light the principles of their distribution.

475. One of the hardest problems in machine translation is the organization of the machine memory: should the machine remember separately only whole words (= the "lexical" organization of the machine), or should it remember separately the stems and the affixes (= the "grammatical" memory of the machine). Scholars are not in agreement as to the choice of technical procedure in this matter.[15]

Languages have many grammatical characteristics, and whatever particular type of technical procedure may be adopted, these must be stored in the machine. This presents many difficulties which are not only technical but also linguistic. In connection with the latter, the greatest problem is usually the inadequate treatment of particular fields of grammar. For instance work with machines requires a detailed knowledge of syntactic phenomena, and in fact linguists are just beginning to construct effective theories and methods in this branch of study.

476. The demands of machine translation compel linguists to develop further their theoretical knowledge in a variety of hitherto inadequately investigated fields of linguistics. The practical aim of enabling the results of linguistic research to be correctly used for work with machines imposes on linguists the necessity of formula-

---

[15] For example the staff of the Seattle (U.S.A.) centre for machine translation are in favor of "lexical organization", while Soviet specialists are predominantly interested in the "grammatical" type of "memory".

ting their definitions as clearly and concisely as possible. The establishment of a tradition in this respect will ensure theoretical studies of languages of better quality and a more efficient method of presenting practical grammatical rules.

Work with the machine, then, has shown what research in the field of linguistic theory still remains to be done, what has been done with inadequate results, and what has not been completed. All this justifies an optimistic estimate of the value of the work on machine translation. However, the enthusiasm of the pioneers in machine translation is no longer shared by the majority of linguists. They are disappointed by the slow rate of improvement in the translations.

477. Machine translation first began in the U.S.A., and the first system is now at Harvard as a piece of historical evidence of the important break-through in the progress of research. Today there are a number of centres for machine translation in the U.S.A. which are well-known throughout the world. For example the work of the group of specialists at the Washington University in Seattle, which is primarily concerned with working out algorithms (see § 389) for machine translation from Russian into English, enjoys wide renown. The work of the Cambridge (Mass.) group is also outstanding today.[16] One should mention also the group from Georgetown University, the group of scholars from California University and the representatives of the Wayne State University. In all these centres the resources are specially concentrated on studying the linguistics structures of English and Russian. Distributionalism, which originated in the U.S.A. (see above § 332), with its copious elaboration of mechanical methods of analysis, has become an excellent basis for the further linguistic treatment of the above mentioned languages in fulfilling the needs of machine translation.

478. The great competitors of the Americans in work on machine translation are the Soviet specialists. They began to organize their resources for this work later, but with amazing speed, in the course of only four or five years, they produced an excellent staff of specialists in mathematical linguistics whose results have already

[16] The members of this group are drawn not only from Harvard University but also include specialists from the Massachusetts Institute of Technology.

reached an enviable level. In 1955 the Soviet scholars began preparations in connection with machine translation, which concerned only two pairs of languages: English-Russian and French-Russian. By 1959 programmes had been worked out for about twelve pairs of languages. It is thought that U.S.S.R. now leads the world as regards the number of specialists engaged in machine translation. The great centres for machine translation are in Moscow (the Institute for Precise Mechanics, the Electronic Laboratory of the All-Union Institute for Scientific and Technical Information, the Steklov Mathematical Institute) and in Leningrad (the Experimental Laboratory for Machine Translation). Smaller groups of scholars are also employed in work connected with machine translation at the Moscow Pedagogic Institute for Foreign Languages, at Moscow University, and at the universities of Gorki, Kharkov, Kiev, Petrozavodsk, Tiflis and Erevan.[17]

So far the resources of Soviet specialists have been mainly concentrated in two directions: the composition of *glossaries* (i.e. dictionaries in the machine) and on the study of an *intermediary language* in the translation (i.e. the language of formulae into which the human language to be translated is transferred). In their work in this latter field the Soviet scholars have achieved interesting theoretical results.

479. Other European and Asian countries[18] are also developing work on machine translation today, but for the present the leading position in the world in this work belongs to scientific centres in the U.S.A. and the U.S.S.R.

[17] In view of the rapid pace of progress in this field of scholarly activity, it is quite probably that this information (mainly gathered from reports published several years ago) is no longer complete.

[18] The Chinese language has always aroused the interest of the linguistic public because of its specific structure. Hence news of the progress of machine translation in the People's Republic of China has evoked considerable interest in linguistic circles: linguists hope that information which should be forthcoming from a detailed study of the structure of Chinese and its comparison with Indoeuropean linguistic structures would be highly valuable for the further development of general linguistic theory. The first available information about machine translation in the People's Republic of China was given in an article by Lju Jun-cjuan "Issledovatel'skaja rabota v oblasti MP v Kitajskoj Narodnoj Respublike", *VJa*, VIII, 5 (1959), pp. 102-104.

Bibliographical References

480. The first phases of work on machine translation in the U.S.A. are best illustrated by the studies published in the collection *Machine Translation of Language*, ed. William N. Locke and A. Donald Booth (New York, 1955). A Russian translation of this collection was published in Moscow in 1957 with the title of *Mašinnyj perevod* (under the editorship of P. S. Kuznecov).

The voluminous collection *Linguistic and Engineering Studies in the Automatic Translation of Scientific Russian into English. Technical Report* (Seattle-Washington, 1959) contains representative studies from the group of scientists working at Seattle.

A. G. Oettinger's book *Automatic Language Translation: Lexical and Technical Problems* (= *Harvard Monographs in Applied Science*, No. 8) (Cambridge, Mass., 1961) gives an excellent illustration of the results achieved at the Harvard Centre for machine translation.

Concise surveys of what has been done in this field of scientific activity are given by the representatives of the Cambridge (Mass.) group W. N. Locke and V. H. Yngve, the Seattle representative Erwin Reifler and the representative of the Georgetown centre Paul L. Garvin, in the collection of the *8th Proceedings*, under the title of "Machine Translation" (pp. 502-518).

Y. Bar-Hillel gives a survey of the work done on machine translation not only in the U.S.A. but also in Great Britain in *Report on the State of Mechanical Translation in the United States and Great Britain* (Jerusalem, 1959).

There are numerous monographs which give an adequate picture of the results so far achieved in different American centres for machine translation. Those who are specially interested in this subject will find appropriate information in such periodicals as *Mechanical Translation*, a publication of the group working at the Massachussets Institute of Technology. A certain number of further studies may also be specially recommended which have attracted particular attention abroad, primarily in the U.S.S.R.:

V. E. Giuliano (of the Cambridge-Mass. group) – "An Experimental Study of Automatic Language Translation", *Mathematical*

Linguistics and Automatic Translation, Report NSF-1 (Cambridge, Mass., 1959);

M. E. Scherry (of the Cambridge-Mass. group) – "Syntactic Analysis in Automatic Translation", *Mathematical Linguistics and Automatic Translation* Report NSF-5 (Cambridge, Mass., 1960);

V. H. Yngve (of the Cambridge-Mass. group) – "Sentence-for-Sentence Translation", *Mechanical Translation*, vol. 2, (1955), No. 2, pp. 29-37, "A Framework for Syntactic Translation", *Mechanical Translation*, vol. 4 (1957), No. 3, pp. 59-65, "A Programming Language for Mechanical Translation", *Mechanical Translation*, vol. 5 (1958), No. 1, pp. 25-41. "A Model and an Hypothesis for Language Structure", *Proceedings of the American Philosophical Society*, vol. 104 (1960), No. 5, pp. 444-466;

L. R. Micklesen – "Russian-English MT", *American Contributions to the Fourth International Congress of Slavicists Moscow, September* 1958 (The Hague, 1958), pp. 245-265, "Form Classes: Structural Linguistics and Mechanical Translation", *For Roman Jakobson*, pp. 344-352.

For a closer acquaintance with the results of Soviet efforts in connection with machine translation, the most convenient source is the collection *Materialy po mašinnomu perevodu*, Vol. I (Leningrad, 1958), which includes such well-known works as: N. D. Andreev, *Meta-jazyk mašinnogo perevoda i ego primenenie* (pp. 40-60), V. V. Ivanov, *Lingvističeskie voprosy sozdanija mašinnogo jazyka dlja informacionnoj mašiny* (pp. 10-39), etc.

I. A. Mel'čuk, an outstanding specialist in machine translation, gives a survey of the work done on machine translation in the U.S.S.R. in an article entitled: "Raboty po mašinnomu perevodu v SSSR" (Vestnik NA SSSR, 1959), No. 2, pp. 43-47.

The mathematician O. S. Kulagina is one of the world's most famous specialists for machine translation. Her theory as to how the grammatical structure of languages may be most conveniently prepared mathematically for the purposes of machine translation was published under the title: "*Ob odnom sposobe opredelenija grammatičeskix ponjatij na baze teorii množestva*" in *Problemy kibernetiki* I (= *Gosudarstvennoe izdatel'stvo fiziko-matematičeskoj literatury)* (Moscow, 1958), pp. 203-214. This theory is explained to linguists by I. G. Revzin in "O nekotoryx ponjatijax tak nazyvaemoj teoretikomnožestvennoj koncepcii jazyka", *VJa*, IX, 6 (1960), pp. 88-94.

A closer insight into the present level of Soviet achievements in the field of machine translation may be obtained from the various studies published in the periodical *Mašinnyj perevod i prikladnaja lingvistika*, and also in *Voprosy jazykoznanija* (where the material is presented in a particularly accessible manner, specially written for a linguistic public which was only beginning to feel the need to make a closer acquaintance with such a new field of linguistic interests).

Recently the collection *Issledovanija po slavjanskomu jazykoznaniju* (Moscow, AN SSSR, 1961) included the study (pp. 374-382) *Teoretičeskie osnovi mašinnogo perevoda na russkij jazyk*, written by a group of authors: O. S. Kulagina, A. A. Ljapunov, I. A. Mel'čuk, T. N. Mološnaja. Here, clearly and concisely presented, are the latest results of the most eminent Soviet specialists engaged in machine translation, who are particularly interested in the problem of an intermediary language.

Finally, for all those who would like more detailed information about the theory of translation in general, the collection *On Translation*, ed. Reuben A. Brower, *Harvard Studies in Comparative Literature*, vol. 23 (Cambridge, Mass., 1959) is recommended; it contains works by linguists as well as by specialists in literature. For example Roman Jakobson, in his study *On Linguistic Aspects of Translation* (pp. 232-239) expounds his theory concerning the phenomenon of translation: everything can be translated in such a way that the basic message in question remains unchanged, but the *code* (see above § 457) by means of which the message is conveyed must be subject to change in the process of translation – every language has its own specific code; hence translation requires the reshaping of many details, subtractions and additions in the spirit of the new code into which the message is transferred; thus every translation of a poetic text must inevitably become a creative linguistic transposition. In *Principles of Translation as*

Exemplified by Bible Translating (pp. 11-31) Eugen A. Nida advances the hypothesis that a satisfactory translation is impossible not only because of the difference in code (i.e. in the structure of language systems), but because each language has its own cultural background which determines the particular type of metaphorical associations. Williard V. Quine in *Meaning and Translation* (pp. 148-172), applying logical analysis together with the methodological procedures worked out in the theory of information, shows that mutual coefficients between languages can be found in view of the adequate characteristics of sentences present in the language from which and into which the translation is being made, without regard to the differences in their grammatical structures. Finally, Antony G. Oettinger in *Automatic Transference, Translation, Remittance, Shunting* (pp. 240-267) sets out the principles of machine translation with special reference to the existing prospects for the improvement in technique of automatic translation of Russian texts into English.

SUBJECT INDEX

The numbers given refer to paragraphs, not pages; the letter *n* after a number means that the subject is referred to in a note under the text of the paragraph in question.

Academic semantician v. semantician (philosophic semantician)
Acoustic, ~ phonetics: the beginning of its development 216
Actualization: Bally's theory of ~ 266
Actualizer: a linguistic means for ensuring actualization v. actualization
Aesthetic idealism, ~ in linguistics: the formation of the basic ideas on ~ 170; ~ as interpreted by Vossler's school 171-175; ~ as interpreted by the neo-linguists 176-185
Affective linguistics: in the framework of the French linguistic school 161; the ~ of Charles Bally 263
Agglutinative, ~ languages 63
Alexandrians, v. Alexandrian school
Alexandrian school: the main results of the work of the ~ 14
Algorithm: the era of ~ in scholarship 389
Allophone: v. combinatory variant
Amalgamating, ~ languages 63
American linguistics: the pioneers 317; the significance of Boas' works 318-321; Sapir's theory 321-325; Bloomfield and the theory of distributionalism 332-341; the anthropological investigation of language 342-351; psycholinguistics 352-360
Americans, the ~ as a linguistic school v. distributionalists
Analogists: the attitude of the ~ in discussions on the origin of language in the ancient world 9
Analogy: the law of ~ 94
Anomalists: the attitude of the ~ in discussions on the origin of language in the ancient world 9
Anthropological, a term in American scholarship 342 n.
Anthropological linguistics (*ethnolinguistics, metalinguistics, macrolinguistics*): the pioneers of ~ 342-348; Whorf's theory 348-349; prelinguistic and para-linguistic investigations 349; kinesics 350
Antimentalism: the ~ of Bloomfield's theory 329-330
Aphasia, ~ as a subject for linguistic studies 308
Apperceptionalistic, Wundt's ~ theory 83
Approximate method: statistical procedure in machine translation 446

Archiphoneme: the origin of the ~ in the process of phonological neutralization 289

Areal (*geographical*) *linguistics*: ~ within the framework of neo-linguistics 176; its contribution to dialectology 181-183

Articulatory, ~ (*motor*) phonetics: the beginning of its development 216

Assimilation: the phenomenon of ~ according to Grammont 159

Associative: the ~ theory: Steinthal's ~ theory 80

Associative relationships: in contrast to the syntagmatism of De Saussure 383 n.

Bally, ~ 's linguistics v. Geneva school

Basic dictionaries: the working out of ~ 441

Behaviourism: as a scientific standpoint 328; its influence on American linguistics 329

Bilingual: ~ communities and the problem of languages in contact 155

Bilingualism: the inclusion of the problems of ~ in studies of the language of children 160

Binarism: ~ in Bally's syntagmatics 268; ~ in the linguistic method of Roman Jakobson 303-305; the significance of Jakobson's methodological ~ in scholarship today 305-307

Binarity (*dichotomy*): the principle of ~ in the establishment of distinctive (phonological) oppositions 303

Binary: the ~ relationship in syntagms (according to Bally) 268; ~ oppositions in phonology 286; the ~ (*dichotomic*) principle in phonology 303

Biolinguistics, Zipf's ~ 439

Biological naturalism, ~ in linguistics (*Schleicher's theory, Darwinism in linguistics, the "Stammbaum" theory, the "pedigree" theory*): the foundation of the theory of ~ 60-63; the theory of ~ as expounded by Müller 65

Bit, the ~ in the theory of information 460

Bloomfieldians v. distributionalists

Boppists v. comparativists

Bow-wow theory, the ~ (or *onomatopoeic*) theory concerning the origin of language 8 n.

Calculus: language conceived as a ~ 402

Classical stylistics v. stylistics

Classification, the ~ of languages: according to Schleicher 63; psychological (according to Steinthal) 82; conceptual (according to Sapir) 321 n.

Code: in the theory of information 457; in machine translation 468

Code corn, a term applied to dialectal phenomena 155 n.

Code noise, a term applied to dialectal phenomena 155 n.

Coding v. encoding

Combinatory variant (*allophone*): the definition of ~ s according to Trubetzkoy 282

Communicative channel, the ~ in the theory of information 461

Commutation, a glossematic term v. substitution

Comparative grammar: ~ at the beginning of the nineteenth century 53-59; ~ during the time of the neo-grammarians 94-98; ~ in the twentieth century 132; mathematical criteria in comparative historical studies of language 445

Glossematics (*Hjelmslev's linguistics, neo-Saussurianism, the Danish school, the Copenhagen school*): the foundation of the theory of ~ 368-371; the subject of ~ 371; the theory concerning the relations between form and substance, expression and content 372-378; the abstract character of ~ 378-381; the method of commutation in ~ 381-383; the distinction between paradigmatics and syntagmatics in ~ 383
Glossology v. linguistic semantics
Glottochronology (*lexicostatistics*): the origin and significance of ~ 445
Glottogonic, ~ theories before the nineteenth century 8 n. and 42
Grimm, ~ 's law 55

Harvard school: the foundation of the ~ and its relations with the Yale school 236; the importance of the ~ today 309
Hierarchy, the ~ of linguistic phenomena 238
Historical grammar v. diachronic linguistics
Historicism, the ~ of the neo-grammarians v. neo-grammarians
History of language v. diachronic linguistics
Hittite: the decipherment of ~ 440 n.
Hjelmslev's linguistics v. glossematics
Homonymic conflicts, the theory of ~ 150
Homonymy: ~ and its separation from polysemy according to Hjelmslev 376
Humboldtism: the ideas of Humboldt upheld by representatives of ~ 71-75

Idealistic stylistics v. stylistics
Idiolect, a term in modern dialectology 154
Immanent: language as an ~ phenomenon according to the theory of the glossematicians 379
Immediate constituents: in the morphological and syntactical theory of distributionalism 336
Implicit: the relationship between the ~ and the explicit in language (in the light of the theory of information) 463
Incompatible, the ~ tendencies of linguistic development 313
"Independents": the ~ in relation to the neo-grammarians 108; the ideas of H. Schuchardt 108-113
Indian, the ~ grammatical school: the pioneers 16-18; Pāṇini's grammar 18; the epoch after Pāṇini 19; the general significance of the work of the ~ grammatical school 19-23
Individual psychology, ~ in language: according to Steinthal 81; according to Vossler 172; according to the theory of the neolinguists 179
Individual stylistics v. stylistics
Information theory: the field of investigation of ~ 449; ~ as the foundation of cybernetic studies 450-453; the methodological principles of Roman Jakobson in ~ 453-456; the main achievements 456-464
Inner language form: ~ in Humboldt's theory 71
Innovation, linguistic ~ s 64
Instrumental phonetics v. experimental phonetics
Intelligibility: modern phonetic research in connection with the ensuring of ~ 225

Logical positivists v. logical empiricists
Logical symbolism: ~ in linguistics 387-396
Logistic, ~ grammar 394
Logistics: the beginnings of ~ 390; the range of interest of ~ 391-396

Machine translation: how ~ could be used for the universalization of science 465; ~ as a proof of the correctness of the structural method in linguistics 446; the pioneers of ~ 467; the technical aspect of ~ 468; the possibilities of ~ 469; the main problems of ~ 470-476; work on ~ as a stimulus to linguistics 476; the engagement of linguistic resources today in connection with ~ 477
Macrolinguistics: ~ in contradistinction to microlinguistics 342 n. and 438
Marked: definition of the ~ category 288; the opposition of the ~ category to the unmarked according to the principle of binarity 307
Markov's process in mathematical linguistics 437
Marrism: the linguistic training of Marr 198; Marr's main ideas 199-206; Marrism as elaborated by Marr's disciples 206-211; the end of Marrism 211; the results of the epoch of Marrism in Soviet linguistics 212
Mathematical linguistics: the foundation of ~ and its significance today 431-444
Matrix: the ~ in Pike's tagmemics 334 n.
Mentalism: the standpoint of structural linguistics against ~ 231
Metalanguage (the algebra of logic): the beginning of interest in ~ 121; the working out of ~ 388; ~ as a subject of interest for the glossematicians 367
Metalinguistics v. anthropological linguistics
Metalogic: the interest of ~ for metalanguage 390
Metamathematics: the interest of ~ for metalanguage 390
Method, the ~ characteristic of twentieth century scholarship 116
Microglossaries in machine translation 470
Microlinguistics: ~ in contradistinction to macrolinguistics 342 n. and 438
Mixed languages v. Creole languages
Mixture (interweaving), the ~ of languages: according to Schuchardt's theory 110; according to Marr's theory 201
Monogenesis, the theory of the ~ of languages: according to Trombetti 184 n.; according to Marr 199
Morpheme, the definition of the ~ 334
Morphophonemics, an American term; v. morphophonology
Morphophonology: ~ in the programme of the Prague school 298
Motor, ~ phonetics v. articulatory phonetics

National psychology, ~ expressed in language: the beginning of the theory of ~ in Humboldt's teaching 73; ~ according to Steinthal 81; ~ according to Wundt 85
Nativistic theory, the ~ or ding-dong theory 8 n.
Neo-grammarians: the Leipzig school and the foundation of neo-grammarianism as a theory and a method 93-98; the historicism of the ~ 98; the theoretical views of H. Paul 99-106
Neo-Humboldtians: the linguistics of the ~ 77
Neolinguistics v. aesthetic idealism in linguistics

Spectrograph, the ~ in phonetic investigations 222

Speech (parole): ~ in contradistinction to the phenomenon of language (langue) according to De Saussure 259

Sprachbund v. language alliance

Stadialism: Marr's theory of ~ 200

"Stammbaum" theory v. biological naturalism in linguistics

Static linguistics v. synchronic linguistics

Statistical linguistics v. quantitative linguistics

Stenography, the contribution of ~ to the introduction of the statistical method in linguistic research 436

Stochastic process, the ~ in the theory of information 458

Stratification, the ~ of languages: the semiotic ~ of languages according to Wegener 398 n.

Structural, the ~ theory of sound changes v. sound changes

Structuralism: ~ in general in twentieth century scholarship 119-121; the victory of ~ in linguistics 137

Structural linguistics: the theoretical foundations of ~ 230-231; characteristics of the development of ~ 232-234; the basic schools of ~ and their mutual relations 234-237; ~ in the U.S.S.R. 237; the basic programme of ~ today 238; the usefulness of ~ 240

Structure: the ~ of the system at the centre of interest in twentieth century scholarship 119

Stylistic criticism, the ~ of Leo Spitzer 173 n.

Stylistics, different conceptions of ~ : classic ~ 165; sociological ~ 165; individual ~ 166; collective ~ 166; general ~ 166; ~ in the spirit of the conceptions of the Harvard school 168; the idealistic ~ of Leo Spitzer 173; rational ~ (Bally's) 264

Subject: the phenomenon of the ~ in the spirit of Plato's conception 10

Substance: ~ in contradistinction to form according to Hjelmslev's theory 372

Substitution: a methodological procedure in structural linguistics 238; the application of ~ in the elaboration of distributionalism 332

Substratum, the language ~ 183

Suppletivism: the phenomenon of ~ and the problem of the arbitrariness of the language sign 248

Symbol: the use of ~ s in the process of analysis 389

Synchronic (static) linguistics: ~ in contradistinction to diachronic (dynamic) linguistics according to De Saussure 260

Synchrony: ~ in contradistinction to diachrony according to De Saussure 260

Syntagm: the ~ based on the principle of binarity (according to Bally) 268

Syntagmatic relations: ~ in contradistinction to associative according to De Saussure 383 n.

Syntagmatics: ~ in Belić's linguistic theory 195; in relation to paradigmatics according to Hjelmslev 383

Syntax, linguistic ~ : during the epoch of the Alexandrians 14; the development of ~ from the beginning of the present century to transformationalism 418-422; transformationalism in syntax 422-430

Syntax, philosophic ~ : according to Morris 400; according to Carnap 402

INDEX OF PROPER NAMES

The numbers given refer to paragraphs, not pages; the letter *n* after a number means that the name is mentioned in a footnote under the text of the paragraph in question.